THE KING WHO WOULD BE MAN

BRIAN A. PLANK

The King Who Would Be Man
Copyright © 2020 by Brian A. Plank

All rights reserved. No part of this publication may be reproduced, distributed, or transmitted in any form or by any means, including photocopying, recording, or other electronic or mechanical methods, without the prior written permission of the author, except in the case of brief quotations embodied in critical reviews and certain other non-commercial uses permitted by copyright law.

Tellwell Talent
www.tellwell.ca

ISBN
978-0-2288-2641-5 (Hardcover)
978-0-2288-2640-8 (Paperback)
978-0-2288-2642-2 (eBook)

Table of Contents

Acknowledgments v
Foreword vii

PROLOGUE 1

Chapter 1   I'm an Adult Now 11
Chapter 2   Home Sweet Home 28
Chapter 3   Welcome to the Rat Race 59
Chapter 4   Your Time Is Going to Come 71
Chapter 5   Surprises Come in All Shapes and Sizes 91
Chapter 6   You're Making Me Laugh 111
Chapter 7   The King of Hearts 115
Chapter 8   What Is and What Should Not Be 129
Chapter 9   My Boy's Gonna Play in the Big League 141
Chapter 10 You're Fucking Crazy! 157
Chapter 11 PTSD 166
Chapter 12 I Live to Love and Love to Learn 191
Chapter 13 Life, Death, and Other Trivialities 198
Chapter 14 You Can't Bring Me Down 206
Chapter 15 The Never-Ending Lessons 212
Chapter 16 He Started Throwing Stones 221
Chapter 17 Salute the Flags 227

Chapter 18 King of the Castle 239
Chapter 19 Hello Me, It's Me Again 248
Chapter 20 The Real Thing 256
Chapter 21 Yield to Oncoming Traffic 274
Chapter 22 The Struggle Continues 293
Chapter 23 Good Times, Bad Times 306
Chapter 24 The Gift 314
Chapter 25 He Shall Kill 325
Chapter 26 A Self-Righteous Hypocrite 349
Chapter 27 Goodbye 372
Chapter 28 This is the End 385
Chapter 29 I See Your True Colors, and That's Why I Love
            You 401
Chapter 30 Perseverance of Time 407

EPILOGUE 415

Acknowledgments

First and foremost, this book is dedicated to the memory of my father, Donald A. Plank, who sadly passed on January 24, 2018. He taught me what it meant to be a real man, and how to conduct myself as one. I feel you with me every moment of every day. Until we meet again…

It goes without saying that my mother, Carol E. Plank (née Wheeler) has always had my back and pushed me to be the best I could be. She doesn't believe it, but she is one of the most intelligent and wisest human beings I have ever had the pleasure of getting to know. I truly aspire to live up to her degree of integrity, human kindness, and love.

And then there is Terry-Lynn Plank (née Malone), my best friend forever, and one of my unquestionable soulmates. I remember when we first started dating some twenty-five years ago, I asked her to read my very rough manuscript—it was printed by a dot-matrix printer. She anxiously read what I had written. I'll never forget her first written words of relief after realizing that I actually could write: "You shock my awareness."

Lastly, I wish to genuinely thank everyone who I have had the opportunity to meet over the years, the good and the bad, the beautiful and the ugly. If it wasn't for you, I wouldn't be at this amazing point in my life.

Here's to the crazy ones. The misfits, the rebels, the troublemakers. The round pegs in the square holes. The ones who see things differently. They're not fond of rules. And they have no respect for the status quo. You can quote them, disagree with them, disbelieve them, glorify or vilify them. About the only thing you can't do, is ignore them because they change things. They invent. They imagine. They heal. They explore. They create. They inspire. They push the human race forward. Maybe they have to be crazy. Because the ones who are crazy enough to think that they can change the world, are the ones who do.

– Steve Jobs, 1997

Even if they ostracize me and use my name as a curse, they are still using my name — the more hate they spew about me the more powerful I become.

– B. A. Plank, 2018

Foreword

I started writing this novel when I was in my early twenties—over twenty-five years ago. This novel was going to be my magnum opus, the book that was going to get my message out there and was going to change the world. But it was getting too big to publish, especially for a first-time self-publishing author.

This is a fictional novel in a memoir format. It is very loosely based upon a dark period in my life. Some of the characters are loosely based upon individuals whom I have encountered, and some individuals who never existed at all. Some parts have been ripped from the headlines; some parts are from the deepest, darkest corners of my mind; and some parts are based upon reality as I witnessed and felt it.

It's about what it's like to be the weirdo, and a nonconformist. What it's like to be the joker in the kingdom. How difficult it can be to reason with the unreasonable.

It's about how lonely it feels to be the one black sheep in a field that is white and still try to fit in. It's about the feelings of being ignored, teased, bullied, beaten, drowned, and still resurfacing before that last ounce of air is about to expire.

It's about the human condition. It's about human emotions and how they are handled. There is joy and misery. There is success and jealousy. There is modesty and arrogance. There is exceptional and average.

It's about how it feels to suffer from mental illness, be it minor or debilitating. It's how it feels to want to help someone who is suffering, but not know how. It's about labeling and stigmatizing—not just the mentally ill, but all and any group that is different than the mainstream.

It's about how it feels to be mistreated for no apparent reason. It's about vengeance and atonement. It's about war and pain. It's about winning and losing and realizing that the only thing that matters is that the game was played with integrity.

It's about conquering fear with love, trying to take the good from the bad and creating a happy life experience. It's about how easily the fear can overcome the love, but how ultimately the love can shine through.

It's about hope.

PROLOGUE

I often ran alone through the shabby downtown streets in the city. These streets were where we the homeless and the dregs of society were drawn to and called home. We had fast trains shuffling hundreds of thousands to and fro every day. There were numerous long-abandoned subway tunnels below ground—some were filled with the homeless. Others like me were surface dwellers. Airplanes and jumbo jets were endlessly flying above the urban landscape, which was cluttered with high-rise apartments and condos.

Towering high above the ground, these skyscrapers kept the skies overhead practically hidden. I occasionally looked up beyond them. Usually the sky was dingy with thick gray smog, but there were those rare days when it lifted a little and I could see the blue sky laden with grayish white clouds marred by chemtrails. Humans had destroyed this once great and beautiful city, as with most other cities throughout the world.

As cliché as it may sound, the city *was* a concrete jungle. There were no fresh green lawns or trees here. I remembered being a young boy growing up in the suburbs, which were filled with parks, fields, and forests, all only a short bicycle ride from home, and all for us to freely explore. But even the homey comfort and happiness that I recollected was all but extinct, save for the rural regions that skirted the city. The capitalistic perversions of our governments and corporations had exploited the suburban beauty by densely populating it in every available location at outrageous prices, until there were no more parks, fields, or forests to frolic in. This was our city as planned out by our self-proclaimed forward-thinking leaders.

Most humans were sheep (also alternatively referred to as "lemmings" or "sheeple"), and were generally indistinguishable one from another, with their heads and eyes pointed forward. God forbid they looked to the left or right. They moved as directed, with their noses near-buried in the asshole of the sheep in front of them.

Those in charge—the shepherds—were rewriting history over and over, day by day, and the sheep just lapped it up as fast as it could be conceived. Never questioning, they kept moving in the direction they were being herded. The majority were too preoccupied with staying aligned with their fellow sheep to wonder about or seek the truth. Most of the shepherds were sheep as well, they just answered to a higher level of shepherds.

The minority who *did* see through the bullshit and dared question the mainstream were those I referred to as being on "their path to enlightenment." They were the metaphorical black sheep, the ones who stood out and dared stray from the rest of the herd. They often tried to stir up the rest of the sheep. They were a small but ever-evolving group, although frequently discredited by the governments and corporations through public shaming, labeling, and being pushed over the brink of sanity, such that no one would take them seriously.

We, the homeless, we represented *failure*. We populated the grimy bowels of the city; we populated the places where children were warned to never venture into. We were hidden away from the "regular" citizens—they didn't want to be reminded of the worst that could happen, and especially that occasionally it did happen. We were a boil on the ass of a prince.

The bowels were where the broken and ostracized ended up. The mentally and physically ill, the runaways, the forgotten, and the ostracized—all of those who society quietly ignored, those who had simply slipped or been forced through the cracks and been left wandering aimlessly.

The ostracized included the black sheep, those who pushed the boundaries too far and/or questioned the status quo a little too often. No shepherd liked a nonconformist or a shit disturber in their herd, because they continued to openly question and protest the status quo, often trying to entice the other sheep to stray and find their own path. The shepherds would try to bring them back in line, but these shepherds were responsible for keeping the whole herd in check, so they could only spend a little precious time trying to gather the strays before the rest of the herd started wandering about too.

As a result, the sheep left behind tended to roam about, until eventually either disappearing into the bowels or finding their beacon, their path to enlightenment.

Of course, there were always the ill-intentioned strays and shepherds who attempted to lure the herds by selling their snake oil, their instant happiness in a bottle. These individuals destroyed lives with their drugs and promises of a fast track to a Utopian existence.

I eventually found a small group of friends and forward thinkers with whom I could share my ideas as well as disappointments and frustrations. Friends and foes alike came and went. Each had met some purpose, although their roles weren't always clear at the moment they were there. Open conversations with these friends and acquaintances gave me a wider spectrum of mind-blowing opportunities that sometimes influenced how I approached and processed thoughts and logic.

Our constant questioning of the norm brought on a deserved paranoia; we were a tremendous source of fear and a true threat to the shepherds' status quo. Although generally a minority, we were building strength in numbers. However, when one of us was cornered we were typically blackballed and tormented until being driven over the edge, pushed to the bowels to minimize or discredit our influence.

We all came from various backgrounds. Some of us were well educated, some not at all; an education, no matter to what level, did not imply or ensure genuine intelligence, it simply indicated that an individual was capable of learning and regurgitating higher-level details and specifics.

Engaging in critical and creative thinking is the key to genuine intelligence.

Question everything.

This can be accomplished by breaking problems into smaller, more manageable pieces, and then putting the puzzle back together piece by piece, or cluster by cluster.

Although living in the bowels, my deluded mind remained sharp. I continued examining and defining solutions to many societal problems. However, I often felt as if I was alone, putting together a million-piece jigsaw puzzle only to discover that I was missing a single piece. I feared that all attention would be drawn away from the elegant imagery of the assembled puzzle and put on the gaping hole.

Even as this level of thinking was mastered, it was still flawed by our very nature, by our humanity. By our free will. As I've often heard it said, "We are only as strong as our weakest link." That was the bottom line.

In general, the sheep trusted that their shepherds had their best interests at heart and believed that they were being led in the right direction, that one day in the future they would enjoy prosperity and happiness in return for being obedient.

This was an outdated mode of thinking.

The truth was that our lives were constantly a case of the majority being led by the mediocre minority. It was all about profit and power: more money equaled more power. With some exceptions, the shepherds did not have their flocks' interests in mind at all, they had their own situations to consider. The shepherds blabbed of zero tolerance for bullying, lying, and cheating, but *they* were the worst bullies, liars and cheaters. I had witnessed it. I had *experienced* it.

From early childhood, I had always tended to be a well-intentioned nonconformist and unintended trendsetter, and at times a shit disturber. I had been blackballed some time ago, forced over the edge of sanity, driven from the comfortable life of a common corporate success to this lonely life on the gritty streets. I lost all that mattered to me, not just my possessions and my family, but most importantly my *mind.*

My rejection from the corporate world did not occur just because I had been outspoken and shared my experiences and opinions of the truth about our corporation and society, it was also because I had offended and/or embarrassed a select group of the higher-level shepherds. I had laid all the cards on the table for all to see, forcing them look at and acknowledge their own irrefutable inadequacies.

They had to get rid of me. I was dangerous.

Although it may at times sound otherwise, I was not an elitist.

Before and after being shamed and shunned, I always wanted to share my gifts, not lord them over anyone. Still, I had to admit that I had difficulty tolerating the empty stares I received from my societal and professional peers when I shared my theories, ideas, and facts. They readily excused my words and behavior by labeling me "delusional."

All that I really wanted was to help lead my fellow humans toward finding their path. I wanted them to see and react to the truth. I wanted them to open their eyes and see that they were capable of peacefully rising and speaking out, that they did not have to be just another common sheep.

I lived for those rare moments when I witnessed one of the sheep becoming aware.

All that I hoped for from anyone else was that they try in their own way. Was that too much to ask? If so, perhaps my entire argument was moot; maybe I *was* just an elitist. Perhaps I held the bar higher than I should have expected from others.

I couldn't recall how long I'd been on the streets.

It was nighttime. There was no moon out. It was so quiet. Too quiet. I could barely even hear the voices arguing with my own thoughts inside my head. I was safely sleeping in my open-ended box outside on the downtown street.

That's when it happened.

There was a sudden bright light in front of me. The light was warm—this warmth enveloped my entire body. It made me feel like I was floating in space. I was in some state of suspended animation. I could move effortlessly. There were no obstacles or points of resistance. Perhaps this was how it felt to be in the womb. I don't know. I couldn't remember.

I pried my eyes open.

Although blurry at first, I could eventually make out a hand reaching out to me. Everything else was black. I tried to speak, but my lips and throat were so dry that I could not even manage a crackle or a croak.

On the street I had seen so much evil done in the name of survival. We, the homeless, were often beaten and tormented for fun by those who were privileged. Many blamed us for living on the streets—it must have been our own fault, right? I had once been a married man, working as a well-educated professional with a great-paying position and a bright future. But the onset of my mental illness combined with my unrelentingly inquisitive mind got in the way of sustaining my picture-perfect life.

Life on the streets of downtown . . . it wasn't all bad. Sometimes on the coldest of winter nights the police rounded us up and threw us into jail for a night or two; we were well fed and got a good sleep. Most of us respected the rules of the streets. My small clan would share food and money, maybe a bottle of cheap wine, and on special occasions a small bottle of vodka or whiskey. On other occasions, the "good people" were great about keeping us fed, and occasionally sheltered.

But tonight, this hand before me . . .

Part I
The Family Guy

Chapter 1

I'm an Adult Now

She Didn't Seem to Care
Spring 1990

I recall the first time I saw her. It was about a year before we started dating; we were partying at the house of my friends Jake and Dave Prue, brothers from the Black Bass, a small chain restaurant throughout Pennsylvania where I had spent my later teen years working. She was sitting on the end of a big sofa. She was very young, about sixteen years old and *very* pregnant with Jake's kid—so much so that I thought the baby was about to burst out right then and there.

It was almost summertime. I was finishing my first year of four at engineering school at Penn State University. I was getting ready to write my final exams and then I would be working at SM-Steel, a local steel mill in my hometown of Pittsburgh, *and* as a cook at the Black Bass before returning to school for a second year. I was nineteen. Despite my busy work schedule, I always had time to party.

I looked older than my age, so I was rarely carded when I went to buy beer. But because I wasn't twenty-one yet, I had my ass covered with a high-quality fake ID.

At the time I preferred smoking weed over drinking beer, because I was never hungover from weed like I often was after an evening or afternoon of drinking. Of course, being a stupid kid I usually combined the two to intensify my level of intoxication. Nothing felt better than chugging back a dozen beers and then taking a few hits from a bong.

I just recently had a crude tattoo on my left arm covered over by a professional artist, and when I arrived at the party Jake dragged me over to the couch where she was sitting and he implored me to show her my "awesome new tat."

My new tattoo was on my upper left arm. It was a large fiery skull with long hair, a musical triplet crashing through it, and small musical notes floating around it. It represented my dedication to music, both as a musician and as a music lover. I chose to use a skull because it represented that I would always have music in me until the day I died. I kept the tattoo on my upper arm so that I was able to keep it hidden when wearing a short-sleeve shirt—back then tattoos were not generally considered to be socially acceptable.

Her name was Jennifer Albright.

She seemed hardly interested at all.

His full name was Charles Johnathan Albright, but they nicknamed him Chucky. Chucky was born that autumn, a few months after I met her for the first time. I had since left the steel mill and returned to school to start up year two with the books. There was a Black Bass franchise near school, so I continued working while studying.

I happened to be at home the weekend that Chucky was born, so I went with Jake to visit the baby and Jennifer in the hospital the day after he had been born. Jake was glowing; he was so proud to be a dad. But he was only eighteen and had no idea what being a dad meant. He had never been exposed to children, let alone infants. Like me, he was a heavy dope user and hardcore partier. In fact, he revealed to me that when Jennifer went into labor he was spaced out on LSD. He was trying to describe how mind-blowing the birthing was while tripping out. His brother Dave later told me that Jake had passed out during the birthing.

Jake awkwardly picked up the baby and handed him to me. Again, Jennifer showed very little interest in me. I never gave it a second thought.

She was destined to change my life forever.

My First Real Relationship
March through August 1991

Jennifer Albright was just turning seventeen and I was twenty when we started dating.

I was just finishing my second year at school; one more week and I would be back home and off to work at SM-Steel. One random night, just after I'd returned home from school, Jennifer Albright called me. She completely blindsided me; we had never said much more than hello to one another. She was no one to me.

She invited me over to her place for a couple of beers and to play Tetris. I knew that their relationship had been struggling, so I asked her about Jake. I didn't want to get in the middle of whatever they had going on, especially with them having a baby together. She made it clear to me that Jake was no longer with her and hadn't been for a few months.

I was intrigued—was this a romantic gesture or purely platonic? I figured I had nothing to lose, so I walked over.

Jennifer answered the door and invited me in.

Her mother, Julie, was sitting on a pale blue couch smoking a cigarette and watching Jenn play her video game. She had a drink beside her; it looked like rye. Jenn's twelve-year-old sister Shelli was also there, sitting off to the side in a little chair reading a book. Chucky was already in bed.

I sat on the floor beside Jenn. Before my butt had even hit the carpet, Julie started drilling me with questions. I had dated my share of girls enough to recognize the typical hazing that many teenaged girls' parents put young men through. But Julie was in a league of her own.

She cut right to the chase, barraging me with questions. One question of many which stuck with me was: "Would you marry my daughter if you knocked her up?" I thought it odd, as although Jenn was above the age of consent to engage in sex, she was still too young to legally marry.

I seriously considered my response to the question. Finally, I told her, "I would be careful to avoid a pregnancy in the first place."

Julie nodded and asked, "But what *if*...?"

I thought a little more and responded, "Well... I would, but only if we loved one another."

Her mom took a sip of her drink and a long drag from her cigarette.

Our eyes locked again as she told Jenn to get rid of me, right then and there.

Julie had Jenn when she was eighteen herself; she was only thirty-five now. She was a very shrewd and opinionated lady and a bit drunk. I heard what her alcohol-clouded mind was telling me right at that moment: *You're not the one.*

A little red flag was raised inside of my mind. I ignored it. Jenn completely ignored my conversation with her mom; she just kept playing her video game. Julie finally asked Jenn if she was going to let me play. She ignored her mother again.

Julie offered me a beer and smiled. "Get me one while you're up." She pointed toward the kitchen.

On my way to the kitchen, I smiled and said to myself, "Okay, I think I know what I'm dealing with here."

I returned, sat on the couch and pulled out my cigarettes and Zippo lighter, laying them on the end table beside me. Julie looked at me.

We had an interesting chat over a few beers. I didn't care for her all-knowing self-important attitude, but she wasn't mean or uninviting, she was simply a very experienced woman.

Julie was a Native American. She never knew her father. When she was about three, her abusive drunk of a mother died, after which her older sister raised her in poverty on the reservation. She was later adopted by a loving middle-class European immigrant couple—the Albrights—when she was twelve years old. Despite the life that the Albrights had tried to offer her, she was too deeply rooted in her impoverished upbringing to flourish.

Julie was eighteen in the mid-1970s when she became pregnant with Jenn, and although the Albrights tried to be supportive, society shamed young unwed mothers, especially in upper-middle-class suburban families. Upon adopting her, they had thought they were providing opportunities that she otherwise would never have had. They were showing her how wonderful life could be—and she had screwed it up.

Life had been rough over the years for Julie and her two daughters, Jenn and Shelli. They had grown up poor. Julie refused to accept her adoptive parents' assistance. For a few years she distanced herself from them; she was too proud to let them see her struggle.

Jenn told me that the best Christmas they ever had was in 1981, when she was eight and Shelli was about three. Julie had no money for gifts or food; she could barely afford rent. They had Kraft Dinner for Christmas dinner, and they sat around the small black and white television watching Rudolph the Red-Nosed Reindeer, the only show they could access with just an old antenna.

They learned the meaning of love and respect by the way Julie stood by them when they had nothing. After a few years living in the roughest parts of town and dealing with the dregs of society, their financial struggles finally ended when Julie managed to get a full-time permanent union job that paid well at a local factory. That, according to Jenn, made the family cherish and appreciate their future Christmases even more.

It was at that point that Julie reconnected with her adoptive family.

Julie's adoptive parents doted on the girls. Jenn's grandfather found her especially endearing. She was smart and pretty. She seemed to have a good head on her shoulders. She was the reason his old gray eyes sparkled. She was also the reason why his old gray eyes lost their sparkle.

After Jenn became pregnant with Chucky her grandfather refused to see her. She had so much going for her and he felt that she had ruined her future—he didn't want to see her go down the same path as her mother had.

Her heart was broken.

He died before Chucky was born. Jenn felt horribly, and that look of disappointment from his face when she told him she was pregnant remained etched into her brain.

So, there I sat talking up Julie while Jenn continued with her game of Tetris. After an hour or two, Shelli pulled her nose out of her book and went to bring Chucky down for a bottle and for me to see him before I left. This was the first time I'd seen him since I'd visited him just after he was born. He was now six or so months old.

I went home with a strange but quirky feeling. Jenn had barely spoken to me and Julie had already predicted the end of our relationship before it had even started.

In addition to my long, straggly red hair, huge sideburns, and big-ass tattoo, I was the drummer in a metal band. I think that was what initially attracted Jenn to me. I came across as if I was living the rock 'n' roll lifestyle, and she wanted to be a part of it. I had learned that being a musician on the stage attracted a lot of women, but they were usually piss-drunk or high when we were done performing. I felt that I owed it to them to not take advantage of their intoxicated state, although that didn't mean I wouldn't let them go down on me.

Jenn called me again the next day. And the day after that. We talked for quite a while each time and I became quite impressed with her unbridled tenacity; the way she pursued me and worked to gain my attention made me believe that she really wanted to be with me. This dispelled my initial misgivings about her. Nonetheless, it took me a couple of anxiety-ridden dates before I finally worked up the gumption to kiss her.

Since my first kiss, I had a complex about my kissing technique. I was under the impression that you had to literally suck the breath out of the mouth of the girl you were kissing, because Mom had always called it "suck-facing."

None of the girls I kissed had ever said anything, but I was generally left feeling that making out wasn't as fun as it was supposed to be. Jenn was only sixteen and I was twenty, but the difference in age was of no consequence to us, and our parents never expressed any displeasure. When I finally did kiss Jenn, she jumped up and wrapped her legs around me while pressing her soft lips against mine. I began my suck-facing routine and she pulled away.

"What are you doing?" she asked. Her bewildered face was only inches away from mine.

I was tremendously embarrassed.

Jenn giggled. "Relax," she cooed as she tilted her head and looked down at my mouth. She slowly pressed her lips against mine once again, and then licked my lips. I liked it. She told me to do the same to her, and I liked that too. We slowly started making out. Within a few minutes my kissing stigma was gone.

Finally, I understood why kissing was considered romantic and fun.

After that, our relationship took off like an I don't know what. She was very up front and warned me that she wanted to be cautious about having sex—she didn't want to get pregnant again and so we would not engage in intercourse for a long while. Jenn was going to be my first lover so I was just a little more than wanting to get inside her pants, but I figured that I had held off this long from getting laid so there was no big deal if I waited another month or two.

We slept together a week after our first kiss.

The first time we had sex it was rather unremarkable. Although Jenn was experienced, she was used to her partner just rutting on her for a moment or two and then finishing. She had never experienced any deep satisfaction when having sex, and she had little if any experience with foreplay. My attitude was that I wanted my girlfriend to feel as beautiful as she was; giving her an orgasm was the most powerful source of pleasure that I had to offer.

The next evening we made love again. I wanted to be a little more adventurous and compatible with each other in bed, even if it was only my second time having sex. We were in my bedroom and I wanted to try something new, which I had seen in porn many times. She was lying on my bed naked, and I spread her legs wide and licked and kissed her from her lips down to her belly and then to her clitoris.

Within minutes she had her first orgasm ever.

Life was perfect.

I was living with the woman of my dreams.

I had a small family.

Shortly after meeting Jenn I left the Black Bass. It was late April, just after the end of my second of the four school years. I was making killer money when I went back to work at the local steel mill as a laborer. I had decided not to return to school in the upcoming fall term but to stay working at the mill. I knew that I would be laid off at Christmastime because work was slow, and that I would be rehired the following spring. I also knew that Unemployment Insurance would yield me a nice little income during the few months of being unemployed and that this would help take care of my Jenn and Chucky, showing them how it was living the high life.

I worked my ass off so that I could I share my good fortune with Jenn and Chucky by taking them for nice dinners out, trips to theme parks, and adventurous travels to different tourist attractions.

Just having a car to travel in was a luxury that Jenn had never experienced.

I was so addicted to my new life that I all but turned my back on my friends at the Bass without even a goodbye. I had heard through the grapevine that Jake felt quite betrayed by me, and that he had become extremely vocal about it.

One night early in our relationship, Jake brought Chucky home to us from his scheduled weekend visit. He was with his friends in a small gray Ford sedan. After dropping Chucky off, the wheels of the tires squealed down the street and I clearly heard Jake yell out of the passenger window, "Fuckin' slut!" two or three times while the driver honked the horn.

A few days later, Jake's younger brother Dave reassured me that I had done nothing wrong. Jake *had* been out of the picture for several months. But Dave warned me that it wasn't quite as open and shut as Jenn made it out to be. Jake had still been seeing Jenn almost right up to when I came into the picture. But the two had nothing in common except for Chucky. Apparently, Jake had become overwhelmed by fatherhood and his new responsibilities.

To further Jake's issues, he barely even knew Jenn as a person when she got pregnant. They were two young teens who had met through a common friend, and in less than two months she was pregnant. It was out of a sense of obligation that Jake and Jenn stayed together throughout her pregnancy and for a short while afterward.

Jenn told me that the night that she got pregnant was on New Year's Eve. They were tripping on LSD at an Alice Cooper concert. She wasn't on the birth control pill, and they didn't use a condom because when Jake was an early teen he'd been in an accident of some sort and one of his testicles had been badly damaged and was not tended to properly. It had atrophied and the doctors told him he would be impotent for the rest of his life.

Furthermore, he had become jealous of his son. Chucky was taking all of Jenn's time, so in response he had strayed. He began nailing a new girl. When Jenn spoke of this I saw a different side of her. She began trashing this new girlfriend—it was a lot like how Jake was trashing me. At the time I was so blinded by my love for Jenn and Chucky that I barely even noticed this commonality, but still, I wondered: If she was happy with me, why would she care who Jake was screwing?

Dave told me that he had been telling Jake for months to get his shit together or someone else was going to come along and scoop her up right from under his nose. He was right.

Jake's parents, particularly his mother Gwen, insisted that they remain in constant contact with Chucky. He was their flesh and blood regardless of any teenaged bullshit that Jake and Jenn had going on. As per Jenn, Gwen dropped by whenever she felt like it and expected Jenn to spend time with her.

Jenn did not like this. Not one bit. And she was very vocal about it.

Most times Julie would sit down with Gwen in Jenn's place.

I knew the Prues: Gwen and her husband Frank. I had always liked them. Deep inside I was somewhat perplexed. They were good people. They reminded me of my own parents. Friendly. Open. Inviting. Earlier that year, Dave and I had spent New Year's Eve in his basement bedroom getting drunk. His dad even went so far as to check my (fake) ID to ensure that I was over twenty-one—the legal drinking age—before letting me drink my beer in his house. Dave was only seventeen so he wasn't allowed to drink. I would hide a beer in the washroom vanity every time he needed another.

Ironically, that was the same night that Jake and Jenn dropped acid and ended up getting her pregnant.

I was young and in love for the first time. This was beyond any crush or infatuation I had ever experienced.

One afternoon after a couple more dates, I told Jenn that I wanted to bring Chucky along on our next outing.

"That is exactly what I've been hoping for!" She wrapped her arms around my neck. "I want you to be more than just a part of Chucky's life. I want him to call you Dad."

I smiled and told her that I wanted that too. We began to kiss.

We looked at each other with sly sparkles in our eyes and crooked smiles on our faces. Julie was at work. Chucky was at daycare. Shelli was at school. I stroked Jenn's long raven-black hair. We didn't even make it all the way into the house before I was deep inside of her.

We had only been together for a couple of months when I told her that I loved her and wanted to marry her in a year or two when I had saved enough money to afford a big wedding, and even possibly buying and moving out into our own house. She was thrilled with this idea—she said that would be her dream come true. I didn't know that someone could have a smile as wide as hers at that moment.

Chucky was such a great baby. He hardly ever fussed and he smiled and giggled a lot. Within a couple of months, I left the comfort of my parents' house and moved in with Jenn and her family. Well, I unofficially moved in. Jenn was on welfare, which not only ensured there would be shelter over their heads and food on the table, but an extra bit for "miscellaneous expenses" such as liquor and dope. If I officially moved in with her as her common-law partner, with my high wages from the steel mill she would be cut off from her benefits. At the time I never thought twice about it.

Jenn decided that my parents should be Chucky's grandparents. Jenn had never met her own father. All she knew about him was that he was a Native American and that he refused to assume any responsibility for her. Julie was the only other grandparent that Chucky had.

My parents loved that little boy so much. They accepted him as though he was their flesh and blood. Like me, they doted on his every action. I clearly remember my dad lying on their bed throwing Chucky up and down in the air. I don't know which of the two laughed louder. And Mom built up quite the collection of books to read to him. Chucky loved it when Grandma read to him.

Enter the Mullet Man
September 1991

Chucky had been enrolled in daycare since he was a month or two old. This was because of a government social service directed at young teen mothers with the aim of promoting good parenting skills and teaching them how to reintegrate themselves into society.

Jenn returned to high school while I worked at the mill. We had been together for six months at that point. I was proud of her for trying to reopen the doors of opportunity rather than sitting on her ass collecting welfare like some of the girls she had befriended through these social programs.

One day, shortly after she had returned to school, I was off shift and I came home after running a few errands to find some guy with the definitive mullet sitting on our couch while Jenn was in the kitchen making lunch. I went in to see Jenn and she explained that not only was he a friend that she'd met at school, but that he'd claimed to have known me in middle school.

His name was Mike Jagger.

Upon looking at him, I recognized that I *had* known him when I was in middle school.

Mike had been dealt a shitty hand in life. His father was a career criminal and he had instilled some of his less favorable attributes in Mike.

Mike's days and nights were filled with partying and supporting himself by committing petty crimes, such as break and enters, stealing car stereos, and trafficking dope. When he was only eighteen years old he had been busted for a B&E. He had been jailed for three months.

He would be on probation until he was twenty-two. I had just turned twenty-one, as had he a few months earlier, so he just had to keep his nose out of the shit for one more year and he could become legit. Sounds easy, right?

Nope. But as I came to understand Mike I understood why.

Mike openly admired me. I was smart and I worked hard to get ahead in life. He was especially impressed that I was doing it legitimately. Unlike Mike, I had been raised by stable and loving parents. Mike was excited to introduce me to his parents. I think that he was trying to impress upon them that he was turning over a new leaf and not hanging out with criminals any longer.

Mike's parents were divorced. His mother had all but given up on him. She was a miserable woman and had remarried. Mike's stepdad openly disliked him, often referring to him as "criminal trash." As soon as Mike was eighteen his mother kicked him out; it was shortly thereafter that Mike was imprisoned for breaking and entering.

After getting out of jail, Mike's stepdad wouldn't even let him have a key to the house. His mother didn't object. When I learned of what she had been through, first with Mike's dad and then with Mike, I saw where she was coming from. When I did meet them I didn't like that I was treated like just another criminal, but I reasoned that after years of disappointment I really couldn't blame her. But his stepdad *was* an asshole. Mike's dad wouldn't take him in, so Mike got his own apartment and sold dope and stolen car stereos to pay for it.

His father had been bad news and raised Mike to be a lifelong criminal—crime was all that Mike knew. I first met Mike's dad at a party at his dad's girlfriend's house. I took an instant disliking to him. He was cocky to the point of being narcissistic. I sensed that he didn't care for me either. Mike was always unsuccessfully trying to gain his father's approval. His father *looked* like a criminal—he had an age-hardened affect. Mike tried to impress his father by telling him how smart I was; his father seemed even less impressed.

Mike's father worked at the same mill as I did. He was a laborer, and although he didn't know me he knew what the smart guys did. As per the stereotype, they wore fancy lab coats over their shirts and ties and walked around with clipboards. They were always taking notes. They rarely addressed the workers, but they always knew how to do the workers' jobs better than they did. They then returned to their air-conditioned offices and proceeded to determine how the work could be streamlined and/or made more efficient, which often meant eliminating jobs or adding tasks to their already full plates.

Somehow, Mike's mother had instilled a decent set of morals in him. Mike's dad had spent a good chunk of time in and out of jail while Mike was a youth. Mike was rarely violent and his criminal activities were never personal—he would only steal from businesses, never from people's homes. Usually all he stole was cash register money and car stereos. I know that didn't put him high up on the to-be-sainted list, but after listening to some of his stories about his father's behavior, he looked golden.

Mike's proudest moment in his life was from when he was nine years old.

His maternal grandparents owned a little cottage on a small obscure lake way up north just on the States side of Quebec in Canada where his family would go for their summer holidays. Mike often reminisced about the great times he'd had as a child going fishing with his dad, when his dad wasn't in jail.

They would go up to his grandparents' cottage on weekends to go fishing and hunting—or so Mike believed. During the late summer and late autumn days, while the summer crowds were returning home for the winter, his dad and crew went on their annual blitzing of cottages and small businesses. Mike's dad had no conscience. He would trash his victims' homes in search of valuables.

This particular year was Mike's initiation into the family business. His dad had been raising hell there since he was Mike's age.

While his dad and crew were tearing apart someone's cottage, Mike was assigned the role of lookout. His dad had told him that the police were rarely out in this region. There was a small town nearby with a police force made up of about ten officers who were responsible for a vast region of land, most of which was cottage country with a lot of lakes and forests. The lakefront properties served as summer homes for the well off. And that made their properties prime meat for the hungry wolves.

This night, while his dad was doing his thing, Mike heard voices and saw flashlights waving back and forth, beaming through the forest and wooded paths. It was the police. Mike did his job and alerted the crew. His dad and cohorts escaped; unfortunately, Mike didn't.

He was drilled for hours, but he refused to turn in his old man or any of the crew. Since Mike wasn't caught in the act of stealing or inside the cottage, the police had no grounds to hold him. They said they couldn't leave him in the outdoors unsupervised so they had to drive him home.

Mike's dad had never shared any escape plan or identified a place to regroup if they had the cops on their tail. Mike was the worst criminal I knew. He was the *only* career criminal that I knew. He almost always ended up doing something stupid and getting caught.

Back then there were no telephones in the northern towns, so the police took Mike straight back to his grandparents' cottage. His mother was there—she was pissed that his dad was involving him in crime. That was the last year that she was with his dad before suing for divorce.

It never occurred to Mike that his dad would be there too.

The police grilled his dad and family but they couldn't place his dad at the crime scene, so they reluctantly didn't arrest him. Mike's mom suppressed her fury until the police were finished questioning the family and left. Mike's dad said nothing to him, but he later gave him a whooping for getting caught and leading the police to his home.

And that is why Mike claimed that not ratting out his dad and crew when he was nine years old was the proudest moment of his life.

Chapter 2

Home Sweet Home

I'm Going Through Changes
1992

As predicted, after a four-month period of unemployment from January until April I'd returned to the steel mill that spring. But within a short time I started to get bored with my job. The money was great, but I was realizing that there was just no future there for me. At best I would be hired on permanent full-time and from there promoted to shift leader at some point, or even be given an office job. But that could take many years. The guys with whom I worked liked working with me, but they began telling me to get my ass back into school.

    Despite myself, I had always been an academic at heart. The economy was unsteady, and the reality was that I was going to be getting laid off and rehired by the mill regularly, possibly for a few years, until being formally hired. The new autumn schoolyear was approaching. So finally I left all the money and shiftwork to return to school. This time I applied to a three-year co-op engineering technologist program at the local community college. I met with the dean of chemistry and metallurgy and he instantly added me to the program, ready to start in September. I chose not to return to the four-year degree university program because I didn't have the confidence in myself that I would be able to handle the workload.

Jennifer was able to take a high school equivalency test and she was also able to start studying social work at the same community college at the same time as me.

We both thrived . . . at first.

Upon graduation from the community college I would have a diploma and the designation of Engineering Technologist. I specialized in chemistry and metallurgy/materials. The program I was enrolled in was a three-year co-op work program. Because I had completed two of four years in engineering school back in April of 1991, I was admitted directly into the second year of the technologist program, and I was given additional credit for a few of the second-year program courses.

The co-op work terms were one of the key features that attracted students to this institute. We got hands-on training during the work semesters and we got to see how the academic work related to the real world.

I fit in well with my new classmates. I made some good friends and attended a lot of great parties. I was still a chronic pot smoker. I found that a few of the other students liked to drink and get high too. With the reduced intensity of community college compared to the four-year university, I found that I had time to party *and* do very well in school.

I noticed that my anxiety levels were starting to mildly influence my social decisions, but I was able to push through. I was growing nervous of meeting and speaking with new people and attending social events. It helped that the other students were very welcoming. Plus, alcohol and weed were good at dulling my anxious feelings. I went to see my family doctor, Dr. Gantt, about the anxiety. She dismissed it as mild anxiety and indicated that many people suffered from it to about the same degree. She said she had no concerns and sent me on my way.

If she only could have foreseen the future.

While I was getting acclimated to college life, Jenn was also making new friends, and new adventures were opening for her. She was also granted the feeling of freedom for the first time since she became pregnant. She had missed out on her prime teen years and hadn't been able to get the partying phase completely out of her system, although I took her to some dandy parties at which she got pretty wasted.

I failed to notice that Jenn's friends were always around while mine were rarely present.

To succeed in the engineering technologist field in college, you still had to put in the work, just like to succeed at anything. But again, it wasn't nearly as intense as university. I had just turned twenty-two, I had a great life, and I worked hard to ensure that I would open more doors of opportunity. Within the first few weeks of my first semester that September I had finally learned how to learn, and quickly established myself as the class brainer, a title I hadn't held for years.

The significant difference between community college and the four-year university programs was that college seemed like a natural extension of secondary school while university was like a big leap upward from high school. I realized this was the reason acceptance into the four-year university program required higher grades. One interesting statement that one of my university profs had told us in first year was that we were all *intellectually* capable of succeeding in university—if we weren't, we would never have been accepted. But intellect had little to do with the maturity and self-discipline that university required. He followed that by informing the class that almost half of us would be gone by Christmas. I remember looking around the room, trying to identify who would succeed and who would drop out. For as long as I could remember I had been told that I was a brainer and a shoo-in for academic success, so as I was scanning the room I failed to note that I wasn't looking at me.

My First Professional Job
January through April 1993

My mom was always telling me that if I wanted to be taken seriously in the workplace I would need to cut my hair. This used to irritate the shit out of me; I felt that if a company wanted to access my skills they would hire me for my brain, not my haircut. My beard was fine if I kept it trimmed and neat. I knew that most interviewers would see past my physical appearance but that there were those who would instantly make judgments. If they wanted a cookie-cutter yes-man for an employee I was not their guy.

I must admit, however, that Mom did have a good point. I realized that I was closing a few doors. At the time, "teamwork" was the newest buzzword floating through companies and corporations. Teamwork called for *conformity*. The concept was beautiful on paper, but the reality was that there was no place for free-thinkers, and independence was considered unacceptable non-conformance. I was a philosophical, out-of-the-box thinker, the type many employers claimed to want but didn't know how to handle when it counted.

After my first semester at the community college, the time came for my first co-op job placement. I was invited to three or four interviews but I was unsuccessful in landing any of the jobs. Many of the employers waited until the academic session was ending or over before they listed their student positions. Honestly, it was a little nerve-wracking, but the college had a co-op department so we students were applying for jobs that were specifically posted—we didn't have to develop networking skills and/or find jobs on our own. Finally, I was invited to an interview at a steel foundry in a tiny little town in Vermont. It was about a ten-hour drive northeast from my home in Pittsburgh. The nearest major city was Montreal, also about two hours away.

  Before I even agreed to the interview there was a lot of thought and discussion that went into it. I wanted Jenn and Chucky to know that I wouldn't be able to come home regularly. It was winter and a four-month contract position, so I figured I would be able to come home once per month. My parents said that if I wanted they would bring Jenn and Chucky up to see me at any time. The position paid well and would be a terrific foundation upon which I could build my career. Everybody, including Jenn, agreed that I should take the position if I was offered it.

Dad was a big friendly guy. A tall man at six foot four, he towered over most. Especially over Mom—he was a good fourteen inches taller than her. Dad and Mom were the kind of people who many tried to emulate. They were the real thing, the type who would do almost anything for anybody, especially for family.

  Dad and I made the trip northeast to the foundry for an interview. We had a good time; Dad never complained when it came to helping me out. When I was a kid we used to go on a lot of adventures. This was just another addition to the list of good times.

  When we arrived at the town, the first thing we did was scope out the local cuisine.

McDonald's it was.

Next, we shopped around for potential living places. We placed our focus on hotels that were close to the foundry and could house me for four months. This place had to be reasonably priced and either have or would allow me to have a small hotplate for cooking. And last but not least, I needed a color television. The foundry was located in a small town so there wasn't a lot of choice, but as we worked our way down a short list we found one that would not only meet my needs, but they did the cleaning and looked after the sundries including linens, towels, and toilet paper. Each room also had a small bar fridge/freezer.

The rooms weren't huge but would completely suit my needs. I would be living alone for the first time in my life. This included paying for my own accommodations, which meant I wouldn't be able to save as much money for the following academic session as I usually did. The only other point of contention was that my room would not have a telephone, but the office phone was free to use. I decided that this was where I would stay if I was offered and took the position.

Next, it was time for Dad to have fun.

Dad always loved getting to know new people, and he was well known for stopping by people's homes, often unannounced, and finding himself sitting down for a chat over tea or coffee.

Before we had left for this trip he had looked up the address of the local church minister, and we dropped by his family's house to introduce ourselves. I think that aside from meeting his social needs, Dad was trying to establish a safe zone or a place for me to go should I find myself lonely. We were invited in for coffee, but it was getting late and I reminded Dad that we had a busy day coming up. The minister told me that I was welcome to stop by their home or the church anytime I liked. As a rule I did not attend church, so I knew that I would never see them again. Unless Dad found himself up that way again.

I think that Dad was a little disappointed that we couldn't visit longer, but he'd had a nice twenty-minute conversation. That was good enough for him.

We went to a motel that he had booked before we left. We watched a movie and then went to sleep. I needed my rest for the interview, which was scheduled for early the next morning.

We got up early and went out for breakfast. I didn't have money like I used to. I had been away from the mill for four months while I was studying and my reserve funds were used for tuition and books—and dope, smokes, and booze. Dad paid for the entire trip, McDonald's and all.

After the interview, when Dad asked I couldn't recall what I was asked. All I remembered was that it was Nestor Riaz who interviewed me, and that I kept asserting, "That is *exactly* what I want to do!" after each time he spoke.

The next day, just after Dad and I had returned home, Nestor called and I was offered the job. I was on the road to my first professional job within five days.

Nestor later told me he hired me because of my enthusiasm.

As soon as I accepted the position I called the hotel that we had stopped at. I packed up my dope, guitar, and amp, plus some clothing, hugged and kissed my family, and went off for the loneliest period of my life.

It was winter, so I correctly assumed that most people would be cozied up inside their houses, not out partying. There was a small group of townsfolk and tourists who liked to go snowmobiling in the frigid northern winter. But it wasn't really my idea of fun, so I never ventured out to meet them. Besides, the average winter temperature was eight degrees Fahrenheit.

The hotel was owned by two twin French Canadian brothers and a local townie who managed the place. On the rare occasions that I did go to the front office, they would always put on a bright smile and ask me how I was enjoying my new accommodations. They were all great. In addition to the aforementioned amenities they supplied soap and shampoo. I had my little hot plate, which I didn't use much after the first month in favor of eating McDonald's. By the second month, the fridge/freezer was no longer used to keep food but to house my beer and vodka.

For the first month, I had brought an ounce of hash with me to help overcome the very lonely and boring weekends and weeknights. My spare time was spent watching reruns of Star Trek: The Next Generation, getting high, and sleeping. Sometimes I played my guitar.

The hotel owners must have known that I was smoking dope and jerking off, because I didn't put too much effort into hiding my hash pipe or my porn mags. Plus, I went through a lot of bath tissue. I got paranoid a few times because my room was right next to the main office. I feared that they were going to call the police on me for smoking dope and I was going to go to jail.

They never said a word to me.

The paranoia increased a little with time, but it was manageable; I was always able to talk myself down. However, because I was so isolated I realized that I was slowly falling into a depression.

On the bright side, I loved my job. It was my first professional writing position.

My primary job function was to write the company's quality-assurance manuals. The intent of these manuals was to lay out the actions and reactions that the company would take to keep defective products from being sent to the customer. The manuals that I wrote were part of an international system, so that all quality concerns were addressed in a similar manner worldwide.

My supervisor Nestor Riaz was awesome; he was quite possibly the best professional supervisor I had in my entire career. Everyone at the company was great. Here I was, a twenty-two-year-old kid telling department managers, right up to the chief executive officer—the CEO—how they had to do their jobs to satisfy the quality requirements. And they agreed to it!

One week every month I would work my forty hours in four ten-hour days so that I could have a long weekend with Jennifer, Chucky, and my family.

The first weekend visit home was a slight disappointment. I foolishly waited until Friday morning before leaving for home and I ended up getting caught in rush-hour traffic. On top of that, one of the major highways was temporarily closed due to a blizzard. I ended up on the road for over fourteen hours. Jenn and all my friends had gotten together to party upon my arrival. Jenn had even left Chucky with her mother for the night.

I was so exhausted from the long drive that I couldn't stay awake for the festivities, and I fell asleep early in the evening. I didn't even get a chance to make love to Jenn until the next day.

I was happily awakened with my penis inside Jenn's mouth the next morning. We screwed for at least two hours, until Julie brought Chucky home. The rest of the day was rather uneventful. We went to the mall, and later that afternoon we had a quick dinner and visit with my parents. I bought my required ounce of dope from Mike Jagger for the coming month, and before I knew it, it was Sunday morning and I was back on the road heading up north again.

The second visit home didn't resemble the first. I left on the Thursday evening after work, so I missed the rush-hour traffic. Still, I didn't arrive home until well after midnight. Jennifer seemed a little bit distant, and most of my friends had made other plans. Jenn didn't seem as pleased to see me as she was the first visit, nor did she want to make love. This really upset me, because thinking of her near-flawless nude body writhing in sync with mine was one of the things that had kept me going over the past four weeks. Nonetheless, I was excited to see her and Chucky—I figured she was just busy with school and keeping house.

My intuition was telling me that things were changing between Jenn and me, but I couldn't put my finger on anything. Without putting much thought into it, I ever so slightly sensed that Jenn wasn't being monogamous. I dismissed my confusing inner thoughts, once again packed up my requisite dope and other sundries, and went back up north.

Just after my second visit home, I was about halfway into my contract and growing anxious and homesick. I still loved my job, but when I wasn't working all I was doing was getting high, watching television, and masturbating. I wasn't making any real friends at work. We were all very friendly as acquaintances, but I think that I was subconsciously avoiding establishing friendships. Instead I was slowly retreating into myself. I was lonely and bored.

I was becoming deeply depressed.

I had told my parents that there was no need for them to come up and visit, which was exactly the opposite of what I needed. I did call home at least once a week, but the only phone was in the hotel's front office and the owners or their manager was always there, so I had no opportunity to get into any private or personal conversations.

It also occurred to me that Jenn and my parents had stopped calling every week as they had said they would.

Out of sight, out of mind.

A dark cloud was forming over me.

On my third, and last, visit home, I arrived around midnight on the Thursday night. Upon arrival I knew that Jenn had been cheating on me. It's true, you just kind of know. For some reason I believed that Mike Jagger had been nailing her. I got myself so worked up that I finally accused him. Naturally he denied it. For some reason I believed him.

Still, I couldn't overcome that strong disturbing sense of her infidelity.

Mike remained stoic. I think it hurt him a bit that I would think that he would betray me. We all partied our asses off that night.

The next day I woke up around noon. Mike was gone and Jenn was making grilled cheese and tomato soup for Chucky. I asked her if I could have some, but in a snide tone she told me to make my own.

This was new.

I was a little put off, but it wasn't worth starting something about.

I called Mike Jagger to score my ounce of dope for the upcoming month. This time he wanted me to visit with his dad before I left. His dad ended up smoking over a gram of my hash. I was getting *really* pissed off—he didn't even offer a hit to Mike or me. I recognized it as a control/superiority play: he was daring me to call him out. But I recognized that he wasn't the kind of man to piss off. When we left, Mike asked me why I was looking so peeved and I told him. He said nothing; he wanted so badly to be acknowledged and respected by his dad.

I returned up north for my last month and finished my co-op term.

The Manipulative Negotiator
May through November 1993

I was back home for good and it was time to return to school for my next semester of academics. After that first co-op semester ended all my friends had seemingly moved on. It was as if I had been frozen in time for the past four months. I had been smoking a lot of dope for a long time. Considering that, plus having been stuck alone living in that tiny motel room for four months, affected me in some indescribable way.

I knew that I had changed.

I was moody. I was moderately paranoid about everyone and everything. I felt that my work term had been a punishment. I felt like a victim of myself.

Jennifer had left out her journal one night, and so, like the sneaky little so and so I was, I peeked. All that it said was, "I don't know what it is, but [he] is different."

Upon my return, for reasons unknown to me at the time, Jennifer was less than keen to have me move back in with her and Chucky. Although I still spent weekends with her through the week I stayed with my parents. I had been making great money through most of our relationship, and now for the first time I was without. When I was working at the mill I had been paying for her cigarettes, booze, and dope all the time. Suddenly unable to even pay for my own, I looked to her to share her cigarettes et al.

She began to show her true colors. She wouldn't even give me a cigarette when I asked. I was forced to seek monetary help from my parents. Jenn was beginning to reveal a dark, manipulative side. She started to nitpick about the little things. She began using sex as a weapon. If I didn't do something she wanted, she would cut me off. When I wanted to make love to her, she was often uninterested. This sense of sexual indifference was furthered by her insistence that I go down on her every time I wanted to get laid. And she was getting harder to get off. I started to dislike eating her—it wasn't sexy or fun anymore. It used to be one of my favorite activities; now it was work.

She rarely gave me head anymore.

Her reasoning was that she had been sexually abused by one of her mother's many boyfriends when she was younger. I tried to be sympathetic, but when I considered her new account of what she had been through I couldn't make sense of it. She'd had no problem going down on me when *she* felt like it. Throughout our relationship I would often be delightfully awakened with my penis in her mouth. She even asked me to cum in her mouth a time or two. She told me that her abuser would cum in her mouth and slap her if she spat it out. She said she had been traumatized. She also said that she had never told anyone else, not even her mother. It was our secret.

She was on the birth control pill, so we had stopped using condoms early in our relationship. I never gave it a second thought, until I realized after I'd returned from my co-op job her story of Chucky's conception had also changed—now her story was that she *had* been on the birth control pill when she became pregnant.

To freak me out, every month she would tell me that she had missed her period and that she thought that she was pregnant. She had been back on the pill ever since Chucky had been born. I knew that the pill wasn't 100 percent effective, but the odds of her having two pregnancies while on it seemed to me to be low. Still, this would send me spiraling down into a mental vortex—how could I support a family and attend school and build a career? Miraculously her period would come almost as soon as I started to panic. I couldn't rationalize what reaction she was hoping to elicit from me with this new game.

I think that she did it just to be mean.

Of course, I *did* have the option of using condoms.

I was no expert, and certainly in no position to judge, but my gut was telling me that she was full of shit. She suddenly had an excuse for everything. Things just seemed a little too convenient to me. Suddenly she was suffering from arthritis and her joints ached. Suddenly she was too tired to make love even though she was getting over eight hours of sleep every night. Suddenly we couldn't hang out because she had a friend who was in a crisis. She knew that I couldn't call her out, because I couldn't prove that she was lying.

And then there were a few times when she would accuse me of infidelity. I would *never* cheat, even though I was sometimes tempted. I had done nothing that I was aware of to deserve this near-constant bombardment of bitchiness. I didn't know when to say yes or when to say no. I didn't know up from down. I couldn't tell from her belligerence how she wanted me to react.

My instinct was to bury myself under the fluffy pillows and blankets and pray that things would all change back to the way they used to be before I went away. But time changed nothing and my prayers went unheard. My friends and family later revealed that they saw I was struggling but knew that I would be more incensed than open to their attempts to intervene or help. So I just smoked my dope and drank my beer hoping they would numb me enough to deal with her abuse.

Jenn was becoming openly hostile.

She was trying to mimic her mother by being tough and shrewd. But she didn't have the chops to pull it off; she just came across as a selfish bitch. Still, she did manage to bully me into doing what she wanted. She managed to get into my head. She made me feel guilty, like I was the source of all our relationship issues.

I was blindly and willingly allowing her to rule my life, and not just sexually. I was too afraid of losing her to stand up for myself. I thought that being a family man meant putting up with the daily bullshit and pushing through it to be a good provider and to make a good life.

Her family and I had frequently clashed over a variety of moral values and issues. They had grown up in the roughest area of the city because Julie refused her adoptive parents' assistance. Julie and her girls knew poor. It was in their blood. But Julie was also excellent at putting on airs to fit in with the privileged, just as her adoptive parents had taught her.

Jenn's family knew how to lie and cheat others. How to be manipulative. How to play the system. A big issue for me was that they believed and insisted that the government owed Jenn a paycheck to raise Chucky. I believed that the government had provided her with numerous opportunities to get her life on track: they offered free parenting skills courses and free daycare so she could go to school and be reintegrated into the working world. They didn't owe her these opportunities, they were privileges set out for her to take advantage of. My mother wasn't paid to raise me and the government wasn't paying me to go to school.

At least that's how I saw it.

Jenn had somehow managed to gradually isolate me and drive all my friends away without my noticing. She would tell my friends that I was busy when they called. She would belittle me in front of them with snide comments. I was only allowed to hang out with *her* friends. She even tried to restrict my access to mutual friends, especially Mike Jagger.

Jenn and I had only been together for just over two years. It seemed that Chucky was the only true blessing still in my life. And it didn't take Jenn long to break down that relationship. She started demanding a diamond ring in exchange for the title of stepdad, which was a significant level lower than dad, as she had proclaimed when we had first got together.

One weekend Jenn was out of town with her mother and Chucky and I had a couple of old friends from the Bass over. I hadn't seen them since Jenn and I had started dating. We were just shooting the shit when my friend accidentally dropped his glass of water. It broke. We cleaned up the mess and figured it was no big deal—shit happens, right?

When Jenn got home, I told her about it and she freaked out. She yelled at me for over thirty minutes that it was one of the only things her beloved late grandfather had left her. I sensed that she didn't really care about the glass; she was simply using it for an excuse to make me feel bad about myself.

As always, I ignored my gut and continued as her personal doormat.

Jenn was hanging laundry in the backyard and yammering on about God knows what. As her tone began to increase by decibels, Chucky came running to me crying. I'd had it; I finally told her we were done. All I wanted to do was to scoop up that sweet little boy and take him with me. I had to really fight my emotions to avoid doing so, but I knew there would be no easy way out of that pile of shit. I told him I loved him and I left, with Jenn still blathering in the background.

I went back to my parents' house and called Mike Jagger. I was telling him about how bitchy Jenn had become. He agreed that he had witnessed it, and that I had done the right thing by leaving her. I was telling Mike how glad I was to be without her, except I'd miss Chucky. The breakup had happened so quickly it was almost a blur in my thoughts.

While I was on the phone with Mike, Jenn called. I let Mike go and asked her what she wanted. She said she had made a mistake in letting me leave her and she missed me—it had been just shy of two hours. I caved and told her it was cool; I had overreacted as well. I called Mike back and told him what was going down. He simply warned me to be careful.

Chucky was tickled pink to see me back.

I went to Jenn's and we fucked all night.

And yes, she gave me a BJ.

My semester at school went swimmingly. After our two-hour breakup, Jenn seemed to calm down and she was much more tolerable. We were becoming close again. As far as I was concerned, the breakup was a tiny blip on the lengthy tapestry of our relationship.

As my second co-op term was coming up that autumn, Nestor Riaz called me and offered me the same job I had held before. He informed me that my work from the previous term had passed the requisite international quality standards, with the occasional necessary correction. I wanted so badly to go, to escape my life which had seemed to crumble to dust after my first co-op; however, it was for that very reason I had to turn down the offer.

Jenn and my friends, and even my parents, had noted some severe changes in my personality. Being a very passive individual, I shouldered all the bullshit that Jenn was flinging. I never even thought about talking with a friend or family member; I believed it would make me look weak. It was unanimous that returning to the foundry in Vermont could do more harm than good. Mom believed that my concerns began in my late teens, but she later recalled that it was after my first co-op when my mental and emotional health issues began to visibly manifest.

I was convinced that no one else would love me except my parents. I was afraid to be pointed out as the guy who couldn't handle being in a relationship, or who couldn't manage a small family. I felt that I had to suffer to succeed. I had no one I trusted enough to talk about it, so I kept trying to please Jenn.

No pain, no gain, right?

It was late September and the economy was in a recession, so student jobs were harder to attain. I couldn't sit on my ass for four months and the mill had taken me off their callback list once I returned to school. I needed to work, so Mom talked with a friend who worked at the post office—they were hiring for the upcoming Christmas season.

I applied and was hired.

The day before I was to start working at the post office I was invited to a steel-forging plant right in Pittsburgh for a job interview.

My mom was still harping on me about cutting my hair to get a "real" job. I refused, but I had already missed out on one month of work due to the lack of available jobs. I was interviewed by the general manager and the human resources manager at the plant. I was so desperate to get this job that I promised I would cut off my hair if that would make any difference. Both interviewers laughed. I was offered the job, and I didn't have to cut my hair.

Because of the slowed economy the plant wasn't busy; in fact, the days dragged. My job was to check the orders to see if they could be filled and to update the product database when required. The woman with whom I worked was terrific. We spent most of the days discussing life, death, and the universe. I also read a lot of textbooks while I was working to fill the gaps between chat sessions.

Jennifer had once again started ramping up her obstinance and intolerability. She and Chucky had moved into a house with her mother and sister and her mother's new boyfriend Bill. She started telling me she didn't want me living with her. She didn't even want me spending my weekends getting wasted with her. She wanted me to go home to my parents. After a couple of weeks she relaxed on the weekend restriction. Even though I wasn't making money like I was a couple of years back at the steel mill, I was once again making enough to keep her supplied with smokes, booze, and dope.

By this time I had retreated into myself so deeply that I was irreversibly depressed, and anxious about every move I made near her. She would quibble about the smallest of things, and Chucky, who had just turned three years old, was very sensitive to it. Jenn would get angry for the silliest of things; for instance, if I told her that I loved her, or if I touched her ass affectionately, she would yell at me to stop. I knew she was cheating on me—again. I suspected it was with a guy, Dan O'Reilly, who worked with Bill. Dan was suddenly over at their place drinking every weekend.

One Friday night at her place, I had gone to bed early because I was tired from studying. I awoke the next morning to find a half-finished bottle of rye in her entertainment room. I asked her about it and she just sluffed it off by saying Dan had come up for a few drinks. She reassured me that they were just friends.

Red flags.

The next Friday I was at her place again. I had settled into bed, and I awakened around two o'clock to a crumpling noise. I knew

Dan was upstairs in her entertainment room. I pretended to be asleep. I realized that what I was hearing was Jenn tearing a condom from the roll. As much as I wanted to run upstairs and catch them in their carnal lie, I couldn't bring myself to do it. I didn't want to see it, so I just kept pretending I was asleep. I finally drifted off to sleep, despite my certainty that I was twenty feet away from Jenn and Dan fucking like the pigs they were.

The next day I confronted her, and she denied it.

I had become completely withdrawn. All I had was my dope and the word of a two-timing bitch. I had shut out everyone, both friends and family.

One day after work I went straight to Jenn's. When I entered, at about six o'clock, Jenn, Julie, and Dan were all sitting on the couch with beers in hand. I thought that Dan looked a little apprehensive, and Jenn a little too comfy sitting close beside him, but I ignored it.

I think I was glad to that she'd lied to me. It was easier than facing the truth.

The Kids Are Not All Right
Late November 1993

Jenn and I were sitting on her bed talking. It was refreshing: we weren't arguing, we were just talking. I knew that I was emotionally weak, and so I told her that if she was going to break up with me to do it right then. She swore that she wasn't ready to give me up. I told her to be honest, because I couldn't handle it if she broke her word down the road.

She swore she had remained true to me.

I didn't believe her, but for my own peace of mind I forgave her for any and all infidelities that she may have committed over the past two and a half years.

That night I had the best sex of my life.

Christmas and New Year's Eve were only a few weeks away. One day, I asked her what she wanted to do for New Year's. She told me that she was going with her mother and Bill to a dance. I told her that sounded like fun, and her eyes widened.

"I didn't get you a ticket," she responded. I was thrown off kilter. I didn't understand how she could make plans without me—I was practically her fiancé. I told her that I wanted to go, and I wanted to know why she didn't even mention it to me.

"You never want to go out anymore," she said.

She was right. Over the past year I had become very secluded, a veritable hermit. And I probably would have said no if she had asked. But it hurt that I wasn't even offered the opportunity to bow out. I figured it was okay—strange, but okay.

On the next Saturday night just after Jenn had reassured me that we were not going to break up, I had a good heart-to-heart talk with Julie over several beers. We hadn't had a good open and honest talk like we had when we first met in a long while. We were both pretty buzzed.

Suddenly, the conversation turned. Julie took a sip of her beer, pulled out and lit a cigarette, and leaned back in her chair. She allowed a puff of smoke to curl up from her mouth to her nostrils.

"You and my daughter are never going to get married," she said bluntly.

"You are wrong," I responded flatly. "Once we're done school and working next year—"

Julie cut me off. "You and my daughter are *never* going to get married." Again, she took a sip of her beer and a took a drag from her cigarette. "I know my daughter. You are not the one."

I pulled out my cigarettes and lit one up. I moved in closer to Julie and studied her features. She was dead serious.

"You don't understand . . ." I tried, but no matter what I said she refuted me.

"I know my daughter. I know her better than you think you do. You are not the one," she emphatically reiterated.

I believed that Jenn and I were destined to be together forever, and no one, not even her mother, was going to convince me otherwise. I didn't pry for any further details regarding Julie's insight, as my mind was spinning.

Julie was the kind of mother who would stand up for her kids or family no matter what; it didn't matter if they were right or wrong. Guilty or innocent, she always had their back. She'd even defended me on occasion. I didn't have the balls to ask Julie if Jenn had stepped out on me, but I was completely aware that if Jenn had been cheating, Julie knew.

I was in complete denial. I couldn't accept that Jennifer and I were not meant to be, especially after Jenn had just given me her word.

After about an hour my stomach soured. I began to feel waves of gut-wrenching nausea and so I went to bed. Nothing of any interest happened for the rest of the weekend, except I had one of the worst hangovers of my life that Sunday.

On the Monday I went to work feeling content and surer of my relationship with Jenn than I had been in a long time. I felt that I had convinced Julie that Jenn and I were meant to be.

When I arrived home—my parents' home, as per Jenn's insistence—I called Jenn as I had every day.

"It's over," she said when she answered.

I was confused. "What's over?"

"We are."

I began pleading with her. "Can't we meet in person to discuss this?"

She held her ground. "No."

There was a long pause on both ends of the line.

"Does Dan have anything to do with this?" I finally asked.

"No," she lied. "I'm not going to be seeing anyone for a while."

And with that we were broken up. This time for good. I suspected that after Julie and I had talked she had told Jenn to end the relationship because she was being unfair to me.

Near the end of our breakup phone call, I asked Jenn if I could come over and get my things.

"Please give me some time. I couldn't bear to see you so soon. I would be too upsetting—I really do love and care about you. Can I have a while and get back to you?" she responded. She sounded melodramatic. I knew that she was just slinging her shit as usual.

That evening I felt ashamed of myself because I had lost Jenn.

I felt like a loser.

For the first time in a very long time, Mom, Dad, my sister, and I sat down as a family for a meal. My younger sister Ellyn had just entered the working world—she was a dermatological assistant. Unlike me, she could be a squawk box. That night of all nights she just wouldn't shut up. I begged her to leave me alone. I can't recall what she was going on about, but I do recall asking her to shut up with ever-increasing vehemence. She wouldn't stop.

I snapped. I stood up and went to where she was sitting. I picked up her plate of food and dumped it on her. She screamed.

"I said shut the fuck up!" I bellowed.

She shut up for about ten seconds and then started freaking out even more.

"What's your problem?" asked my dad.

"Jenn fucking dumped me tonight! Now are you fucking happy?" I stormed downstairs to my room and slammed the door. I didn't want to talk to anyone. I didn't want to be talked to by anyone. I didn't want to see or be seen by anyone.

I rarely lost control of my faculties, but I felt like a complete loser for having lost Jenn. Once I had cooled down I realized that I had let my devastation and sense of betrayal spill over onto my family. Being the type that didn't like discord or loose ends, I returned to apologize an hour later.

My parents and I talked for hours that night. They tried to reassure me that I was not the first person to be dumped and that I wouldn't be the last. In fact, they told me I may go through the pain of betrayal and having a broken heart several times in my life, and that it never got easier.

The next day at work I was still in shock. How could Jenn, the love of my life, have done this to me? The lady I worked with was a great listener. She reminded me a lot of my own mother. As it turned out, her son had gone through a tough breakup the week before. I didn't know if she was just trying to be sympathetic or telling the truth, but I found it very comforting.

That night when I got home from work, I called Jenn. I was scared shitless over what she was going to say. I had decided that I wasn't going to beg or try to change her mind. I asked her if I could come over to collect a few of my school supplies. She said she would prefer that I didn't, but after some emotional arm-twisting she agreed to it.

I went to her house and walked in as usual. I remember wondering if I had to knock now. No one else was home. There was a small plastic garbage bag containing some of my schoolwork sitting at the front door. Jenn was in the kitchen but came out when I called for her. We sat down. For the first time in a long while she looked happy. I asked her if I could go upstairs to collect a few things. She told me she was on the way out and that there wasn't enough time. I began to feel bitter.

She started asking me if she could keep some of my things. I was still in love with her and she was being so nice and sincere, so I agreed. As for the rest of my stuff, she asked for a couple of weeks before I came to pick it up. I stupidly agreed. I even let her keep my beloved first typewriter.

She said, "All I want for you is someone that makes you happy."

"*You* make me happy," I insisted.

She kept shaking her head in disagreement. "Think about it. You've been miserable for months now."

I had no firm ground to stand upon. Even though I disagreed with her I realized that we couldn't be together if I was the only one willing to participate in the relationship.

Her response to my next request left me in a state of disbelief.

"Can I still come to visit Chucky?"

"No," she said flatly. "I would prefer it if you didn't see him anymore."

I felt as if I had been punched in the throat a dozen times.

"I was forced to deal with multiple stepdads as a child, every time Mom had a new boyfriend. It really messed with my head. I don't want Chucky to go through that," she went on.

I knew that she was full of shit. As I'd learned over the past years, she was an ace at suddenly making up convenient stories of disturbing events that she supposedly had experienced. Because these were sensitive issues, I felt it inappropriate to call her out on her bullshit. She had learned how to play my heartstrings; of course the absolute last thing I wanted was for Chucky to have to suffer.

But it was so close to Christmas, and Chucky was integrated into every facet of my life. My family had been looking forward to seeing Chucky's face when he opened all his gifts. Jenn halfheartedly apologized, saying she felt it would be inappropriate.

I asked around and investigated what my rights with respect to Chucky were. I even consulted my parents' attorney, Truman Kush. I was told that because I had no biological relation and Jennifer and I were not married, and had never officially or legally lived together, I had no rights whatsoever. It was hard on my entire family. I suffered deeply, not just for losing Jenn but more so for losing Chucky.

On the Friday night after the breakup I went down to Mike Jagger's place. Mike also considered himself to be a good friend of Jenn's. He kept insisting to me that the breakup was in no way my fault, and I had done nothing wrong. I was depressed and loaded—a bad combination. I may even have been crying a little. Maybe a lot. Mike even started to get angry with me; he was very insistent that I had done absolutely nothing wrong.

At the time I couldn't understand his anger.

I didn't understand why Mike was so persistent about my innocence until after a few months had passed, when he confirmed my suspicions that Jenn had been cheating on me while I had been up north the previous year.

Apparently she had gone so far as to have bragged about it to him. She had brought home a strange man she had met at a bar, just for a one-night stand. He told me that she had done this a few times. Mike claimed to have expressed his lack of approval to her. Mike had always held me up on a bit of a pedestal because I had what it took to live a clean and successful life. He told me that she was downright wicked to have done that to me.

I asked him why he hadn't told me earlier. I wanted to know why he was protecting her. He claimed that it was me he was protecting. He believed my knowing would have made it harder for me to heal and move on. I wasn't sure if he made the right call, because I had already questioned her integrity and commitment. Sometimes I thought that if I'd known for sure that she had cheated I could have had closure earlier on. At the same time, Mike was correct: I would have despised her for lying to me, because now that I did know, I *did* despise her.

Most of my friends from what seemed a lifetime ago, even my immediate family, came out after our breakup and said that they didn't really like Jenn, and more so they didn't like to see the way she treated me. I remember when Jenn and I had just started seeing each other, one waitress friend at the Black Bass asked me in a somewhat derogatory tone, "Why are you going out with that girl?" A lot of the Bass crowd who were my friends claimed that they were able to see through Jenn's facade. When I had left the Bass to work at the steel mill and be with Jenn and Chucky, I had abandoned an entire group of friends.

I asked a few of them why they didn't say anything. My question was answered with a resounding "would you have listened?"

And the truth was no, I would not have.

Unfortunately, the more I heard about how poorly she treated me, the more it only made me feel like a greater sucker. But everyone loved Chucky; he was such a great kid. I think that I missed him more than I missed her. I felt a speechless pride when I was commended for my positive influence on his young life.

Regardless of how hard I tried to find myself a way back in with my old friends, the ones from the Black Bass, it was too late. I went to a few parties with some of them. I met a few women. But nothing panned out. I became—remained—depressed and dejected.

I returned to school for my next academic semester. Despite my depression I still excelled at my schoolwork. I think that being with my college buddies and working on my schooling was a good distraction.

Before I knew it, the semester was coming to an end and there was a new dawn on the horizon. A new page was being turned in my life.

I was about to get my first real taste of the corporate world.

Part II

I May Be Dumb, But I'm Not Stupid

Chapter 3

Welcome to the Rat Race

Watch This Video
Monday, May 2, 1994–Friday, May 6, 1994

After another successful term of studies at the college, it was time for my third work term.

Kyle Kerns was one of two gentlemen who interviewed and hired me to be his technical assistant at W.V.H. Steel, a steel-forging plant located roughly between Pittsburgh and Penn State University. This was where I was to spend the rest of my career in the engineering field. Kyle was also new to the company; he had only been hired three or four months before hiring me.

On my first day, Kyle gave me a quick tour through the plant and introduced me to a few key players with whom I would be interacting, including his brother Dave, one of four shift leaders.

Next, he sat me down in his office and planted a huge safety manual in front of me.

"Read this," he said.

It was straightforward. I had worked in manufacturing facilities, so I wasn't as green as a lot of college or university kids my age were.

After lunch, Kyle took me to a small room just off the front office where one of the human resources employees was chatting with three additional new hires. She invited me to have a seat, and within minutes she proceeded to put a videotape into a TV/VCR. What we watched was a twenty-minute presentation given by the current owner/CEO.

By the end of the video I was hooked.

W.V.H. Steel was a small family-owned steel-forging plant located in Erie, Pennsylvania, just about two hours north of Pittsburgh. The company was named after its first proprietor, Wallace Van Horne. Its doors opened in 1910 and the plant quickly became one of the city's well-known manufacturing employers, especially for their contribution during the Great War.

Wilson Van Horne, the grandson of Wallace, was born in 1935. He had been groomed since birth to run the family business. He attended Penn State and graduated at the top of his class with his Bachelor of Science degree in mechanical engineering in 1958. At an incredibly young age, he inherited the business from his father in 1960, the same year as his one and only son, Richard Wallace Van Horne, was born. Like Wilson, Richard was intended to one day inherit the company.

Wilson was a very astute engineer and businessman. He was known for his totalitarianism approach to running the company. He surrounded himself with yes men to boost his ego. With Wilson's tenacity and foresight, the business began to grow from a family-owned operation to a highly regarded mid-sized manufacturer.

It was summer 1985. Wilson was at a business convention, where he sat in on a presentation given by an enthusiastic middle-aged man named Kent Oswald. Kent was a motivational speaker and corporate advisor for small to mid-sized manufacturing businesses such as Wilson's. Kent was promoting an exciting new business philosophy for effectively running an efficient and profitable manufacturing operation.

This new concept was "teamwork."

It was the latest trend that companies were just starting to embrace. It was becoming so popular that by the late '80s/early '90s most post-secondary educational institutes began to include it in their curriculums.

The key to a successful team meant that open communication and trust between team members was implicit. This required the inclusion of a diverse group of members with varying skills and capabilities to ensure as many details as possible were covered. The teams had to be adaptable and flexible to changes, and an atmosphere of confidence and creative freedom to foster the best in each member was needed.

Wilson and Kent developed a profound friendship. Kent was persistent but not overbearing. Ultimately, through numerous passionate conversations and examples, Kent was able to usher Wilson to a new level of understanding, a new paradigm of running his company. Kent showed Wilson that the sum of the whole outweighs the sum of the parts, and by listening to others and considering their opinions the best decisions could be made.

Wilson realized that he would have to surround himself with a management group that comprised dedicated, open-minded thinkers right from the top level down, a group that would be a team and lead by example. The hardest part for Wilson was that he would have to trust his management team and accept their decisions and ideas.

This did not just happen overnight.

Kent joined Wilson's senior management group as a strategic advisor. He personally coached and worked with them to get them to function as a team. It took a few years for Wilson to reach the point that he could let loose the reins and trust his senior management team implicitly. As Kent had expressed to him, Wilson eventually realized that given the opportunity, his management team would apply their various skills, not their ability to nod in agreement with his every word. Of course, Wilson reserved veto power over any decisions that were made. He was a businessman, not a socialist.

Wilson and his team established a new incentive program that was based upon concepts above and beyond manufacturing output and efficiency. There was now a human element included. His goal was that the teams would work together and cooperate with one another to improve the safety, improvement, output, and efficiency of the plants.

Teamwork.

In early 1992, W.V.H. Steel reached a critical junction: the company was either going to expand or fold. An opportunity to manufacture a new product in a reasonably untapped niche came to be. Wilson and his senior management team chose to take the risk and expand. They bought an old defunct forging plant in a small city east of Pittsburgh, about three hours southeast of the original plant in Erie and one hour west of Penn State. Wilson invested almost all his existing capital and incorporated the company to fund his endeavor. The new plant started to produce by late 1993.

It was at this new plant that I was hired to work for Kyle. The commute was about an hour from my house to the plant but the traffic was generally good, and I always hit the drive-thru for coffee and a muffin and enjoyed the drive with my music cranked.

I wanted to work in an environment in which I was inspired and encouraged to be my best, be listened to, and where I could have the opportunity to make some real change in the working lives of others. But it was Wilson's blatant conviction to upholding these ideals that truly won me over. Right then and there I decided to become an active part of his company.

I was never afforded the opportunity to chat with Wilson for more than a minute or two, but I came to know his personal assistant, Cassie Andrews, quite well, and she told me that Wilson had a soft spot in his heart for me.

This new approach toward operating his business was a reality that many of Wilson's long-term employees from the original plant had difficulty with. Wilson had always been a dictator, now he was asking for input on decisions. This new business philosophy frightened many of them, as the traditional autocratic boundaries were suddenly blurred. Many of these employees became quite territorial and unwilling to listen to or share their knowledge with new and younger employees for fear of becoming obsolete.

Unfortunately, teamwork looked better on paper than in practice: it required a great deal of patience, dedication, and selflessness. I found that there were very few of us who truly comprehended the concept and how to effectively implement it.

I still believed in Wilson's vision. That was what I cared about. What bothered me was that most of my leaders didn't.

Not even his own son.

I was only twenty-three years old, and I watched Kyle like a hawk. He oozed confidence. Within no time I learned that he was a player; in a few short months he had already mastered the company politics and was well on his way to the next rung on the corporate ladder.

The only complaint I had with Kyle was that he would take credit for my work. Instead of giving me or whoever deserved it the credit, he would say things such as, "I did this."

I spoke with a few others in the department and they explained that this was just how Kyle was; it was nothing personal. And it wasn't; in fact, I genuinely liked him.

Just to satisfy my curiosity, I performed a little experiment and found that if I tried to take credit for even the tiniest hints of *his* work, he was quick to correct me. I always wondered if he'd made the connection.

I was destined to meet many different personalities during my tenure at the company.

One day, after getting my payroll, tax, and contract paperwork in order, I was returning to my workstation and there she was. She was leaning on a yellow rail that separated the plant from the main office, smoking a cigarette. She was a tiny woman: she stood at about five one and couldn't have weighed more than ninety pounds. Her hair was long and blond. She had the most amazing twinkle in her aqua-blue eyes. She acknowledged me instantly. I don't know what exactly it was about her, but a spark was lit within me.

Although she didn't introduce herself, I later learned that her name was Katharina McMann, but went by Kat. I knew instantly that one day I was going to make her my wife.

One Fine Day
Saturday, June 18, 1994

One Saturday morning, Chucky's dad Jake called and invited me to go to a record convention. We no longer harbored any resentment toward each other; Jake explained how Jenn overlapped her boyfriends to ensure she was never alone, never caring that she had just stepped on the back of the old boyfriend. She wouldn't let one man go until she was sure that the new one was going to work out. He explained that he was now reaching out to me because he had a complete understanding of what I had been going through.

As soon as he explained it, a lightbulb went off in my mind as I recognized her pattern of behavior. I wish I could have said that it made it easier to get over my ill feelings toward her, but at the very least I hadn't been put through the wringer just because of some quirk or fault that was specific to me.

I happily agreed to go with him, and when he picked me up he had a special surprise for me. He had brought Chucky.

We went to the record convention and had a blast. I bought some records, and then we took Chucky for ice cream. As Jake was dropping me off I turned to say goodbye to Chucky, only to find he was sobbing.

"What's wrong?" Jake and I asked.

"My mommy told me you don't come see me anymore because you stopped loving me." His almost-four-year-old voice trembled. His bottom lip was quivering as he cried. His little brown eyes looked straight into mine. I choked back tears. In fact, I think one may have escaped from the side of my eye. Jake and I passionately reassured him that was not true.

Every day I thought about that sweet little boy's face covered in tears. I wished Jenn could feel the pain she had created with her lies. The irony was that she specialized in childhood social work in college—she if anyone should have known better. To avoid messing with Chucky's head, she had messed it up anyways.

I just hoped that he would outgrow it.

Brian A. Plank

The Reality of the Relationship
Mid-July through Mid-August 1994

Several months after Jenn and I parted ways, I was at a local café when I ran into the young lady with whom I had shared my first kiss when I was fourteen. We ordered our coffees and caught up on what we'd each been up to since we were kids. I thought that she was beautiful as a teen, but now she was one of the most gorgeous young ladies I had ever met.

After a couple of mediocre dates, I was so greedy for her affection I convinced myself that she was my soulmate. One night we went out for dinner. She was wearing a long flowing orange dress. I was breathless as I stood in her doorway watching her walk down the corridor toward me.

She was a very passionate woman. I knew that she wanted me to make love to her. As per my luck, I'd had diarrhea before we went out, and thought that I could put off making love to her to a later date when I felt better. After dinner, I stopped by my house to use the bathroom. Still feeling a bit queasy, I made a hugely regrettable decision: for reasons only God knows, I threw my supply of condoms into my dresser drawer. I had forgotten about how passionate she could be. Besides, I didn't want to get excited and shit her bed.

While we were engaged in foreplay, she never removed anything more than my shirt. She was stroking my penis through my jeans. I decided to up the ante and remove her dress. All she was wearing was a frilly pair of white panties.

Her pussy was so wet and smelled so good.

I gently touched it, and I heard her suck in her breath with a hiss and sigh with excitement. I licked her through her underwear. All I wanted to do was remove that thin layer of underpants and taste her.

But she never unzipped my jeans, so I stayed away from her pussy and concentrated on every other part of her body. We made out for a couple of hours.

My diarrhea had gone into remission, but by then it was too late.

I had the worst case of blue balls in human history.

A few nights later she abruptly told me that she thought that we would be best as just friends.

I was crushed. I never found out what she truly tasted like. I never learned how it felt to be inside of her. Not making love to her was one of my greatest life regrets.

After our short relationship ended, I struggled to figure out where I'd went wrong. I called Mike Jagger. I stated that regardless of being friended by her I was in love with her. I became convinced that I was destined to be single forever. First Jennifer, now her.

Putting his criminal upbringing aside, Mike was ingenious when it came to moral and ethical issues. We were sitting in his apartment downing beers while I was going on and on, and he plainly stated, "You're not in love with her. You're in love with the *idea* of being in love."

Right then and there I was over her.

Fucking brilliant.

The Sellout
Thursday, August 18, 1994

Mike Jagger and I met for coffee every day after work. It had only been two short years since I had worked as a laborer at SM-Steel where Mike's dad worked. Now I was working as a student in a professional environment at W.V.H. Steel, while Mike held a job as a dishwasher in a small restaurant in the local mall.

We would discuss the past day's events and the ridiculous and outrageous things that our coworkers did. After our daily fill of coffee and commiseration, we would go the local video-rental store and get movies. Usually around midnight I would go home, sit in my car and get high, and then go into my room where I was still living with my parents and do a little bit of writing before masturbating and going to sleep.

I remembered that during my first work term in Vermont I had watched a show on TV where Jason Newsted of Metallica had cut off his hair—I think I may have shed a sentimental tear or two. Slowly, I was seeing all of my heroes from the '80s cutting off their hair. Everyone was doing the unthinkable and getting crewcuts, and soon going so far as to shave their heads completely. It was the '80s in reverse. My last holdout, Mike Jagger, had recently cut off his long hair too. I was openly disappointed in him.

I was among the last holdouts of an era.

After three months into my work term, I was trimming my hair and my hand slipped, and I cut off a notable chunk of hair. I was still able to tie it back, but according to Mike it was still quite noticeable. As usual, we went out for coffee and movie rentals. Mike was laughing at my missing chunk of hair.

I remember him looking me seriously in the eyes and stating, "It's time."

I nodded.

I let Mike shave my head.

When Mom saw it she squealed with delight and complimented Mike.

The next day I showed up at work and the first thing I did was head straight to Kat's cubicle. I had done some work with her, and we'd had a few nice little chats during smoke breaks. There was chemistry, as I had noted upon our first meeting, but nothing suggestive of a relationship had come up.

I was standing before her smiling nervously. I took off my hardhat.

She turned toward me and her jaw dropped.

"Oh my GOD! What did you do?" she asked.

I could feel my face flush. I handed her a file and nervously walked away. It was a long while before I admitted to her that she was the very first person outside of my family to see my new look.

When I went out into the plant I was greeted with cheers and jeers, but most of all shock. Some of the guys later told me that they hadn't even recognized me at first. I was teased for being a sellout.

One of the upper-level managers stopped by, and I asked him if my long hair had ever bothered him. I knew that I couldn't ask him that when I had long hair because it could lead to a case of discrimination.

He admitted that it *had* bothered him. He commiserated and said he'd had long hair when he was my age, and that he knew how it felt to have to "sell out."

I hated it when Mom was right.

First Impressions
September through December 1994

Toward the end of my co-op term, Kyle told me that he was looking to hire someone for a new permanent position, a process engineer, in his department. He said if I wanted the job it was mine. I thought long and hard. Ultimately, I reasoned that if I took the job I would have a high school diploma with a smattering of post-secondary education at best. I decided that the best play for my career was to return to school to finish my final semester and graduate from college. At the very least I would have some credentials. Kyle merely smiled and went into his office.

A couple of weeks later, Kyle had a stream of young engineers parading through our workspace as he was interviewing them. I witnessed a blur of suits passing by me, but I noticed one in particular. He seemed quite likable. He was a big lumbering guy wearing a black blazer and slacks with a blue turtleneck sweater and polished black shoes. He said hello to me and had a firm but not overbearing handshake, something that I respected, as if it defined a man's level of confidence in himself and his respect for me.

His name was Sidney Stanford, and Kyle hired him.

As my work term was ending, I had a brief discussion with Kyle about working weekends to keep my foot in the door. I had hoped for an office position, but instead he immediately called the shift leader who was on duty. I was hired to work on the floor for two twelve-hour dayshifts every other weekend.

I returned to school and worked my weekends at the factory.

I was chummy with most of the guys in Kyle's department, and when I had a chance during my weekend shifts I would visit with them. They all claimed that Sidney Stanford was an asshole, in addition to many other descriptive terms of endearment. Not one individual claimed that he was a reasonable or even tolerable person.

Chapter 4

Your Time Is Going to Come

Precedence
Monday, December 19, 1994

At the end of our last college class, our professor, Dr. Dali El-Lim, gave a little speech about the future and the diverse opportunities that could open to us as college graduates. Toward the end of his speech, he singled me out.

"You—you should go to a four-year school. You could do it."

A chill ran down my spine.

I knew that Dr. El-Lim had a sturdy network within the steel-forging sector; he had started his career almost forty years earlier working at the very plant I was currently working in. Although the plant back then had a different owner, the basic manufacturing concepts were still applied.

Dr. El-Lim had taken an interest in me from day one. I had no idea just how deeply his fingers were immersed into the academic and corporate worlds. I later learned that he had even used his influence to spread my name and endorse me to the highbrow players in the steel-forging industry as early on as my second work term. I later learned that his influence was so deep that Wilson Van Horne himself had specifically requested that Kyle Kerns interview me.

I was just a kid in my early to mid-twenties, so I was pretty clueless as to how these players operated and just what it meant to be on their radar. I'd heard of the importance of networking—which was also a new up-and-coming concept—but I was starting to have more serious bouts of social anxiety, such that I stopped going to conventions and tradeshows.

I just somehow knew that I was meant to do something of significance, something that would really help people. I had known this for as long as I could remember, but I didn't know how a young college boy could pull anything meaningful off, especially at a steel plant. So I let those feelings fade away. But in the back of my mind I kept that seedling of a thought ready for when the time came.

Educationism
Wednesday, December 21, 1994

I had kept in minimal contact with Kyle Kerns while I worked in the plant on my alternating weekends. Unbeknownst to me, Dr. El-Lim's influence was once again unveiled almost instantaneously. The very day after my last college exam before Christmas, an enthused Kyle called me at home and offered me a job as a laborer in his department. I was quite surprised and excited, but in the back of my mind I felt like I was meant for better things. I know that sounds arrogant, but I wanted to maximize my exposure to the teams so that I could have a greater impact.

I quickly learned that almost everyone with a four-year degree or higher looked down on the rest of us. Plant management opted to promote workers from the floor into technical and leadership positions. Degrees and diplomas were not permitted to be displayed, even though they were considered when it came to wages and levels of responsibilities. It was a part of the team concept: each member had their place, but having a piece of paper did not imply having more influence or power.

Unfortunately, most of the university-educated employees viewed themselves as much more capable than the college graduates. Not without exception, technologists like me were somewhat recognized, but our knowledge was equated with hands-on work experience and the academic portion overlooked. Plant management put an emphasis on work experience. University graduates had no idea what college graduates were capable of. At the time, it was a common opinion that community college graduates were not as smart.

When I first started working for Kyle, I asked several of the plant techs that I'd been introduced to where they went to school, and they looked at me strangely and told me the name of their high school. This surprised me, because from my experience junior engineers and technologists started at their level.

I worked with several older individuals who had been working at the plant for over twenty years. They were regarded as the experts of the plant. These veterans knew the inner workings and details of everything that occurred in the plant at a hands-on level. Often, they openly expressed a clear contempt for the new generation of engineers and technologists.

I was a university-capable technical thinker with a little bit of university education, "only" a three-year college diploma, and "only" three or four years of manufacturing experience, so my thoughts and opinions were not readily listened to, regardless of the potential depth of understanding that I had.

I had to admit, I was only twenty-four years old and had a lifetime of learning ahead of me.

Anyways, due to union precedence, even though Kyle was the departmental leader he was told by human resources that he couldn't just hire me into his department as a laborer. I would have to start at an entry-level union position like everyone else. With that said, Kyle hired me back into his department in the student position again. This was a temporary solution, but it gave Kyle another four months to figure something out.

We Are in Need of an Intervention
January 1995

The atmosphere throughout the department—and the entire plant—had changed significantly since I had started there only eight months previously. An "us against them" attitude was blooming between the union and management.

I believed that with my college education complete, all I would have to do was continue learning and gaining technical experience. I had never been directly exposed to corporate politics before. I only knew what I had witnessed of Kyle. I had no interest in getting involved in that end of the business, I just wanted to do my job.

The moment that I was formally exposed to Sidney Stanford was the very moment that I was formally exposed to politics. Sid *was* an Asshole with a capital A. Even Kyle joked that a part of his job was cleaning up after Sid's messes.

From midway of day one I realized that I had never met a more selfish person in my life. Sid's arrogance and know-it-all attitude were baseless—he had no experience. This was not the same man whose hand I had shaken four months earlier. He was cocky and arrogant but he couldn't back it up.

When I returned, Sid's first acts were meant to vet me out as a friend or foe. Except for our level of education, I was everything that he wasn't: I was good at my job, I got along well with almost everyone, I was generally respected. And I was smart.

I was a team player and he was a glory hound. Never the two shall meet.

He quickly identified me as a threat, so he went with foe.

The concept of working with me soured Sid's palate. He did not regard me as a peer. Rather, Sid likened himself as Kyle's equal because of his four-year engineering degree, even though Kyle held two undergrad degrees, was working on his MBA, and had over ten years of manufacturing experience.

Sid, like all other self-centered egomaniacs, would convincingly speak as if he sincerely gave a shit and was genuine when dealing with someone else's concerns or feelings, but he proved time and time again that he had no intentions of doing anything unless it was self-serving.

He always wore a cheesy grin when he talked to one of his underlings and he refused to share the workload with me, even though Kyle had recommended we "work things out." I started to grow a little fearful, even paranoid, and thought that perhaps Sid was trying to push me out of the department, or possibly even the company. If I had nothing to work on, why would they keep me?

The irony was that Sid wasn't doing anything but talking a big game.

Well, in truth he wasn't just talking, he was also busy putting up roadblocks to prevent success everywhere that he could; not just to me, but throughout the department. For instance, when I was about to launch a new process improvement that I'd been working on for several months, Sid suddenly put a stop to it with no good reason. Thousands of man hours and dollars were wasted, and Sid didn't even blink an eye.

Somehow Sid had managed to impress the plant management team. I had to admit, he *did* have a charismatic affect and a convincing tone. Just like he had shown me when we first met.

It was as if his job was to prevent me from doing mine.

And Kyle never intervened.

She Had a Nice Life
Friday, March 31, 1995

It was a wonky day from start to finish. It began with a crippling migraine and finished with a throbbing concussion.

I had been suffering from migraine headaches for over three years. They generally lasted anywhere from one to three hours. The term that my doctor used to diagnose them was "cluster headaches."

The headaches always started with a tight feeling in the back of my neck. Then for approximately fifteen minutes they would come in increasing waves of intensity until the entire left side of my head was throbbing. The left side of my face would droop and my left eye would become red and enflamed—it felt as though someone was poking a hot blade behind my eye. All I could do was smoke cigarettes and drink cold water, preferably in the dark, until the pain started to recede. After the headache was over, I would be physically drained with a need to sleep for an hour or so. Although medicated, sometimes I had as many as two or three of these headaches a day.

I tried to hide my headaches from my coworkers. Sid started to accuse me of being lazy, so I finally went to Kyle and human resources with a doctor's note so that it was a recognized disability.

On this day, after my headache had sufficiently subsided, I went to the kitchen and picked up the daily newspaper. I always looked in the obituaries, even though I never knew any of the people listed in them. It was an inside joke that I shared with my dad: we would check the OBs to make sure we weren't in them.

I turned the page and there it was: Julie Albright had passed away.

There were visitation hours set for that night. Despite our differences, I felt obliged to make an appearance at the funeral home to pay my respects. Julie and I hadn't always seen eye to eye, but there had always been a mutual respect, if not friendship, between us.

Because of my headache I was already late for work. Because it was registered as a disability, I could come in late and make up the time later. Back in those days I was putting in up to sixty-hour weeks anyways, so it wasn't ever an issue. Kyle generally let me set my own hours, and despite his own personal thoughts on the issue Sid learned not to push it either. Although I don't think that Sid could even count to forty, because he never put in a full week's worth of work through his entire time with the company.

Once at work, I called Jake to find out about what had happened to Julie. After our messy breakup, Jenn and I had no contact with each other. My only source of information was Jake, and I didn't speak with him often either. Jake had never mentioned the cancer. The only thing I knew for certain was that after we'd broken up, Dan O'Reilly and Jenn officially became a couple. They had been together for just over a year.

Apparently, she had been diagnosed with breast cancer a month into the new year, just after Jenn and I had split. She'd had a double mastectomy followed by intense chemo and radiation therapies. The treatment, although successful, took its toll on her.

Two months later she learned that she was no longer in remission and decided to go on untreated. Instead, she had downed an entire bottle of oxycodone and a six-pack of beers.

Jake told me that the then-four-year-old Chucky had been the one who had found her lying in bed, cold and dead. Chucky wasn't going to be at the visitation; according to Jake, the poor kid was quite distraught over the loss of his Nanna.

I arrived at the funeral home around 7:30 p.m.

Julie had been cremated, so only a silver urn surrounded with pictures of Julie and her family were at the front of the room, which was moderately cluttered with people who had come to pay their respects. I looked around and the only people I recognized were Julie's family, including Jenn, Shelli, and Dan plus a couple of their cousins from out of town.

As I headed toward Jenn and Shelli, Dan stepped in front of me.

"You're not welcome here," he said.

I studied his features and tried to read his body language. I recognized that he was trying to be the family protector. I wasn't afraid. I ignored him and pressed on toward the mourning family.

"I said, you're not welcome here," he emphasized. Again, I ignored him and moved forward. I could smell the reek of whiskey on his breath. As I brushed by him, I felt his hand on my shoulder and he swung me around. Before I knew what was going on, I felt his hands pushing on the back of my head as he brought his knee crushing into my forehead.

I'd always had a high tolerance for pain, but I saw only black and went down like a ton of bricks.

Dan dragged me outside into the cool spring air and went back in. Shelli came out and apologized on her family's behalf. She helped me up. We talked for a few minutes and then her composure changed.

"I would be strung up by the neck if I was heard saying this to you, but Rusty looks just like you," she whispered. Jake must not have mentioned to me that Jenn was pregnant, because if he did I would certainly have remembered.

My head was throbbing. I asked her what she was talking about. She explained that Jenn had a baby in August the previous year. She said the baby shared my features, particularly his nose and eyes and the same thatch of thick red hair.

He was born Russel Daniel O'Reilly on August 5, 1994.

When he was born, Jenn had insisted that Dan was the boy's father and declared so on the birth certificate. Dan had not objected and contended that he was in fact the father.

My head was reeling with pain. I knew I was concussed but I managed to get up on my feet. My legs were wobbly and weak. I even threw up a couple of times. I took a few paces back and forth and let Shelli's news sink in. I rested my hands on my knees and leaned over to catch my wind. My vision was blurred and I was nauseated—I could tell that Dan had really done some damage to me. It felt as though he had possibly fractured my skull. At least there was no blood.

I asked Shelli to pass on my condolences to all of Julie's family and friends. Shelli returned to the visitation and I stumbled to my car, and although I probably shouldn't have I drove myself to the hospital.

They kept me overnight at the hospital. My skull was not fractured but the doctors said I had a severe concussion. I spoke with the police, but in the end I decided not to press charges against Dan.

Once at the hospital, I did the math: the last time Jenn and I had slept together was approximately nine months before Rusty had been born. At the same time, that was when she had started screwing Dan. So there *was* a chance it could have been Dan's son.

I was cogitating on Shelli's words. *The baby shared my features, particularly his nose and eyes and the same thatch of thick red hair . . .*

Could it be?

I had a son?

No One Is Home
Early April 1995

Except to pick up my belongings, I don't think that I had spoken more than a sentence or two to Jenn since our breakup. With all that had happened at the funeral home, I hadn't even had the opportunity to express my condolences to her. I had barely even seen her.

The first time I called her I was at work. She answered, but as soon as she heard my voice she hung up. I tried calling two more times before I decided to stop trying. I wasn't sure if she didn't want to talk because she was grieving for her mother's passing or if she wanted to avoid the Rusty issue.

I assumed a bit of both.

I knew that Dan would be at work and Shelli should be in school, but Jenn might be home alone. I left work early just to be sure. My thinking was that if Jenn was confronted face to face she would have no choice but to talk about our child.

When I arrived at her house there were no cars in the driveway. That was good—it meant that Dan was out. Jenn had never learned to drive, and Shelli was only sixteen and just starting to learn. I knocked at the door and saw a hand pull the door-window curtains to the side. Next, I saw Shelli's face peeking through the window of the door.

I heard the deadbolt click, and Shelli was standing in front of me.

"Is Jenn home?" I asked.

Shelli signaled me to give her a minute. She returned and came outside with a coat on and slippers on her feet. She pulled the door behind her until it was almost closed. She asked me for a cigarette.

"Is Jenn home?" I asked again as I pulled out a cigarette for each of us.

Shelli put her finger to her lips. "She's sleeping," she whispered. She lit the cigarette. I lit mine up as well.

"Can you wake her up?"

She shook her head. "No, but I can go get Rusty. Wait a minute."

Shelli and I had always gotten along great; we had a special bond and she was like a little sister to me. I knew that if Jenn knew that we were talking she would give Shelli shit, let alone if she knew that I was about to meet my son.

The door closed again. I watched as the curtains gently swayed in the breeze, and before they could settle the door was reopened and there was this beautiful little face beaming up at me from Shelli's arms. He was swaddled in a soft down-filled light-blue blanket. Just as I had been told, he was an infant version of me.

She handed him to me. I instantly fell in love. His tiny little hazel eyes blinked at me a few times until opening wide and meeting mine. I felt as though I were looking in a mirror. There was no question about it: Rusty was my son. I kissed him gently on the forehead and passed my child back to Shelli and left.

As soon as I got home, I sought out my parents' counsel. I hadn't mentioned Rusty to them earlier because of the hurt they had experienced with Chucky being pulled from their lives. Now that I had seen my son and was convinced that he was mine I told them about him.

They were thrilled at the idea of having a grandson.

I hopped on the phone with Truman Kush as quickly as I could. I had dealt with Truman before when I was investigating my visitation rights to Chucky after Jenn and I had split.

I explained my situation to the lawyer and he explained the basic process to me. It could take a few years.

Truman told me his retaining fees and said he would begin the following day. This was going to be costly. I wasn't making very good money but I decided that I could figure something out.

I knew that Jenn and Dan would fight to the bitter end before admitting the child was mine.

Corporate Politics 101 – An Introductory Course
Late April 1995

It was a few days before my second student contract was coming to an end, and once again the plan was that I take on an entry-level union job. Kyle let me know that he was working on a plan to keep me in the office, but to just go with the flow for now.

I was called by Kat McMann to come finalize the hiring details. As always, I was tickled pink for the opportunity to go see her, even if it was under professional circumstances. At that time she worked in HR and a part of her job was to guide new recruits through the hiring process. I couldn't help myself; since our initial meeting I'd had a bit of a crush on her, although I would never dare let her know.

At the same moment that she was giving me directions to the clinic where they would take the requisite blood and piss test, the plant manager, Milan Esteban, interrupted us by telling her to discontinue all hiring. My stomach lurched a little and a wave of anxiety overtook me. Kat gave me a look of surprise and sympathy and tried to speak up, but she was overpowered and silenced.

It was too freaky to be mere luck. The plant union leader happened to be standing there, and he pulled Milan aside and told him what he had just inadvertently done to me. That day there was an angel on my shoulder, or a devil—it all depends upon how you look at it.

The next thing I knew I was sitting in the Milan's office, and he said of course I had the job; I was the last hire into the union. He went on to tell me how much I would love working twelve-hour shifts, and all the other wonderful opportunities I would have ahead of me. He told me that in a year or two, when I was ready, I could approach Kyle about working in the office for him again. Milan was another typical engineer who seemed dismissive of my college education and experience.

I thought, *Fuck that.*

I hastened to see Kyle. I wasn't an engineer, but I knew what I had to offer and that attaining a community college diploma was not just an easy, mindless endeavor. I refused to be underemployed. To quote a former fellow worker's words, "I went to school so that I only had to wash my hands after I pissed, not before *and* after."

Kyle reacted quickly. He used his influence on the higher-ups and the union, and the very next morning they presented me with a new plan. They offered me a four-month contract position as the department trainer.

My new position was to write the job procedures and then train the workers in the department to perform the tasks required. This opened a whole new world to me. To train the workers, I first would have to learn and understand the process or function that I was teaching them. I gradually became an expert in almost all the department's operations.

One bonus was that I would not be working *for* Sid, I would be a part of the plant training department. Unfortunately, I would still have to work *with* him.

I'm not sure how or why, but I was beginning to feel a little inferior. The world was mine for the taking, yet I was becoming deathly afraid of being unemployed. From early on I had been programmed into believing that I was fortunate to be awarded the privilege to work for this amazing company—W.V.H. Steel—which just brimmed with enthusiasm and endless opportunities.

What I believed in and what kept me there was Wilson Van Horne's values and morals.

When signing this contract, I realized that it was not an equitable trade, although I did realize that I was the one who had insisted on a skill-based position rather than joining the union. Now my skills were being used, but the remuneration was significantly lacking. I was young and aiming to please. I foolishly believed in the good intentions of my leaders. At the time, I failed to consider the mounting legal costs for my custody case with Rusty.

For every action, there is an equal and opposite reaction.

I loved being the department trainer. I focused my work on the lab, in which I had the most experience from my schooling and work-term experiences. Plus, Sid had no idea how to run any of the lab equipment, so he didn't interfere too much. That is not to say that he didn't stick his nose into my business when he could. I trained all the department's workers how to run the lab.

It was a success.

The day my department-trainer contract ended I was finally hired as a permanent employee. By this time Sid had finally relinquished a part of his little Machiavellian empire and allowed me to oversee the lab, procedures, and data management for the department. My wage was minimally increased, despite my clear and precise logic that I should be earning more. My argument was simple: If I was teaching the union employees how to do their jobs, I should be making at least the same as them.

On the bright side, I was now entitled to benefits.

Kyle was too busy playing politics with upper management, and he knew based upon reliable intel that the HR leader, Liz Stone, could and would be a sneaky little serpent, capable of making his life miserable if she felt her domain was being encroached upon. So he kept his nose completely out of personal *and* personnel issues.

Something Wicked This Way Came
Late June 1995

Not a day went by that I didn't think about Chucky. I hadn't initiated contact with Jake because I wanted to respect Jennifer's wishes, regardless of how I felt. I liked to think that during my time with him I had been a strong role model and helped instill good moral values in him.

It had been nearly a year without having seen Chucky when Jake called and asked if I wanted to come over and visit with him. Jake's family was familiar with and sympathetic to the problems and issues I'd had with Jenn denying me access to the boy, and with Rusty.

Without a second thought, I responded, "Hell yeah!"

Chucky was four years old and about to graduate from junior kindergarten. Apparently, he still occasionally asked about me. It turned out that Jake's mother, Gwen, the "evil" grandmother who used to randomly stop by to inconvenience Jenn, was the one who had suggested that Chucky and I could get some closure by bringing us together to say a final goodbye. I was so grateful to her, and Jake's entire family. They could have been catty or just plain shut me out, but they wanted to see Chucky and me smile together one last time.

I played with Chucky for a couple of hours. He had grown so much.

We hugged. He was "too old" to kiss me.

That was the last time I ever saw him.

Along with the pain of being separated from Chucky always in the back of my mind, I kept reminiscing and dreaming about my son, Rusty.

How I wanted to be hugging his warm little body while he was swaddled in blankets. Watching him grow from an infant into a toddler and being there when he took his first steps. I dreamed of one day teaching him how to throw and catch a ball. How to drive a car. How to treat a woman. How to raise his own family someday. Just like my dad did for me.

Money was already getting tight, but I was doing my best to keep up with the lawyer's fees.

About a Girl
Early July 1995

One afternoon I was sitting in front of my computer, working away, when I received an e-mail from Kat McMann.

"How's it going?" popped up on my computer screen.

I quickly responded.

And simply put, that was how it all started.

We e-mailed each other back and forth for an entire week. We didn't do our jobs at all; we didn't do anything but chat online. We asked each other about our dreams and goals. We asked each other about our work environments—we learned a lot about some of those people with whom we worked. We shared some of our life philosophies. Our likes and dislikes.

Finally, near the end of the week, she asked me out for beer and pretzels. I had wanted to ask *her*, but I had been through sexual harassment training and I was deathly afraid of losing my job for flirting or asking one of the women out in case I was misreading the situation.

That Friday we had our first date. We were planning to go out for a coffee and a bite to eat; instead, we simply sat on the couch in her apartment and talked for something like four or five hours. It ended with a sweet little kiss and a promise to talk on the phone the next day.

It was the best date I had ever been on.

She never did say what had prompted her to e-mail me that one afternoon.

Mike Jagger and I were planning to attend a record convention that Sunday. All that I could talk about was Kat. I asked Mike if he minded me inviting her. He shrugged his shoulders and gave his consent. Kat showed up with a girlfriend to even out the playing field.

The date went horribly.

Kat and her friend were not record collectors, and they were clearly bored. On the other hand, I was in heaven with all that sweet vinyl surrounding me.

We decided to go for hamburgers after the convention. Kat and I both had butterflies in our stomachs, to the point that neither of us could eat. We were quickly falling in love, but it felt as though our connection was slipping through our hands. The entire day had been just plain awkward. We both thought that this potential relationship had just ended.

I knew what I wanted. I'd been through enough of the games that men and women play. So I called Kat that night and we both chuckled about the day's happenings.

We made plans to go for coffee after work the next day.

That was the start of an amazing roller coaster of a ride, a lifelong relationship.

The first time I met Kat's family, we had only been together for a few weeks. She had told me a great deal about her family. She had an older sister, Emma, who was married with three young kids. She also had an older brother, Gavin, who was also married with two young kids. Her mother was a sweet woman; she and her eight siblings had emigrated with their parents from Holland to America after the Second World War.

Kat's parents had separated when she was eighteen.

Her father was alive but had fallen down the path of being a bitter drunken recluse.

That day we attended a barbeque at Emma's house. I was wearing a sleeveless hoodie and hadn't thought about it until I met Gavin. I apologized for not covering up my tattoos. He just shrugged it off and told me not to worry about it.

They were great people.

Everyone almost immediately saw that Kat and I were soulmates, except for her stepfather, Len. The first words he ever spoke to me were: "Where do I know you from? I've worked in the jails—is that how I know you?"

He didn't even start with a hello.

Kat had cautioned me that Len was a jerk, so I just let his words drift. In his younger days he had used to grope at Kat and even come on to her. He would grab or smack her ass. When he had started living with her mother, Kat was eighteen years old. She was thirty now.

Back when he came into the picture, Len was a heavy drinker. Apparently, her mother liked to party too. One night while he was drunk, he came into Kat's room and tried to touch her and stuff his tongue down her throat. She fought him off and told her mother the next morning.

Len never drank again. It was never spoken about again. But the occasional slap and tickle and innuendo never really stopped until I came along. Kat had no tolerance for his behavior. She often expressed that she had lost a bit of respect for her mother for not kicking him out of their lives. Emma and Gavin rarely spoke of him, but the unspoken consensus was that he was an asshole.

Emma joked around with me as we were leaving. She winked at me and smiled as she told her kids to start calling me "Uncle."

She saw it. We were meant to be together.

Rusty's First Birthday
Saturday, August 5, 1995

I had only met him once before. My beautiful son, Rusty.

It was his first birthday. Jenn and Dan were having a big party for him. I never received an invitation, not that I was surprised. The only way that I had learned about the party was through Shelli.

I wanted answers.

I wanted to hear Jenn acknowledge that Rusty was my son. I wanted to know why she was keeping him from me. I wanted to know why she was denying me parental rights to my child.

I called her. Often. But she would rarely if ever answer or respond to my calls. When she did answer, her words were spat out so venomously that I could hear the crackle of her spit hitting the phone receiver. She would shout and scream obscenities at me. She went so far as to physically threaten me and my family if I didn't back off.

On occasion I would hear Dan O'Reilly in the background, egging her on.

I called my lawyer and he told me to keep a detailed log of dates and times when Jenn and I spoke, and when she would issue these threats of harm and violence.

Although we rarely spoke, when we did she was highly illogical and cruel. Sometimes I suspected she had been drinking. It didn't take long before I had a sizable log of her threats.

Chapter 5

Surprises Come in All Shapes and Sizes

The Shot Heard Around the World
Early Autumn 1995

Chucky's birthday was in late September. He was just turning five and starting kindergarten. I thought of him and Rusty every moment of every day. Rusty was already one year old; I had only held him once so many months ago. I firmly held that I should have been entitled to visitation to both children.

I had been screwed out of access to Chucky.

I had faith that Truman Kush would at the very least get me access to my own blood: Rusty. I was suing for joint custody. Truman told me we needed to focus on getting proof of relation and then visitation before seeking any form of guardianship.

As expected, Jenn and Dan were not cooperative.

Already the legal fees and court costs were starting to rack up, and I was beginning to wonder how long I would be able to afford to continue with this lawsuit. Truman had warned me that it could take a few years, and so far it had only been a few months.

Jenn and Dan had sought out legal counsel as well. Even with the two boys, they were able to afford the legal fees. Dan made great money working at a union job, and Jenn had finished college and was now working too. Dan's parents were retired but sitting on a lofty little nest egg and helping Jenn and Dan as well.

Their lawyer must have been quite good because he kept mine busy—at least that's what I reasoned based on his bills. I began to wonder if their legal strategy was to hold out until I could no longer afford my lawsuit.

If that was their plan, it was starting to work.

Within six months from this point, I had to drop my case due to lack of funds.

In late October, I started sniffing around the old university schoolbooks. I was sick and tired of being ignored because of my lack of credentials and experience. Experience would come with practice and time, but I could do something about my credentials—I decided that I was going to take some engineering courses starting in the new year. From my previous university experience, I simply hoped that I would avoid embarrassing myself by passing and exceeding the 60 percent grade average cutoff.

As I worked through the old texts, I realized that I could and did understand them, and I realized that I would succeed. I wasn't going to let anyone victimize me in the name of educationism ever again.

I discussed my plans and goals with Sid. He flat-out denied me his support, telling me that I didn't have what it took to succeed, and he needed me around all day to do my—meaning his—job. That didn't bode well with me at all.

The company had a continuing education policy, so I went over Sid's head to see Liz Stone. I was told that this policy wasn't intended for individuals to earn degrees or diplomas, it was intended for skill upgrades and short-term education. However, there were a few individuals working on their MBAs, including Kyle Kerns, and so we hashed out the details and I was approved to take two courses per semester, with the understanding that I would make up the time that I missed from work to attend class.

So far, Kyle had been the only one trying to keep Sid from tearing the department apart, and he wasn't doing a very good job at it. Kyle had his eyes set on brighter horizons. As expected, one day in the early autumn he finally made it up to the next rung on the ladder. Sid and I were simultaneously pulled up after him. Sid was now the department leader, and I was automatically moved up into Sid's process-engineering position.

Now I formally reported to Sid, which I was less than pleased about. The required aptitude for my new position was high but I knew that I could do it. About a week or two after Sid and I were getting settled into our new roles, I approached him about getting paid more for my new position. He said that I did in fact deserve a raise and that he would investigate it.

Over the next while, Sid occasionally updated me. He excused the delay by calling it an "us against them" political situation. He claimed that HR had no idea what we did or what kind of impact we were having on the company's bottom line. It was all red tape and political bullshit that he was dealing with just to get my salary looked at, let alone amended.

He also told me that he hadn't received a pay increase with his new appointment either.

I felt sympathetic to Sid's quandary. We both deserved equitable pay and neither of us had an advocate to speak on our behalf. I decided that I would be a voice for the both of us. I went to speak to Liz Stone, the serpentine HR leader.

Liz and I knew each other in passing, and she had always been pleasant with me. She was a very attractive woman in her late thirties/early forties.

By that time, Kat and I had been dating for a few months. She affirmed the gossip that Liz was a very dangerous lady. Kat had worked for Liz in HR and warned me about approaching her. She said that Liz had her pretty little fingers in every nook and cranny of the office and plant operations, and she would twist my concerns and comments if and when she saw fit.

Liz was rumored to have attained her position by inventing her credentials while sleeping with the right people. She claimed to have earned a four-year psychology degree and her certified human resources practitioner designation. Kat, unbeknownst to Liz, had access to her employee records, and she couldn't find anything confirming Liz's credentials. It seemed that Liz was just a smooth-talking player.

All the staff job descriptions were available on the company's internal computer network, so I printed a copy for my current role and Sid's former role. They were identical.

"Of course you should be getting paid for the work you do," Liz aped Sid, but with a touch more sympathetic grace. She used an I-really-care-and-want-to-help voice. I looked deeply into her eyes—they were big and brown. I was sucked right into believing that she would investigate and correct my issue.

I was trying to teach myself how to read people. What I was learning so far was that sometimes I could anticipate the feelings and responses of others by their body language and mannerisms. For instance, it didn't take me long to determine that Liz was damned good at being insincerely sincere. Her tell was she would clear her throat every time she was about to be disingenuous.

After a few days, Liz called me to meet in her office. She went on to tell me that my job description had been scrutinized by Sid and her and that my salary was exactly what it should be. I knew more or less what Sid had been making when he was in my role, and my pay was a lot less. This information was readily available on the company's intranet—specific earnings were not posted but pay ranges by job classification were. The main reasoning why I made less was because Sid had his engineering degree and I didn't. I understood that; I didn't completely agree because there was very little that Sid had done that I wasn't doing or was capable of doing, but I did understand.

My platform was that I was doing the same work as Sid had been doing, and that I should be compensated in some way for that. I still wasn't making much more than I had been as a student.

I also learned that Sid had done absolutely nothing for me. Without clearing her throat, Liz revealed to me that Sid had never approached her about adjusting my salary. The only activity started when she contacted him and they reviewed my job description a couple of days earlier, as I had requested.

She also informed me that Sid had crossed a lot of my listed duties off from the description. Mr. Stanford had royally fucked me up the ass while all along telling me he was helping. As if that wasn't enough of a kick in the balls, I learned that Sid had received a significant raise when he became department leader—his feathers were ruffled because he didn't earn as much as Kyle had. Sid was simply self-centered and had overestimated his skillset.

I wasn't sure why Liz had shared all of this with me. I liked to think she was letting me know that Sidney Stanford was insignificant in the big picture.

Later, I insisted to Sid that I would not do the listed tasks that had been struck from the list if I was not going to be satisfactorily remunerated. He sternly informed me that I was not irreplaceable. I was incensed enough to speak with Liz, but for the first time I saw the empty black within his eyes and I was truly afraid of him. I realized Sid's true power over me.

Despite Liz and me bonding, my argument for an increase in salary went unheard for quite a while. I was somewhat bewildered; these managers were behaving as if the money was coming out of their own pockets.

I wondered if this was a game that they were playing, or if it was a test of my loyalty.

Unlike many, I liked Liz Stone. Through our discussions, my intuition clicked in and I knew that she saw something different in me versus what she was used to seeing in others. Unlike almost everyone else, I believed that she truly recognized my potential and saw my sincerity in wanting to make the workplace a better place to be. I believed that she and I had made a deep, although unspoken, connection.

I believed that she saw I could be a force to be reckoned with, although I had yet to recognize it myself. Based upon all the rumors and hearsay—and more importantly my instinct—I concluded that she wanted to be on the winning team. She wanted to revel in the accolades and admiration with me when I did reach my peak and arose as a phoenix from the ashes. So she put me on a pedestal and whispered praises to me.

I believed that, like me, she simply yearned to be a part of something bigger and better than herself. And it was that desire that drove her to keep on top of everything. It was just a shame that she chose to manipulate others to satisfy her own goals.

She referred to me as a genius on several occasions. This suggested to me that somebody higher up was expressing appreciation for my work; she had to have heard it from somewhere. And I knew it wasn't coming from Sid or Milan.

Using the term *genius* to describe me was always a personal point of contention. For all my life my intelligence had been noticed and lauded by adults. I knew I was smart, perhaps even a genius, but using that word opened all kinds of doors—some good, some not so much.

Speaking of genius, some people refused to admit or recognize it and sought to make me out a fool. Being smart and being skilled are two different things. I remembered being at a friend's bachelor party a few years back, and he introduced me to some of his college friends as a genius. They automatically started drilling me on what computer-programming skills I had. I knew only a few. They knew a lot. I let them think that I wasn't so smart. What they failed to realize—and I felt it inappropriate to point out—was that I had the potential to learn those skills if I so chose.

Some people saw it as an opportunity to build up their own sense of self-worth by putting me down. I once attended a short series of doctoral lectures. I was able to comprehend the general concepts presented, and I told a friend who had a PhD. She told me that I was grossly overestimating my knowledge and understanding, and that she was quite offended by my stating that I understood. She said that the people who had presented the lecture material had been working on those topics for years, if not decades, and there was no way that a "lowly" undergraduate student like me could understand. In turn, I explained my interpretation of the concepts in detail to her. She simply nodded that I was correct. More to the point, I wondered what made her think that she could understand these concepts any better than me. I concluded that it was just because she had a PhD. She realized that I was as smart or even smarter than her, but she opted to put me down rather than accept that I could grasp higher-level concepts. The irony was not lost on me—she had not been doing research in these fields either—so I wondered what made her think that she would understand any easier or better than me.

Some people chose to ignore and/or exclude me from putting in my two bits on a subject. I knew what I knew. And I knew that with time I could learn that which was unfamiliar. I wanted to share my intelligence—I had a gift and I wanted to inspire and be inspired. By blocking me from giving input or the opportunity to think and speak about a topic, I would be unable to help down the road. Many thought that because I was a brainer, I believed that I was better than others. That was so untrue! All I ever wanted was the opportunity to help others, be it in technical, social, or emotional ways. By excluding me they got to take on all the praise and glory.

But I was never in it for the praise and glory.

I tried to always recognize my fellow humans' accomplishments. By shutting me out they were risking the achievement of an even better outcome.

Or not.

And then there were those who recognized and praised me for my God-given gifts. These people were from a spectrum of demographics. Ironically, that was the worst—it made me feel insecure and inadequate. I held myself to the highest of standards. I was deathly afraid of making a mistake, failing, or letting them down in any way. When I was in school, the teachers came to expect a certain caliber of performance from me.

My high school English teacher always built me up to the class about my writing skills. He would often read my prose to them.

Most of the other students were indifferent or fine with it, but some grew jealous and some even became angry with me, to the point they would tease and bully me.

At the same time, I couldn't help but like it and feel good when my successes were noted.

After getting no help from my peers or supervisors, I did a little bit of homework. Being the armchair psychologist that I was, after poring through numerous articles I concluded that Sid was a narcissist. He met all the criteria, behaviorally, mentally, and emotionally.

I learned that the basic characteristics of a narcissist included: a distorted sense of superiority, an overestimation of skills, never taking responsibility for or accepting or admitting that mistakes were made, and a complete absence of sympathy and empathy.

Next, I researched how to deal with narcissistic people. I found that there were no tried and proven recommendations. In fact, the only real advice was to not deal with them at all, if possible.

Anything I tried to accomplish was overruled as soon as Sid could assert his power. Even if a project was near completion and serious time and money had been invested, he would renege on his approval. And he didn't just do it to me.

Still, for some reason management kept him around.

Where I Belong
January–April 1996

As planned, that January I returned to university on a part-time basis.

I remember my first day back on the campus. I had just attended my first university lecture in about five years. Passing time before my next lecture, I was alone relaxing on a brick wall in a little alcove with a coffee and a cigarette. I took a deep drag from my cigarette and looked around dreamily. I felt an overwhelming sense of calmness and peace.

"This is where I belong," I whispered to myself.

I was twenty-five years old and in school blasting my way through my courses like I never could have believed. I had secretly set some pretty lofty goals for myself but never really expected to meet them. If you were getting grades in the 65 to 75 percent range in engineering you were doing well, and I was consistently getting marks above 90 percent.

I started to wonder if they had dumbed down the course material since I had attended a few years ago. But I started to talk with other students, and they were typically getting grades in the standard range.

After my first semester I was anxious to know exactly how well I had done, so I went to see the prof who had taught one of the courses I had taken. He showed me the course stats. One student had achieved a 98 percent final grade. I was just behind him with a 97 percent. This was a faculty-wide course, meaning that every student enrolled in Level 2 Engineering had taken it.

There were 400 to 500 students in the class.

The next closest grade was 78 percent.

He told me that in developing the exam he had never expected anyone to score over 80 percent. This other student and I had destroyed the curve.

That night I wept tears of joy.

I was accomplishing much more than those who had come before me. I felt unbeatable. I was an invincible force. I was finally starting to recognize the potential that others saw in me.

"I can do it," I repeated over and over as I let the tears fall from my eyes.

The Flight of Icarus
Winter 1996

Over the previous several years, W.V.H. Steel had thrived. For a few years senior management had been doing their due diligence and researching behind the scenes. They listened to their customers, monitored the modern manufacturing trends, and concluded that to continue prospering the company needed to broaden its global presence and diversify into new manufacturing/processing fields.

This meant expanding into Europe and China, which meant dealing with language barriers and differing approaches to problem solving. It also meant learning and mastering new technologies and processes.

It was a massive and bold endeavor.

The Think Tank Division—the TTD, as we called it—was to be created to hit these goals.

Based upon my experience, my personal feeling was that they were being obtuse and overly aggressive, and they were going to spread the corporation's resources too thin. More so, I didn't have faith that the right people were in place for such a grand expansion. There was too much politicking and the wrong people in the wrong positions to lead such projects.

But then, I wasn't a part of the senior management team.

Senior management announced their strategy to the employees. They also announced that there was going to be a shuffling of some people in the plant to improve productivity and efficiency.

Several managers were moved to different positions. Some were promoted to corporate, some were shifted to different departments.

The first step was replacing Milan Esteban with a new plant manager. Milan—a fully accredited professional engineer—was promoted to establish and lead the Think Tank Division from ground zero.

By the start of the new year, while Sid pissed around I was more or less running the department—in action, not on paper or in any official capacity. For over a year now, each time anything involving my department went awry in any way, Sid was suddenly on holidays and I was formally in charge. On a typical day, all Sid did was hide in his office and play with his computer, unless there was something going down that he believed would make him shine to his leaders.

I made no bones about my degree of dissatisfaction with Sid as a leader, even to Sid himself. There were those in power positions who saw the damage that Sid was doing to me and the department. I was not a member of the union, but I was informed that the union leader had unofficially approached Dave Kerns and raised their concerns about Sid's treatment of me. So finally, one morning, Dave asked me to Liz's office to discuss what they feared was Sid's constant harassment and the emotional and mental impact it was having on me.

I knew that a war was starting inside of my mind, but I didn't realize that it was becoming outwardly obvious.

At long last, here was my chance. At last I could possibly get Sid out of the department, or even the company.

Instead, I sang nothing but praise for him. That was how fucked up I was becoming.

Unfortunately, despite all the grief he caused me, Sid's antics intertwined with his mock-sympathetic tone. He still had me believing that deep down he wasn't such a bad guy.

Sid was screwing up every which way he could. As one of his last moves as plant manager, Milan finally caved under pressure from upper management and brought in Dave Kerns as our temporary department leader. This meant that Sid had essentially been demoted. Sid and I were now peers, although I know that wasn't the way Sid saw it.

Dave told me that he saw right through Sid and had since first meeting him. He assured me that others saw the same thing as I had and that senior management was aware of Sid's antics. Dave Kerns made no bones about it: they were trying to squeeze Sid from the department, if not the company.

For the first time in a long time I breathed with a sense of relief. I was not alone.

I believed that Sid knew his time was coming to an end.

Suddenly, we were pals. He began manipulating me. He would "confide" in me. He started bad-mouthing the new plant leadership at once. He tried to turn me against them by lumping them together with the good old boys, the guys who had worked their way up from being sopping-wet nothings to the top-ranking manufacturing experts, those to whom hands-on experience superseded education. It was in Sid's best interest to make me look like the source of our department's issues.

I knew that he would never take accountability or apologize for his ways. He no longer had Milan Esteban or Kyle Kerns to save his pathetic ass.

He was fucked.

Liz Stone always seemed to be right there when the shit was going down. Sid was an asshole, and even though I had failed to admit that he was harassing me, management was preparing to let him go.

Talk about good timing. Or bad, depending upon who you spoke with. Milan immediately saved Sid's ass and hired him into the TTD as chief engineer. He also gave Sid a significant increase in his salary.

There was a deep sigh of relief throughout my department on that day: no more Sid!

Plant management's plan had been to remove Sid from the plant and promote me into the department leader position. Although I had proven over and over that I could do the job, I found myself feeling very insecure and anxious about formally taking on the role.

Dave Kerns returned to his previous position as plant operations manager. A department leader from a sister plant was brought in to mentor me and help build up my confidence. My new mentor immediately got me my long-awaited raise and trained me how to run the department properly.

I was a natural-born worst-case-scenario thinker. I saw the potential in every situation for a worker to get hurt or worse. I would do my due diligence, but I knew that that would mean a lot of red tape for management and the union. I could not just let things go.

Everyone but me thought that I was ready to step up.

After a lot of soul searching, I turned down the job.

With that, HR posted the position and hired a non-technical guy named Ron. When Ron first started, he called me into his office and asked me what exactly it was that I did. I explained what I did, but he didn't get it. I started to lose it. I didn't understand what he wanted from me.

He quickly attempted to calm me down. All he wanted was to understand, not to undermine, as I had been so accustomed to. I still recalled what he said as clear as day: "I think that working for Sid seriously fucked up your head psychologically."

That was the second time within a month that Sid's influence on my emotional and mental well-being came into question. But it was the first time that my emotional acuity was outright brought into question by someone else.

At the time I had no idea how spot on Ron was.

I had started going a little squirrely because of Sid. Every word out of his mouth was making me question my own thoughts. He had been a tyrant. He would avoid addressing issues by jumping onto tangential subjects or blaming someone else. The most ironic part was that while he was busy slandering me to others at an ever-increasing rate, I was running about asserting that he was a great guy, that he was simply misunderstood.

In retrospect, I know that I suffered from Stockholm Syndrome.

I had a few sympathetic ears, but it seemed as though no one would or could help. Instead of looking at my successes I began focusing on my failures. I began to feel undeserving of anything better.

My problem was that I cared.

To me, my role was much more than a job, it was an opportunity. I could share and improve the working lives of my coworkers. I felt that I had so much to offer, especially now with Sid no longer dwarfing all my achievements.

I didn't need nor want to be put on a pedestal.

I wanted to be liked and accepted and respected for my sincerity and integrity.

I learned that the saying was true: You can't please all of the people all of the time.

Soft whispering voices were starting to echo through my mind. This just confused me more. It seemed that whenever I had a conscious thought there was this whisper of disagreement. I thought that it was just my consciousness and subconscious acting in concert to reason out problems and/or questions.

Ron quickly came to believe that he wasn't being paid equitably for his new position, so after two months with no changes to his salary he returned to his old job.

I felt that my skillset was best suited to technical work, not managing people, and so Dave Kerns bit the bullet and took on the departmental leader position again. This time it was a permanent solution.

The Big Boys Are Smiling . . . Smile Back
March 1996

I had been at W.V.H. Steel for just shy of two years. I remember wondering where I would be in ten years after Kyle had first hired me. I started to believe that I would be as revered and accomplished as him. The only difference was that I had little interest in climbing the corporate ladder. I just wanted to be where I could do the most good.

Little did I know that the higher-ups had an interest in me.

When I had first returned to school in January of 1996, I had a scheduled weekly meeting with the chair of our department, Dr. Leo Wilder. We hit it off instantly. The first time we met he mentioned Dr. El-Lim. I was shocked to learn that my old college teacher was even aware of my career progression; I hadn't seen or heard from him for about two years.

Dr. Wilder and I discussed a wide variety of topics, mostly geared to academics. I remember telling him midway through the semester that I was going to be at the top of the class, and that I would achieve an A+ average. He suggested that perhaps my goals were a little bit too lofty, but as the marks started rolling in he began to see my potential and appreciate my tenacity. He told me outright that I was blowing his mind with mine.

One of Dr. Wilder's hires, a brilliant young Irishman named Dr. Phil Lang, taught a couple of my courses. I scored 97 and 99 percent in his courses. I thought that it was just dumb luck—of course I had studied my ass off, but I felt as though I hadn't really struggled with any of the material or concepts.

Phil took an instant interest in me, personally and professionally.

I recall the day. It was in the late winter 1996. Phil and I were standing outside one of the university buildings chatting after a lecture. I was smoking a cigarette—it tasted so sweet in the cool air.

Phil posed the question to me: When it came down to it, would I choose a career in the private sector or in academia?

I thought about this long and hard for a good while.

The thought of attaining a PhD and doing research in academia did intrigue me. And the corporate world had done nothing to entice me into staying—quite the opposite. The only real question was: Would Kat and I have to suffer financially while I focused on school? And what of Rusty?

Phil also suggested to me that it was time to get involved in the non-academic workings of academia. In other words: the academic version of politics. I attended a meeting or two and I realized that I just plain disliked any politics and wanted nothing to do with it.

For such a smart kid, it took me a while to learn what was going on. I was being tested by the powers that be in the academic world.

The academic boys' club was keeping an eye on me too.

Together Against the Rest
May 1996

Like everyone else, Kat and I knew that we were meant to be together, so after almost a year as a couple we got engaged. We set our wedding date for August 11, 1996, just a few short months after our engagement.

While the wedding planning was going on, I was busy attending classes and kicking ass at work and in school.

I decided that I wanted to accelerate my education, so Kat and I discussed it and we saved up our money and put in a request to HR for me to take an eight-month sabbatical for the approaching fall/winter term. I discussed it with Dave Kerns and Liz Stone, who were both completely supportive. We made all the necessary arrangements, including hiring an engineer and technologist so that I could take the sabbatical without leaving the department deficient.

We're Not Angry . . . We're Just Disappointed
June 1996

Although we constantly spoke of him, Kat and my parents had yet to meet Rusty. Shelli had shared some snapshots of him and let me have them for our wallets. My family was behind me 100 percent. I tried to keep my financial woes away from them, but they were expecting news at any time. I broke down and explained to them that I'd had to drop the lawsuit a few months back.

They weren't pissed at me as much as they were disappointed that I hadn't asked for help. I hated it when I disappointed someone. It made me feel like I had promised to exceed their expectations or live up to some standard and didn't even come close to hitting the mark. At least if I made a mistake and pissed them off, I could ask for forgiveness without feeling unworthy.

Dad had retired from SM-Steel in 1991. He took a buy-out package. My parents were wise and met with a financial advisor. They had a nice little nest egg for their retirement. They were both still young when Dad retired—he had been only fifty-two.

They wanted to travel and see the world, so they started painting houses to make a few extra bucks. They used the painting money to fund their travels. They were living the American dream.

When I admitted that I'd dropped the case for Rusty because of the mounting legal fees, Kat immediately volunteered to help pay for the lawyer and court. She looked forward to being a stepmom. We already had a joint checking and savings account, but I had not dared touch that money.

She told me that her money was our money.

Our savings had already been spoken for. They were intended for our upcoming wedding and my sabbatical.

After a couple of days, my parents told us that they had done some refinancing and offered to front us the money for the case. My sister Ellyn also volunteered to chip in what little she could afford. We were all very excited.

As soon as the money was transferred into our account, I called Truman Kush and told him to pick up on the case where he had left off.

Truman explained that there was still a lot of work to do before moving forward, but he was in the process of initiating the paternity DNA testing. He said he would let us know as soon as he heard anything, but that it could take up to six months.

It took six months.

Chapter 6

You're Making Me Laugh

Satisfaction
June through August 1996

There are those who incite, and even more who perpetuate rumors and lies, but what motivates them to do this?

And who doesn't like a good story?

I liked to think that everyone liked me. I tried to like everyone I met. Unfortunately, some people just left an almost immediate bad taste in my mouth. And therefore it was only natural that I must have had the same effect on some others.

I may have been naive but I wasn't stupid. At work, school, or in social situations, I knew that there would be those who didn't like me. Some didn't like me for my job; some didn't like me because I didn't act or dress a certain way; some may have just plain disliked the nose on my face.

I knew that there were rumors and stories about me that went around.

Everyone had a story about everyone else.

Even me.

And it drove me fucking crazy.

I remember an episode of a long-ago television show. This wasn't an original concept, but it helps me make my point. The protagonist gave a comical presentation to a small, isolated group consisting of twenty targeted adults. He could not see or hear them during his presentation. Afterward, each member of the group was asked to fill out a brief survey based on the experience they had just had.

The next day our character was shown the tabulated survey results. Nineteen of the twenty gave glowing reviews. Before anyone could do anything, our protagonist set out to find the one individual who didn't give a good review, so that he could find out where he had gone astray. He became fixated, even though the overwhelming majority had given him praise. It nearly drove him crazy.

After a great deal of shenanigans and hilarity, he met the person and confronted him.

"I just didn't think you were funny," this person said.

From there, our main character set out to make this one individual laugh, to no avail.

"I just don't think you're funny," this person said again, despite our character's numerous attempts to evoke a chuckle or even a smile.

That main character had obsessed on the negative and ignored the positive.

I saw myself in that main character; it was as if he was me.

In the movies or on television shows, it was not just the well-intentioned clever guys who won the audience over simply on principal; rather, they usually won them over because they were clever enough to outsmart their opponents without having to lower or betray their integrity. Everyone loves it when the underdog comes through in the end, that was what made the stories satisfying.

That's what made them heroes.

By taking the high road in all my doings, I felt that I embodied an inner strength that most people don't have or are too insecure to let show.

Maybe it made them jealous.

Sid reveled in making me look incompetent to overcome his own insufficiencies.

Too bad it didn't all just end there.

Here Comes the Bride
August 1996

It was Rusty's second birthday on the fifth. Jenn and Dan had married the previous day, and the Albright and O'Reilly clans were meeting at the O'Reillys' to celebrate the wedding and Rusty's second birthday.

Once again we were not invited. Not that we would have attended even if we had been asked, because of Dan's prior violent assault on me.

We insisted on giving Rusty a couple of presents for his special day.

We had sent out the wedding invitations, booked the hall, and hired a caterer with time left over for some just-in-cases. It was going to be another three weeks until my sabbatical started. I just wanted—needed—to leave the workplace and immerse myself in my studies. We had planned a simple wedding; about 120 people were expected. Neither Kat nor I wanted to be married in a conventional church, so one of my parents' friends married us in the same hall as we were having our reception in.

Mike Jagger was to be my best man.

At two o'clock on Saturday August 10, I was standing in front of the flowery white arches waiting to see my bride. She was as beautiful as ever. Her father was unable to attend due to poor health. We knew that this would be likely ahead of time, so Kat had arranged for her mother to give her away. Len offered to do it, but Kat said, "No fucking way!"

We let Len emcee the reception.

By three o'clock we were married and out in the summer sunshine getting our wedding photos taken at the local botanical park. After that it was party time and then off to our honeymoon vacation for two weeks.

And before we knew it, we were off on a new chapter of our lives.

We took a two-week vacation from work, but only went away for one. We drove up to a small romantic bed and breakfast in Niagara Falls, on the Canadian side, to see the sights and shop. It was a terrific time in our lives.

We had reserved the second week of our vacation for relaxing and enjoying each other and our families. My parents had gathered and kept all our wedding gifts, waiting for our return from our vacation. They had also picked up our wedding photos.

We went to Kat's parents and had lunch the day after we returned, and we went with them to my parents' house to open our wedding gifts. We really cleaned up.

Chapter 7

The King of Hearts

Tick-Tock
Sunday, September 1, 1996

My parents called us and invited themselves over for dinner.

After dinner Dad sat down in the living room. Mom joined him on the couch and held his hands.

Mom and Dad had been on a ten-day Caribbean cruise while we'd been on our honeymoon. Dad had never been in great physical health, but Mom was determined to make him work off some of the extra calories that he had stacked up at the all-you-can-eat buffets on the ship. So she insisted he walk up and down the ship's stairs rather than use the elevators.

Dad went along with her, and in addition to his physical exhaustion he also noticed a slight tickle in his throat. Mom kept him on this rigorous adventure for the entire ten days that they were away.

When they arrived home, Dad noted that he still had that little tickle. Figuring he had caught a bug, he called our family physician, Dr. Gantt, and booked an appointment for the next week.

When the doctor checked him out, she heard some irregularities. She didn't seem overly concerned, but she was going to refer him to a cardiologist for further testing. Within a week Dad was in the cardiologist's office. He was put through the wringer with all the stress tests they had him go through.

The next day the cardiologist's office called and told Dad he was scheduled for a quadruple bypass the next week. The doctor told him he was in grave danger.

They told us about Dad's condition. They added that the cardiologist was very confident that, while this was a serious procedure, he would be fine.

Kat and I were speechless. Dad was only fifty-seven years old. We had never even thought about one of our parents having serious medical issues. Kat's father had poor health, but because he was a recluse and had been a mean-spirited father, she never thought of him as family.

A week later, Dad had his surgery.

Mom, Ellyn, Kat, and I all sat in the waiting area during the entire procedure.

After the operation the cardiologist informed us that the arteries connected to his heart were all over 97 percent blocked. They had only done a triple bypass because one of the arteries was completely blocked. The heart condition that Dad had was referred to as the "widow-maker." Mom felt terrible—the doctor told her that he was surprised that Dad had been able to walk around on the ship, let alone climb the stairs without having a heart attack.

Dad had a full recovery.

A Little Bit of Luck, a Little Bit of Karma
December 1996

We were all sweating blood by the bucket as we waited for Truman Kush to update us regarding our lawsuit against Jennifer Albright the previous June. He had proceeded to have the DNA testing done. He admitted it was a struggle, as Jenn and Dan refused to cooperate.

After the longest six months of our lives, the DNA test results finally came in.

Rusty was unquestionably my son.

Now armed with the proof of fatherhood, the next step was to get the court to give me visitation rights and ultimately custodial rights. Truman did some quick legal finagling and I was awarded monthly supervised visits, beginning in January.

In late December, after I had finished my final exams, I learned that my position at the plant had been formally given away to one of my former students—my protégé, Macy McBride, an energetic young lady who shared my passion for statistics.

Macy was good, *really* good, and I had promoted the hell out of her to plant management, but I was concerned that I wasn't going to have anything to return to at the end of my leave. We had hired Macy and an engineer to keep the department functioning before my leave started, but I never thought that my role would be permanently filled.

Panicked, I contacted Dave Kerns, and he assured me that I would likely be joining the Think Tank Division, the one for which Sidney Stanford was the chief engineer. And if not, they would find something for me in the plant.

Before I left for my leave, I had visited Sid several times because I was completely enthralled with the high-end engineering work that he was doing. Sid would brag about how he was one of a few engineers out of dozens—most of whom had advanced graduate degrees—who understood the mathematics that was required for his job.

Milan had hired two additional engineers to help Sid with his workload. They both had studied and understood the math that was required for the job. Sid refused to be exposed as an incompetent individual so he disregarded their work. Despite their attempts to notify Milan of Sid's abuse, nothing changed.

I knew exactly how frustrated they must have been. Sid had made it look so easy.

Too easy.

To me it looked like he was just playing with his mouse on an overpriced computer. I didn't believe that it was as easy as Sid made it out to be. I knew that he was not as intelligent as he would have liked people to think. I also knew that he was lazy. I understood the basic concept of the computations, but it would take a lot of time and practice to learn.

I never did learn how to do it.

Neither did Sid.

As it happened, some of our customers had been starting to complain that errors and failures were being introduced into the system. These errors were all made by Sid. Finally, he was called out by upper management on his bullshit ego and logical fallacies with no one to save his ass, not even Milan.

I learned that Sid left our company with his tail between his legs.

No matter how much shit he had put me through, I still thought he was a decent guy and that he had my best interests at heart. I got hold of him and invited him out to the company Christmas party. He begged off, stating that the newly appointed vice president of technology, Rick Van Horne, would be pissed to see him because he had suddenly left the company, leaving them in a lurch.

Even at his lowest point, Sid could not admit that he had fucked up.

I soon learned that an old professor friend of mine, Dr. Royce Pincer, had been hired on as an engineering consultant to fix Sid's numerous costly mistakes. Milan was so enamored with Royce that he was offered a new full-time position—he was asked to head up a research and development department in the TTD. Royce was about forty-eight years old by then and very experienced and accomplished.

The Razor's Edge
January 1997

It was the first court-appointed monthly visit I had been entitled to.

We were scheduled to meet at the Children's Aid Society, or CAS, at three o'clock. Jenn had reported that I was a "heavy drug user," so I now had to give biweekly urine and blood samples for narcotics.

I knew that Truman was working to get me increased visitation, and ultimately some form of custody. However, having to prove that I was not a habitual drug user added many more months to my plight.

I'd heard of and met so many men that wanted nothing to do with their biological children. Yet here I was *wanting* a relationship and being denied it. Jenn was becoming quite adept at villainizing me to the courts. Every time she came up with something new, it was *my* credibility and integrity that was challenged. I couldn't understand why the courts so readily took the mother's word over the father's.

Jenn and Dan came strolling in with Rusty at 3:35 p.m. There was a small room with a table and chairs surrounding it. Jenn and Dan were not allowed to be in the visit, but there was a big window so that the parents and family could view the proceedings.

The court officer was a stoic overseer. He was about five eleven and a healthy 200 pounds. He stood nonchalantly by the door to the room for the entirety of the visit.

I asked him what was to be done about their tardiness—they were thirty-five minutes late. He assured me that it would be documented and that the courts would be given notice.

When I met Rusty, my eyes widened. I crouched down and called to him.

"Come to Daddy," I beckoned.

A confused look crossed his tiny little face, as he looked to the side through the glass partition at Dan, who was his daddy as far as he knew. His tiny pink fingers were wet and slimy with his saliva as he continued to suck his thumb. I remembered seeing Chucky eat his finger in the exact same way.

He took his gooey hand from his mouth and pointed to Dan.

"Daddy," he said.

I didn't know what to do or what to say. I didn't want to confuse the boy, but I did want to assert my parental rights.

"We are both your daddies, Rusty," I explained.

He looked at me for another moment.

Tears filled his eyes as I attempted to give him to hug. He squirmed, so I decided to let it go for the time being. He kept looking back at Dan through the window—"Daddy."

I let go of him and he went running to the window.

I checked the clock on the wall—it was only 3:50.

The court officer stood there, completely ambivalent. Dan moved from the window to the door and began to turn the handle. The court officer moved to the door and told him that I still had ten minutes left to visit.

There was a small box filled with stuffed toys in the corner of the room, so I went and picked one out. It was a little stuffed dinosaur, a brontosaurus.

Rusty was still sobbing as I approached him with the toy.

"Do you like dinosaurs?" I asked him as I playfully danced the toy around. "Don't you want to play with Daddy?"

Rusty was shaking his head back and forth and crying out for his daddy—Dan.

It broke my heart.

My eyes moistened a little. I shrugged and indicated to the court officer that he could go.

I quietly whispered to him, "I love you, son," as I watched him disappear with Jenn and Dan.

I couldn't understand Jenn's malicious disregard of my feelings. I couldn't comprehend her spite toward me. The only thing that I could think of was that she was trying to overcome her own guilt for how she had treated me by belittling me. Likewise, I couldn't understand why Dan O'Reilly would take on Rusty as his own, when the boy clearly was not.

Visibly Rusty was my son, yet Jenn and Dan maintained that he was not.

Kat and I moved into our new house at the end of December, and we had a blast. We were located about a fifteen-minute drive from work. Kat and I had everything packed and ready for the movers to arrive at nine the following morning. That night around nine, our parents, my sister, and Kat's brother and sister all showed up and started moving our boxes from the apartment to the house.

Early the next day when the movers arrived, all that was left was the big stuff.

Our families and most of our local friends came out to help unpack and organize our new home. I was so excited—we owned our own property!

It was Tuesday, January 7, 1997, 5:17 p.m.

I was busy preparing dinner when Kat got home from work. The air outside was cold and crisp. Snowflakes were lazily dropping from the pale gray skies above, twisting and turning in the breeze until they found their destined landing spot somewhere on the frozen ground.

The phone rang.

I didn't recognize the phone number on the call display. Normally I wouldn't have answered, but I felt eerily compelled. If it was a solicitor, I promised myself that I would hang up immediately.

It was Shelli Albright.

Dan O'Reilly was dead.

He had been in on the afternoon shift. As usual he'd started fifteen minutes early, out in the lunchroom with a black coffee and a donut that had come from a vending machine.

His job was to cut off the rough ends from the steel sheets that were being rolled into coils. When cut, these ends dropped into a large rectangular scrap box that was destined for the much larger scrap pile. It was a boring and relatively uneventful job.

Dan hated it, but it paid fantastically.

To overcome their lack of fulfilment with their jobs, Dan and his coworkers would get high when the supervisors were out in their offices doing their paperwork and whatever else they did to ensure that their fingernails stayed clean and their bellies well filled.

Sometimes the steel scrap in the box would get twisted and it was necessary for Dan to loosen it so that it lay flat in the box. That is what happened at 4:20 p.m.

Dan picked up a long piece of rebar and tried to loosen the twisted piece.

It wasn't working, so he climbed up on the side of the scrap box and tried wriggling the piece out from a different angle. He started really reefing on the sheet, and it was starting to yield.

That's when he slipped.

The steel piece was as sharp as a razor and almost sliced Dan's left leg right off.

His coworkers had come running when they heard him screaming. They all knew that the safety procedures dictated that the workers *never* climb up on the scrap box, but they did it all the time. The proper way to get the twisted sheets flat was considered too laborious by the workers. Everyone knew this could happen but had just taken it for granted that it wouldn't.

Dan's femoral artery had been severed and there was blood spurting everywhere.

The plant emergency safety crew had been called in, but by the time they arrived Dan's coworkers had freed him and watched him bleed out on the cold concrete floor.

The police and fire departments had also been called.

Dan was pronounced dead at 4:40, just twenty minutes after he had started trying to loosen the sheet. The police dispatched a car to the Albright house to give the family the news.

According to Shelli, Jenn had fainted when she heard the news.

I asked Shelli if I could come over and watch over Rusty, but she told me that the O'Reillys were already on their way over.

I asked Shelli what she wanted me to do. We *were* in a legal battle, after all.

She just responded that she thought that I should know.

I discussed what had happened with Kat when she got home. Her primary concern was Jenn's well-being. I believed that she was trying to relate to Jenn—that was how she would have felt if something so tragic had happened to me.

Selfish as it may be, I was more concerned about Rusty.

We discussed calling our lawyer to fight for full-time custody. It had only been a few short weeks since I'd had my first visitation with Rusty. We decided that out of respect for the O'Reilly family we wouldn't call our lawyer until after Dan's funeral.

We didn't go to the visitation or the funeral.

A week later I called Truman Kush and told him to move forward to seek joint custody.

Oh Boy, Is This Great!
Friday, March 7, 1997

In early March I received an e-mail at home inviting me to come in to meet with Dr. Royce Pincer to interview for a position in the new R&D department. I was thrilled, but also a little skeptical because the management, especially Milan, had a habit of hiring people who were not well suited to their assigned positions. I knew a little about Royce as an academic and as a friend, (really more like an acquaintance), but not at all as a coworker/supervisor outside of academia.

At the start of the interview, Royce smiled and told me that he recognized me from seven years ago. He even remembered that I got a B+ in his course, even though I was a lazy student and hadn't even bothered to study much. I shook his soft fishlike hand, which I would usually find disturbing, but I paid it no heed.

Royce then told me that he had been asking around about me.

"All good, I hope," I said with a smile.

"For the most part," he bluntly replied.

His answer raised a tiny red flag in my mind; however, I quickly dismissed it.

Royce, Milan Esteban, and Rick Van Horne made it a stipulation that I keep up my schooling upon joining the R&D team. He promised me time for my studies, and said that when I had completed my undergrad degree he would help set me up in a master's degree program, perhaps even a doctoral program.

He even volunteered to be my personal career coach and mentor.

I was on cloud nine.

That evening, just after I'd eaten my dinner, Royce called.

"We have a couple of minor concerns," he revealed.

"We?" I wondered. And then I could hear Milan filling Royce's mind with skepticism, which had most certainly come secondhand from his buddy Sid Stanford.

"I felt as though you were interviewing me as much as I was interviewing you," he said. "You also came across as being a little"—he cleared his throat—"cocky. There are concerns about how you will fit in as a team player."

My heart sank and my mind raced. I took a few deep breaths to calm down and avoid having a panic attack. For a fleeting moment I didn't say anything further to him, but what I had really wanted to learn from him was whether *he* was a team player. And I wanted to learn how he approached problem solving.

I cautiously answered him, "I've experienced that in most cases the team approach to problem solving is not carried out as it is intended. In fact, my experience suggests that the problem-solving methodology at the company has been lacking."

"That makes sense," he responded, sounding unconvinced.

"I am 100 percent behind the teamwork concept. I didn't mean to come across as cocky; that is so not me! I know that there is a lot I need to learn from you and the others in the division. I'm going to work my ass off for you and the team."

"We have a lot to learn from you as well," he said. He seemed satisfied at this point.

Royce had also answered my questions adequately, so I was satisfied.

With those issues clarified, he seemed genuinely excited at the prospect of our working together. We talked on the phone for over two hours, each feeding from the other's enthusiasm about the future.

He offered me the job as a research assistant. He said I would be an "engineer in training."

Royce was offering me the opportunity of a lifetime. He told me that I would be a part of a team of superstar engineers. Another member he was adding to the team was Dr. Shane Wulf, a well-known engineer and former tenured Ivy League professor. I was very excited about this; I felt that as academics they would be a positive reinforcement on my studies. I had done extremely well in my undergrad degree up to that point, and I was confident that I could and would sustain my academic success. And with the tutelage of Royce and Shane I looked forward to applying all the book and classroom learning into being a superstar and really letting my talent grow.

I could hardly contain my excitement.

Part III
The Highway to Hell

Chapter 8

What Is and What Should Not Be

Can You Keep a Secret?
March 8, 1997

After I accepted the job offer, Royce invited me over to his home the following evening to relax over a couple of beers and to take a break from life in general.

He lived in a cozy little townhouse in the suburbs, about an hour's drive north from his work. The spring thaw would soon be beginning. In a month or so, the bright colors of the foliage and flowers would come alive, promising new hope and a refreshing perspective on life.

The door to Royce's home only had a single deadbolt on it—he didn't even carry his key with him. Although he did usually lock his door, he kept the key in a small black mailbox beside the door. There wasn't even a little peephole in the door. I was surprised by the lack of security.

Once inside, the condition of Royce's dwelling came as no surprise to me. His living space was tidy and well organized; everything was just as prim and proper as he was.

The walls were painted a neutral beige. There were two twin brown wingback chairs, each with an ottoman and a floor lamp, all completed with a plain wooden coffee table set between them. There were books sitting neatly on all the available shelves.

A small fifteen-inch tube television sat idly upon a plain little TV stand—I didn't even notice whether it was plugged in. Royce didn't strike me as an avid TV watcher.

There were even more books placed on the coffee table and underneath the television. Royce had several first editions of the classics—Royce's pride and joy were his books. He told me that along with the classics he was a big sci-fi fan.

Where there were no bookshelves, there were plaques and framed certificates speaking to his numerous accomplishments from the past twenty-five or so years. Most of the plaques were posted in his study, which was also home to a desktop PC with a printer.

Being as well read as he was fused my certainty was that he was going to be a terrific mentor and career coach for me. He was very interested in my academic and professional goals. Royce encouraged me to continue soaking up as much knowledge and experience as possible. He casually shared numerous details about himself and asked me my opinions. He was interested in me as a person.

Although prodded by my lack of credentials in the workplace, the true reason I had restarted this journey into engineering and the study of the sciences was not for money or prominence, it was the simple joy that could be derived from stretching my mind until it reached its limit, and then stretching it a bit further.

To me math and science were an art form.

This was the one significant difference between the two of us: Royce was not a philosopher nor a dreamer. He preferred concrete facts over conjecture and hypotheticals. He was in it for the accolades and recognition—and the money.

Royce once told me that, "Nothing is a fact until it can be proven mathematically."

My immediate intuitive reaction was that feelings could not be calculated.

His face resembled the Augie Doggie and Doggie Daddy cartoon characters: his jowls drooped with deep lines exaggerating his sagging cheeks and little wattle of a double chin. His brown eyes looked tired; dark circles were hidden by the thick metal frames of his glasses. He was only forty-eight years old but his face looked much older. He had a haunted look to him. I surmised that he had been put through the wringer a time or two.

Royce always had a warm smile for me, despite his moodiness. He complained about work quite a bit, but I didn't know anyone who didn't.

Kat had met Royce, and she agreed that he was a good man. My coworkers and colleagues from work also spoke highly of him. I also asked around the university, but only a few of the professors remembered him. Those who did spoke well of him.

As I got to know him better, I began to realize that my intuition into his peculiar affect was spot on. Royce had some deep and dark secrets—deeper and darker than the average Joe. Within a short time, he revealed one of the pivotal experiences that had changed his life forever.

It started with his relationship with his father when he was a boy. Royce described his father as an "Nazi-like genius" who had been a strict work-oriented son-of-a-bitch tyrant, incapable of love and with no apparent sense of compassion or empathy. His father's approach to raising his son was setting the highest of standards and then coming down hard mentally and emotionally when his son didn't meet or exceed his expectations.

Royce revealed that the foremost reason he had earned his PhD was because his father had demanded perfection and insisted that his son outperform all others, thus leaving a brilliant legacy in the Pincer namesake. Royce admitted to me that try as he may he couldn't live up to these expectations, but he worked his hardest and had fared quite well.

He never said if his father was satisfied.

His father, Evan Pincer, had served in the Second World War and gone on to earn two engineering degrees while working and raising Royce. Evan was a proud member of Mensa. Royce didn't have the requisite IQ for Mensa. Although he wouldn't admit it, I could tell that he felt ashamed and inferior that he was not the genius that his father had expected him to be.

Royce would often put down Mensa, stating that having a high IQ meant nothing. Having a high IQ, I tacitly sat still and let him rant.

Royce was a very clever man and came across as such. He presented as a man on his path to being enlightened. His views and opinions were vast, just not as philosophically deep as others like his father. I believed that as an *applied* mathematician and engineer he probably was a genius.

I don't know when I'd realized it, but I was an empathetic and sensitive individual. That was what had made me so different than the other kids and the other workers throughout my life. Royce quickly picked up on the notion that I was an empath. Within a few short weeks of our budding friendship, he expressed to me that he had grown to the point he felt comfortable enough to reveal some of his innermost fears and traumas to me.

I saw red flags everywhere. I had an odd feeling that he was planning to fill my head with nonsensical noise for reasons beyond my grasp.

As usual, I ignored my intuition.

Abigail, 1957

Royce explained to me that he had inherited mental health issues such as depression and anxiety from his mother. He went on to share his significant childhood recollections and how they had affected him, helping mold him into the man he was today.

He was born on May 9, 1949. His mother, Abigail Pincer, doted on him, while Evan had little to do with him during his formative years. Any expectations of his son were relayed through his mother. His demands were quite simple: meet and exceed his expectations.

Abigail tried to raise Royce to be the best person that he could be, to be the man she thought Evan would want him to be: brave, strong, and revered. She had to make Evan look good, so she forced herself to whitewash her mental wounds and drove herself to be the belle of the ball, always smiling and chatting up anyone who would listen. Because she suffered from extreme anxiety and extensive bouts of depression, it didn't come easily, but she was committed to her family and so she pushed through.

Royce would often find his mother alone in the front room siting in her rocking chair and sobbing. When he would ask her what was wrong, she would brush away the tears, sniffle a little, and smile at him, insisting that she was fine.

On the surface she seemed so happy.

She had it all: a respected husband, a beautiful child, and a lovely home.

Yet depression took her mind into places only God could stomach. Still, she always wore that cheery smile that her husband and friends had come to expect.

After years of masking her anxieties and depression, she hung herself.

It was June 14, 1958.

A nine-year-old Royce found her body hanging by a knotted bedsheet from the rafters in the front room of their house. Mere seconds after Royce's discovery, his father arrived home from the office.

Royce was crying. He ran over to his father and wrapped his arms around him. His father pushed him away. Royce looked up to his father and saw nothing but a look of loathing. He was unsure whether his father's disgust was directed at him for his crying or at his mother for giving in to her weak mind.

Royce explained to me that this was the first time he had been introduced to the suggestion that the display of emotions was unacceptable. He also learned that having mental health issues was a revolting sign of weakness.

My parents, Dad in particular, had raised me to believe that emotions were a part of life and we should not be afraid to express them. For a brief moment I felt as though Royce was suggesting to me that there was no place for emotions in his presence.

I ignored my doubtful thoughts.

Can I Get an Amen?
June 15, 1958

The night after Abigail's suicide, Royce's father came into his room at about ten p.m., reeking of whiskey. He simply hovered over his son, swaying drunkenly, just looking at the boy. He mumbled to himself, and after about twenty minutes he left, closing the door behind him.

Royce had pretended to be asleep, but he was awake and quietly grieving the loss of his mother. He recalled shamefully turning away from his father to hide the mournful tears running down his cheeks. He swore he heard his father say "amen" before he left.

This behavior reoccurred on a few evenings over the next couple of weeks. Royce informed me that he had eventually concluded that his father's nocturnal visits were his way of expressing his love to his son. He was disappointed that his father had to get stinking drunk before having the gumption to show any love or affection for him.

Evan kept a collection of service revolvers and handguns which he boasted had been heroically hand-picked from Germans he had killed during the war. They were kept in a tall curio cabinet behind the desk in his study. Each gun apparently had a glorious story that went along with it, but Abigail had always insisted that Evan spare Royce his tales of barbarism with which the guns were associated.

Royce explained that he had never shown any interest in the weapons; he was more invested in his science-fiction novels and comic books. However, in hindsight he realized that his father had wanted him to be interested. He wanted his son to hear his war stories and to pass them on to future generations of Pincers.

Usually, his father was not one to reveal any emotion but anger. And his father had a great deal of pent-up fury. Although financially and socially successful, Royce didn't learn until his father's funeral a few decades later that his father had suffered silently from severe bouts of depression due to post-traumatic stress disorder—PTSD.

Royce was "soft." He wore thick-lensed glasses and sported a close-cropped crewcut. He would never be considered intimidating by anyone. He had one or two friends, but essentially lived his life through his books. His father would become enraged when Royce would show up at home displaying any evidence that he had been abused or bullied by the other kids at school. Evan wanted Royce to be a real man, not the little bookish wimp that he was.

But Royce was an observant and clever boy. Rather than embrace violence he watched others and slowly trained his mind to predict behaviors and outsmart the bullies using his intellect and wit. It was all he had.

The Summer of 1958

At his father's behest, Evan's sister—Royce's Auntie Tee—and her youngest son Cameron were asked to come to stay with Royce and his father for the summer following Abigail's suicide. Auntie Tee agreed, and believed that Cameron could indeed be a significant influence on Royce, who was naive and lacked life skills.

They arrived the day after school had let out for the summer.

Auntie Tee stepped up from the get-go. Not only did she take over as the household matriarch, she also immediately immersed herself in as many local women's community and charity groups as she could.

She was often asked how Royce was faring, and she always responded that he was a "good boy" and that he was "flourishing despite his loss."

Cam and Royce shared Royce's bedroom. There was only the one bed plus an old army cot that Evan had pulled out. Royce was instantly assigned the cot, although Cam did offer him the opportunity to wrestle for it.

Royce meekly smiled at his cousin's goading while he set up the cot.

Royce would also have to wrestle for a pillow.

There were still over eight weeks of living with his cousin to look forward to.

When they first arrived, Cam instantly began to harass Royce—physically, verbally, and emotionally. Royce was small for his age of nine and Cam was a big boy—he was thirteen and pubescent.

When he was in a particularly cruel mood, Cam would taunt Royce that his mother had taken her own life because "she couldn't stand to look at her ugly son's face." Cam came up with many other belittling dandies to torment Royce over the following summer months.

Being young and impressionable, Royce heard enough slights against him that he started to believe that in some way Abigail's death was his fault. His father was unapproachable. He was too busy to deal with childish trivialities such as emotions and matters of the heart and he expected the same of his son; still, he recognized that Royce was a young child and unable to emotionally process the misfortunes that life was throwing his way, and that was why he had brought his sister and nephew to stay with them in the first place.

It was time for Royce to "man up."

Cam's father, Toby Fisher, was a cattle farmer. Cam at thirteen was the youngest of seven boys. The oldest was twenty-five. His six older brothers—all built like military fortresses—had no issue with "guiding" and/or "correcting" Cam with force if he stepped out of line. As a result, Cam was one tough bugger too. The boys all left school when they were fifteen or sixteen to help Toby run the farm. Reading, writing, and arithmetic didn't fit with the Fisher boys.

Cam's older brothers had him drinking whiskey straight from the bottle by the time he was ten. Royce's father always had a significant amount of whiskey lying around, so it didn't take long before Cam was getting Royce drunk. They also fooled around with cigarettes—Cam was a habitual smoker but Royce never did take to it.

Often Cam would wrestle and/or pummel Royce into submission. Cam would punch and push him, often leaving scrapes and bruises. That was how Cam's brothers had helped toughen *him* up, and so that was how Royce was going to learn. Royce, being the wimp that he was, always conceded defeat, and while crying he begged for his cousin's mercy. This only seemed to increase the intensity of the attacks.

Regardless of Cam's obnoxious tendencies, Royce was determined to win him over with his wit and intellect. But Cam only responded with further violence.

As the summer proceeded, Cam became unbearable.

Royce simply wasn't improving. Cam was a constant threat to him, yet he refused to fight back. He would curl up into a ball trying to hide his vulnerabilities from Cam. His father would not hear of his son being a coward and Auntie Tee ignored Royce's reports of Cam's brutality, because they had hoped that he would build up some self-confidence and learn to defend himself.

Toward the end of the summer, Cam punched Royce in the side of the head, knocking his glasses off. Cruel to the end, Cam stepped on and broke them. Over dinner, Evan inquired about his son's disheveled appearance.

Royce unconvincingly lied and told him that he'd fallen.

Cam was smugly grinning.

Auntie Tee looked at Cam. "What did you do?"

Cam looked at Royce and then back at his mother. Still smiling, he shrugged.

Finally, Auntie Tee suggested to an enraged Evan that Royce had been punished enough by her son's cruel acts. Evan didn't fully agree, but his sister had raised seven boys so he temporarily deferred the boys' punishments to her.

Still unable to leave it at that, Evan looked Royce in the eyes and told him that he was "disappointed in you and ashamed you're my namesake."

Upon hearing this Royce began sniveling. Evan reached across the table and slapped him.

"You disgust me!" bellowed Evan.

Royce hobbled away from the table to his bedroom and swore that Cam would never best him again.

Royce later learned that after dinner that night, Auntie Tee had taken Cam aside and told him no more bullying, that this time he had gone too far. She and Evan had known what Cam had been doing all along and they were hoping that Royce would toughen up, but with this last incident they finally realized that Royce was never going to be like Tee's boys—Royce was "delicate."

The next morning after Evan left for work and Auntie Tee had left for a ladies' church meeting, Royce snuck down to Evan's study and retrieved a revolver from the display. It was loaded. Royce removed all but one bullet from the revolver and spun the cylinder.

It was time for a game of Russian Roulette.

Cam was awakened by the cold weight of the barrel pressed against his forehead. Royce smiled and pulled the trigger. The hammer slammed down with a loud click.

Royce jumped.

Cam soiled himself.

"Fuck with me again and there might be a bullet in the gun the next time," seethed Royce.

Royce looked at the revolver—the next chamber in the cylinder held the single bullet.

He reloaded and returned the gun to his father's display and continued with his day as if nothing had happened.

Cam never bothered Royce again.

Auntie Tee and Cam left the Pincers on the Friday of the Labor Day weekend that summer.

Chapter 9

My Boy's Gonna Play in the Big League

Dangling Participles
Monday, May 5, 1997

It was my first day on the new job.

I looked forward to working with other professionals from different countries and cultures. I also looked forward to flexing my academic muscles and learning and developing new technologies. This was a very exciting time to be working at W.V.H. Steel, and here I was standing on the crest of the leading wave.

Royce was my hero in every sense of the word. He had been working as a high-level mathematician/engineering consultant for over six years. After finishing his PhD, he had worked for two semesters as an assistant professor, which was when I had first met him, but the academic life didn't "grow on him," as he put it.

I was convinced that with his God-like potential he could learn all our company processes and details faster than I could teach him. Still, because of this lack of in-depth knowledge he had hired me for my applied experience, plus Dr. Shane Wulf, who was one of the steel industry's top lauded researchers.

The R&D team was formally established on that day, Monday, May 5, 1997.

Upon meeting him, I knew that Shane was simply one of the most gentle and compassionate individuals I was ever to encounter. He was also high up there as one of the most ingenious men I had ever met. He was a small man with a full head of spiky brown hair. He sported a mean goatee. He was very lean, and clearly in very good physical condition.

Shane, like me, cared. He cared about the work and he cared about the people. He was a good listener and candidly gave me technical and personal advice when asked. Plus, he allowed me to vent when I was overwhelmed by anything. That was not to say that Shane kept his opinions to himself—if someone did something wrong or started to stray, be it work, personal, or political, he would be the first to stand on principal.

He brought me up short on several occasions. I liked and respected him. A lot.

The first time Royce snapped was during my second week with the team. Around noon, I was getting ready to head out to school. Royce and I were both exiting the office building when he casually stopped and turned to me.

"Next term we'll have to review your course times."

I was stopped short. I immediately felt guilty about leaving for my class. I wondered if I should skip class that day. I decided that I shouldn't. I was consumed by the intent behind his comment.

As soon as I returned from school I went to see him.

"Is there an issue with me attending classes?" I asked him point blank.

He leaned back in his chair. "No."

I wasn't convinced.

"What about your comment about reviewing course times?" I asked with concern.

"Well . . ." he waffled

"I *did* tell you that I was planning on taking a course," I stated.

He nodded. "I shouldn't have said anything to you. That was wrong of me," he said.

I took a deep breath and sighed with relief. "Good."

"But—" he started. And then he shook his head. "Nothing," he mumbled.

"But what?" I pressed him. If I was doing something wrong, I wanted to know.

"Well . . . your class times aren't at the most ideal. But don't worry about it."

I felt a slight wave of relief.

"In my old position, noon was the ideal time for me to leave." I felt as if I should be defending myself against him. I wanted to ensure there were no misunderstandings.

"Well, it is not the optimal time now," he snapped.

Another wave of guilt and panic raced through me. I felt the blood flushing my cheeks as my stomach lurched. I felt like a little boy about to be scolded for speaking out of turn. Royce leaned forward and clasped his soft milky-white hands together. "I'm sorry. I spoke out of turn."

Briefly, I felt as if I was sitting with Sid Stanford again—I didn't know what to do or what to say. This was a new side of Royce, one that I had never expected. And then I recalled him telling me about holding that gun to his cousin's head. A chill ran down my spine as I imagined the click of the hammer smashing down on an empty bullet chamber. I realized that I was sitting across from a man who had confessed to being capable of doing terrible evil.

Once again, he assured me that it was no big deal and it would all work out.

I put my recollection of the vengeance-ridden Royce child out of my mind.

Set Up for Failure
June–July 1997

A few more weeks into my tenure with the R&D team, there was an engineer that Royce forbade me to speak with about our team's work. Royce didn't give me any further details. A little red flag went up within my mind, but again I was too smitten with my new career—*life*—journey to pay attention. But for a millisecond, I thought it peculiar that Royce was being so negative about one of our colleagues.

But I was devout; I didn't want anyone blocking our team's mission.

His name was Gunther Steinmann.

As per Royce, Gunther was a young German engineer who knew nothing about steel or forging despite having a master's degree and a few years of experience in the field. To me, if Royce said it then it must be gospel. I was instantly convinced that Gunther, a man I had yet to meet, was incompetent.

When I did finally meet Gunther I found him to be quite friendly and knowledgeable. If there was any one thing that I didn't like about him it was his ego, but I was growing used to educationism and I was working hard on closing the gap by finishing my degree.

I was pleasant with Gunther, as he was with me, but as per Royce I didn't reveal an iota of information about what the R&D team was working on. In truth, after meeting him I was at a loss as to why Royce had been so disparaging of him.

Later, I learned the reason: Gunther had successfully countered Royce's professional opinion on a project when Royce was presenting it to senior management.

Gunther had simply embarrassed Royce.

I assumed that there had to be more to that story, because a gentleman like Royce—a man who stood for integrity and intelligence—would *never* smear another's reputation over something as piddly as being embarrassed over making a mistake.

For the first few months, the R&D team consisted of the three of us plus an administrative assistant, Helena, who joined us in late May. It was great, although I must admit I felt a wee bit naive and intimidated by the grandiosity of my two coworkers' experience and achievements. And how fortunate I felt to be working with two PhDs! I thought it was like going to school for a living.

One of our primary directives for the TTD was to map out and implement a master plan aimed at restructuring the company's approach to manufacturing. The onus of the success was on the corporate engineering team led by Milan Esteban and the R&D team led by Royce.

This would be no small task.

Rick Van Horne had been put in charge of the TTD. He was promoted to VP of Technology. Milan and Royce reported directly to him.

W.V.H. Steel was a hands-on experience-oriented manufacturer, and at the plant level, as I had faced, the skills and talents of educated people were often ignored solely on principal. Arrogant engineers like Sid Stanford had done nothing to dissuade others from thinking this way.

That was another great thing about Royce: we were likeminded. Not only were we good friends, but we shared a common vision for the team and company. I found our conversations very engaging. I could tell that Royce did as well.

In late July that summer, Royce hired two more PhDs.

Royce had made it crystal clear from the beginning that the R&D team was not going to be an "ivory tower" team; we were going to get down and dirty in the trenches and prove that we weren't just a bunch of pencil-pushing stuffed shirts.

Royce referred to me as an "engineer in training," and it didn't take long for it to be made known where my place in the TTD was, academics and skills aside: I resided at the bottom and would have to work my ass off to prove myself to the rest of the team.

I had no issues with that.

As a result, I did a lot of physical work with a lot of blood and sweat poured in. I never complained once. Many of my former coworkers from the plant joked that they hadn't seen me work that hard since I had first started as a college student a few years prior.

One day I arrived at work to discover that Royce had moved Shane and the other two PhDs into his office with him, leaving me all alone with my tiny desk surrounded by several new desks to be occupied by students in the fall. I was puzzled by this move—there was plenty of room in Royce's office for me as well.

On several occasions over the next few weeks, I would walk by Royce's office and find the team discussing one of the projects that I was involved with. These impromptu meetings happened frequently, as often as three or four times a day, and no one ever bothered to call me to join in. This resulted in a lot of miscommunication, redundancy, and frustration on my behalf.

We were supposed to be a *team*. With every discussion they had, I was falling that much further behind. I was miffed—Royce had questioned my ability to work with a team and now he was preventing me from being a participating member of the team.

For a moment I recalled how some people dealt with my genius: they ignored me.

I felt that I was being set up for failure.

At first I was consumed with my education and future career path. Upon hiring me, I'd been told that my schooling and work were meant to be complementary. After a few months, Royce quietly and politely advised me that other members in the TTD were beginning to question my dedication to the team and to the job.

I felt horrible; that had never been my intent.

It wasn't that I didn't do my job—in fact I did it well—but I realized that what I spoke about most enthusiastically was advancing my education and career. Royce told me that I spoke of work projects as if they were secondary to my education and career path.

I saw Royce's concern and agreed that I would change my behavior immediately.

I thought that the case was closed.

After a few months I was getting bored. It seemed that most of what I did was general labor. I knew that was not the case. It had to be said: Shane and the other PhDs were amazing for helping me with the manual labor. The only thing that frustrated me was that I was not getting to use my academic skills as much as I'd thought I would.

As it was, I had been doing more engineering work in the plant as a technologist.

Toward the end of that summer, Kat began working on her master's in education.

After a few months I was starting to get a bad feeling in my gut. There was something off about the R&D team, but I couldn't put my finger on what. When I closed my eyes and thought about it, all I could see was an endless scourge of red.

That's My Boy!
Sunday, August 3, 1997

I had been showing up at the CAS religiously at three p.m. every first Sunday of every month, just as the family court judge had ordered. Rusty was turning three in a couple of days and I had only been able to take a few minor steps to gain my rights to see him. Even though Kat and I were now financially sound, my parents still helped pick up the costs of our lawyer.

Just before Rusty's third birthday, Truman Kush called to inform us that I had been awarded weekly supervised visits. I was disappointed that the visits still had to be supervised and were still limited to an hour, but I was going to take what I could get.

And despite my drug tests having been consistently proving otherwise, Jenn insisted I was a drug-addled junkie.

Ironically, since Dan had died Jenn had taken a mental nosedive. She had always liked to party, but now she was using alcohol and weed to help with her grief. Jake, Chucky's father, had witnessed what was happening and had called CAS. According to Jake, Jenn was *never* sober anymore.

CAS responded quickly and saw that Jenn was falling apart. Jenn was burning through Dan's savings. She was spending all her money on booze and dope. Apparently, she had quickly developed quite the coke habit. Jake and the Prue family had petitioned the family court for full custody of Chucky, and eventually they won—Jenn was declared an unfit mother.

With Dan O'Reilly being documented as Rusty's biological father, his parents had been given custody of him until the courts were finished with my case. We were growing frustrated with how slowly the process was moving. We had submitted to their tests. We had scientific proof of parenthood.

Unlike Jenn, the O'Reillys complied with the court order, so I started seeing my son every week. I thought they knew they were fighting an unwinnable battle over Rusty but they remained resilient. I didn't know how much money they had in their coffers, but they were keeping us tightly wound.

One or all of Mom, Dad, and Kat usually went with me to my visitations. Sometimes my sister Ellyn joined Mom and Dad as well. They were not allowed to hold or talk with the boy. This was very distressing but they played the hand that they were dealt, knowing that sooner or later things were going to change.

What the O'Reillys didn't yet know but my lawyer's investigator found was that, not having money left for cocaine, Jenn had elevated her drug use and had started using crack. That was some serious shit.

She was becoming a junkie.

Our lawyer told us that despite Jenn's situation Rusty *was* being taken care of—the O'Reillys really did care for the boy and were raising him as if he was their blood. Rusty was almost three years old and I had only seen him a handful of times because Jenn and Dan had blocked us. At least now Dan's parents were showing up promptly as per the court order.

The O'Reillys were always present during my visitations as well. They eventually started to engage with my family. I think that they became friendly because of their mutual concern for Rusty.

Still, the one thing I desperately wanted Rusty refused: to call me Daddy.

Shush! We Don't Talk About Mental Health in the Workplace
Late August 1997

At the time I knew very little about mental health issues. I didn't even realize that I was in the beginning throes of many trials and tribulations.

I was concerned for my friend, Royce—he was not acting "normally."

I did some extensive research and connected a few dots. I started to see that Royce's behavior fell under the umbrella of "manic depressive." I learned that when in a manic state he was more prone to outbursts. I had initially interpreted this as assertiveness, although his angry outbursts did cause me to wince with fear, and lately he was starting to take things too far. He was raising his voice and having little fits of rage.

I also noted that when he was in a depressive mode he was apologetic and self-deprecating. I had attributed this behavior as his humane, gentle nature and quite likely a carry-over from the troubling childhood which he had described to me.

I mentioned my research and conclusions to Shane. He sternly advised me to keep my thoughts to myself. I knew that Shane wasn't generally so blunt, so I decided I'd best heed his advice.

But I still wanted to help my friend Royce.

Kid Karma
Friday, August 29, 1997

I learned that Sid had been fired from the new job he had taken on after leaving W.V.H. Steel the previous December. As soon as I could I e-mailed him to get the lowdown. He told me that his supervisors at his new job had given him a glowing review after his first six months, and then suddenly after another few months they fired him "without cause."

I knew exactly what the cause was; I had lived it: Sid Stanford was a narcissist.

You cannot reason with a narcissist; I had tried and failed. Sid was unable to change because he was unable to admit that he had faults. He was always right, and if he was wrong he was *still* right, it was just someone else's fault.

After learning of his dismissal from this latest job, Milan issued an e-mail to the TTD, asking if he should rehire him. The two particularly bright engineers who had worked under Sid responded that they would quit if he was rehired. I never even bothered to chime in; I knew it would make no difference to Milan.

With all that had happened over the past three years, Milan still couldn't see through Sid.

Sid decided to go into business for himself. He had written a computer program to collect data for the steel-forging plants that operated as ours did. His program would eliminate a great deal of paperwork and help streamline the process. Sid's program was not the only one available in our industry. I had to admit that, despite my history with him, it was a good piece of software. He had Macy McBride (who was in my former plant position) and her managers 99 percent convinced to purchase his software. I warned her that

Sid was not trustworthy, but she had all her ducks in a row and was ready to proceed.

Before purchasing the software, the IT department requested that Sid give them a copy of the computer coding in case something went wrong or if something happened to Sid, rendering him unable to correct the program. Stubborn unto the end, Sid refused.

The plant purchased a software package from a more stable developer.

Without going into detail, Sid fell flat on his face.

To make matters even worse for him, no one in the industry would touch him.

Karma is a bitch.

Although I tried, I never heard from him again.

I still felt bad for him.

Teamwork Defined
Tuesday, September 9, 1997

It was the day after Labor Day. The plant was just starting to produce again, following their annual two-week summer shutdown. The company was abuzz with bright new faces, both students and permanent employees.

The TTD was also growing. It now comprised four fully functioning subdivisions: the design team, the special projects team, the corporate engineering team, and the research and development team. In addition to the two engineers whom he had hired to work under Sid Stanford, Milan had hired a small group of eager and competent engineers to fortify the corporate engineering team's skills. He also hired a sizable group of young bright-eyed co-op students.

The other TTD leaders, including Royce, followed suit. Royce had already hired the two PhDs in July, and now a small group of college and university students were beginning on this day.

Except for some poor leadership choices, the TTD was a massive mental force to be reckoned with. It truly was becoming a world-class team, or it at least had the potential to be.

Since moving the rest of the team into his office, Royce was omitting me from more and more of the technical work and discussions. One of our team's projects required some high-level assistance, so they met with a group of professors from my school. I was about two thirds into level 3 of my degree and still actively taking courses.

I was not invited to join my team. I felt as though I'd been slapped in the face by Royce.

Many of the professors from my department were present.

When they returned from the university later that day, Royce casually told me that Dr. Leo Wilder had told him and the team that I "belonged in academia, not the corporate world." He also told me that the group of profs collectively agreed.

I thought that Royce was complimenting me.

But when I looked at his face, I realized that he was pissed off.

When I first started meeting with Royce, he always expressed excitement for my academic achievements. But as of lately if I mentioned how well I had scored on a test he would show little to no interest.

When I would try to approach Royce about applying more of my technical skills on the job, he would raise his voice and talk over me, stating that I was not the only team member who had found such a level of success in school. He would further go on to emphatically state that he had graduated with his PhD "with distinction," which was the grad school equivalent of Dean's Honors. What I later learned was that Royce had not completed a doctoral thesis like most other PhDs; he did a project that required him to apply some very high-level math skills.

To me it didn't matter. The bottom line was that he had a PhD.

I never knew that we were in competition, but I learned that Royce was threatened by me.

Since moving the rest of the team to his office, I had become so far behind that it wasn't funny. With the new students now filling the desks around me, I felt even more out of touch. I approached Royce once again.

"Well, you *are* just a student," Royce told me flatly.

His eyes burned through mine. I could feel him crawling around the innards of my mind. That made his response even crueler. He knew he had me. He was experiencing my essence and savoring it. He was showing no mercy.

I was so shocked with his blunt lack of tact that my mind went into panic mode. Just a student?

From the beginning I had sworn to myself that I would show him what I was capable of, but he had started throwing out roadblocks along my path to success. I was so busy chasing my own tail that I couldn't keep up.

Although he had initially come across as something of a sensitive and empathetic individual, Royce best understood facts. I needed to put my feelings into numbers that he could comprehend.

Yes, I was a student, however…

Later that day Royce approached me and apologized for his "student" comment.

He had not moved me into his office because he hoped that I would rise to the occasion and lead and mentor the new influx of students. He expressed that he believed in my leadership abilities, and he wanted me to help coordinate and watch over the students. Although my wounds still stung a little, I felt a lot better about the situation. This sounded like the Royce I knew, and of course I was completely convinced.

The only thing I couldn't figure out was why he had made the move in July, almost two months before the students were starting. I was so far behind in our projects that there was no way I could give the students projects to work on.

I should have had "sucker" written across my forehead. I'd fallen right into his trap.

We still socialized occasionally, but as time passed Royce seemed to be growing distant if not disinterested. It was as if he was no longer interested in being friends. Naturally, I concluded that the problem was me—somehow I had always seemed to push others away. I couldn't get a fix on his intent. One day he was my strongest supporter, the next I needed improvement.

I felt as though I was overreacting. As I had been told many times over the past few years, I just needed to thicken my skin.

Usually after an angry outburst he apologized later, and when he finally did apologize his behavior was self-deprecating. He would often commiserate with me, revealing that he too often lacked confidence in himself at times.

I knew that it wasn't in his job description to entertain me or give me any special attention, or even to try to bring out the best in me, professionally or personally—that was all on me. At the same time, he had promised me that he and the team would work with me to become an engineering "superstar."

I started to wonder: maybe they had been correct to question me in the first place; perhaps I wasn't a team player. In many team situations, I tended to play the role of the Devil's advocate—not to be an asshole, but to promote deeper and more detailed discussion about a topic. I did this to ensure that a good idea didn't get swept away with all the crappy ones. I was just approaching issues with a critical mind.

Unfortunately, this approach was more often neglected than embraced.

Royce rebuked me for working against the team with my questions and comments.

I remembered back when Kyle Kerns had interviewed me for the student position. He asked me how I functioned in a team environment.

I had been raised understanding the autocratic management approach: there were echelons of authority. You did your job and you kept your mouth shut. Attempting to be quick on my toes, my response to Kyle was that I would speak my mind but go along with the consensus. Kyle turned around and asked me quite tersely, "But what do you do if you are right?"

I was left speechless.

I never did learn the correct answer.

And to frustrate me even more, I *was* often right.

Chapter 10

You're Fucking Crazy!

An Atypical Intervention
Monday, September 15, 1997

It was about two a.m. I had just slipped underneath the covers. I had just closed my eyes, and that's when I saw it.

My mind was filled with unfathomable wonder. I felt a deeply embracing calmness and warming peace. I opened my eyes to witness an ethereal body dressed in long, flowing, white and liquid gold garments, fluttering in the air. I tried reaching out to touch it, but my body was limp. I tried to call out to Kat to awaken her, but only soundless plumes of warm air expelled from my lungs.

Though it burned through my eyes, I couldn't look away.

And then there was a deep voice clearly speaking directly to my mind.

Tomorrow, your life will change forever.

I was mesmerized.

As suddenly as it had appeared it disappeared.

The warm peaceful feeling remained, calming me as I regained my faculties. My mind was filled with questions, but I was not panicking.

I just knew that this was real. I rolled over and clung tightly to Kat. I wondered if I should wake her and tell her of this experience or if I should keep it to myself—at least until morning.

I was so filled with amazement and wonder that I chose to wake her up. I told her what I had seen and experienced. She was so sleepy that she just mumbled something dismissive and pulled the covers closer to her chin, tightened her grip on my arm and snuggled in for a good night's slumber.

Kat always left for work around the same time I got myself up, so I didn't get a good chance to share the details of my vision that next morning. Once at work, I went to her cubicle and quietly revealed what I had experienced. She looked at me with alarm and asked if I had possibly hallucinated it.

I swore that it had been real.

Although the "angel" had left an overwhelming sense of peace and tranquility, I had been on edge all day. I was anxious to learn what this life-changing experience was going to be.

After work that day, when I entered the house Kat was standing at the doorway. I couldn't get a read on what she was feeling. She looked a little apprehensive and afraid. She'd had a doctor's appointment that afternoon but I had thought nothing of it. Now I feared the worst. The image of the angel from the previous night was still singed into my eyes. I thought the most horrid things—Kat had cancer, or some other life-threatening illness.

We looked at each other for what seemed to me a millennium.

We remained speechless, until finally I approached her and put my arms around her frail body. She was trembling.

"Whatever it is, we'll get through it," I said, trying to reassure her.

I was trying to reassure myself as well.

Finally, she whispered into my ear, "I'm pregnant."

My first thoughts were of panic. This was definitely a life changer.

I let go of her and pulled out a cigarette, lit it, and tried to wrap my head around the implications of her words. I couldn't help but keep thinking of that angel. I could tell by the look on her face that she was thinking the same thing. At least now we knew that I wasn't hallucinating.

We had planned on having kids but now we were both busy with work and school. We hadn't really spoken about trying to have kids recently. We weren't using protection, but we weren't making a conscientious effort to start a family either.

"I have to mow the lawn," I said and hastened out the door, leaving Kat standing in the doorway. My mind was reeling. Everything about my life had just changed forever, just as I had been told.

As I started on the lawn I felt overcome with emotion.

"I'm gonna be a dad!" I exclaimed.

This was indeed a blessing. I looked to the sky and thanked God. Kat had a condition that made it very difficult to get pregnant. The doctors had remained optimistic, but they were quite blunt about the reality that we may never have children on our own.

We were still waiting to hear when Rusty was going to be with us. But this news temporarily trumped that situation. Kat was excited to be having a child of her own, in addition to being a mother to Rusty.

I left the mower in the middle of the front lawn and ran back into the house. Kat was sitting in the front room, sobbing. She was afraid that I was angry with her. My heart broke. But when she saw my excitement, she held a tissue to her eyes one last time and cautiously stood up. She had never looked as beautiful. We hugged and began planning our new life.

The only people we told about the pregnancy were our parents. Otherwise, we decided we would wait until the first three-month period had passed before making it known.

I never did finish mowing the lawn that day.

Mind Over Matter
September–October 1997

Since early childhood I had experienced déjà-vu and discovered that I had the occasional ability to see or sense the future. I came to understand that when I opened my mind to these psychic experiences, my soul was communicating in harmony with my mind, indicating that my life was moving on track. It was a very warming sensation, although it could also create a great deal of unnecessary anxiety when I tried to figure out what the message meant.

It was always accurate, although often not in the way that I necessarily wanted it to be.

Since I had started working for Royce I had been experiencing déjà-vu on an extremely frequent basis—much more than ever before. This led me to believe—to *know*—that I was meant to have Royce in my life, but to what end I did not know.

With Kat being pregnant the future was suddenly in question. The baby was due around late May. We discussed it at length and decided that I should accelerate my studies. We had no idea how much time we would need to spend on a new member in the family. I had my experience with Chucky, so at least I wasn't walking into this situation completely blind. We knew that our parents were 100 percent behind us in our new journey.

We also had Rusty to think of.

My schooling was the one thing in my life that I had complete control over.

I approached Royce about taking another leave. He was ambivalent. I spoke with Rick Van Horne and then Milan Esteban about it, and they were both in favor. With their support, Royce reluctantly threw his hat in the ring and it was a go—within two months I would be a full-time student again.

One of many offensive messages Royce sent me that really sent me on a spin was that "most people get their education done properly in the first place before joining the workforce; they do not depend on their employer to fix their screwups."

This stirred up a mixture of emotions.

My initial feeling was that I was a failure for not getting things right the first time. I had wasted two years in university when I was a kid. But when I thought about it, I realized I had never regretted any of my choices; each one had brought me right to where I was supposed to be.

And suddenly I was somewhat incensed by his comment—who the hell was Royce or anyone else to say that I didn't get my education right the first time? I had earned a college diploma and gained a lot of experience because of it. I *had* gotten my education right in the first place. Just because I hadn't done it his way, who the hell was he to comment on my life choices? It was *my* education and career!

At the time, I failed to realize that I was being guilted into feeling that I was being a burden to the team. Without recognizing that this was a cruel attempt to make me question myself, I started to feel incompetent and undeserving. This reinforced and increased my resolve to be the best that I could be. I began to feel even more indebted to Royce, the team, and the company for allowing me privilege of advancing my education.

It had started with the occasional helpful tip here and there. Slowly it turned into little snippets. And then it became snide comments. Before long, it grew into outright rants.

It was always about the same thing in one way or another: my schooling and my work priorities.

The more criticism I received, the harder I worked to address these issues.

I was determined to be the best of the best, to be a superstar.

Royce's list of my faults evolved with time, until it seemed to take on a life of its own. One minute he would made me feel as though I *was* a superstar, the next minute I was a pain in the "collective ass" of the team.

Before long I started to feel confused and trapped. Was it me, or wasn't I supposed to continue with my schooling as a condition of my working on the R&D team? At the same time, I didn't want to be a burden to them.

What really bothered me was that Royce, Rick Van Horne, and our HR rep had met several times to review and approve my schooling and work expectations prior to even interviewing me for the R&D team. I pointed this out to Royce early on, and he made up a lame apologetic excuse for his comments.

I could tell that he knew he'd contradicted himself. And as he'd proven time and again, he did not like being wrong. I had seen Royce in action when someone crossed him or made him feel like a fool; it was not beyond him to smear his antagonists' reputations. Take Gunther Steinmann for example.

I was starting to see the narcissist in Royce.

Although most people intuitively dismiss it, there is a third side of the coin. That is where those one-in-a-million individuals like me came in, the weirdos, the non-conformists, and the free spirits. But who would be willing to place a bet me?

I was instantly addicted to the maniacal corporate monster, even though every day was a brutal reminder that it was an unhealthy environment in which to attempt to thrive.

And then came my hero, Royce.

It seemed that he had it all, a kind soul, brains, and experience, and he was offering *me* the career opportunity of a lifetime. All that I had worked so hard for, all my dreams and goals, were about to come true. In reality, I had to manipulate my way through his endless physical, emotional, and psychological trials and tribulations. I had to learn to trust my instincts. My very sanity was at stake.

I had known for quite a while that there was something seriously wrong with me. Not the usual weird-kid stuff that I'd grown up with, but perhaps an actual illness. I was stuck in a quandary—my brain wouldn't turn off. I started reminiscing and questioning every awkward and uncomfortable event in my life that I had ever suffered through.

I think that I had known I wasn't well for a few years, as far back as my days with Jennifer Albright. Somehow I just ignored my symptoms as best I could, and I managed to keep on chugging along.

Mom had made mention of my emotional acuity as early as my teen years. Others later claimed to have suspected it, although I had never admitted to anything. Coworkers, friends, family. I felt like a weakling. I had no balls. I was a little pussy.

I was made to feel like a weakling. Like I had no balls. Like I was a little pussy.

Finally, it dawned upon me: I was seeking answers to questions that I couldn't even properly postulate at the time. I wanted to know why my ideas were being ignored. I wanted to know why some of my peers seemed to be working against me rather than with me. I was trying to understand the nature of humankind. I couldn't accept the status quo. The response of most of my friends, colleagues, and supervisors was to "just get over it." With time, I could feel their lack of empathy; I would feel the rolling of their eyes as I approached.

When I wasn't at work, I would ponder these questions with Kat. She too had no answer.

I knew that I was more sensitive than the average Joe, but that was part of what made me unique. Unfortunately, those traits that made me a unique person didn't fit in with the bloodthirsty rat race called the corporate world—at least that's what I was being conditioned to believe. I was led to believe that my continuous search for the answers to my questions left many thinking that I was just a nuisance. Royce outright told me that I was a "high-maintenance complainer," and that should it come to it I would be the first from the team to be let go.

I was under a constant state of stress; how much of it was self-imposed? I couldn't tell. I had been putting all my odd feelings and thoughts aside and now they were beginning to possess me. I believed that I was supposed to take it all in without reacting. Men are built to ignore their feelings. I thought that all men felt the way that I did until they learned to thicken their skin—I was becoming convinced that this was what separated the men from the boys.

It was a rite of passage.

I *had* always been a late bloomer.

I wondered if it was normal to hear voices speaking and arguing with each other inside my head. I concluded that this was just how a person rationalized and reasoned.

I believed that I had to persevere. I could never show any sign of weakness.

I had to be like the nine-year-old Royce. Fierce. Unrelenting. Fearless. Determined. I had to put the gun to my tormentor's head and pull the trigger. God help me if there was a bullet in the chamber.

Although I was now beginning to question my very sanity, for the previous several years I had never considered that I might have had a mental ailment. I believed that I was extremely blessed and that I'd been given a gift. Through school, I'd generally been referred to as "gifted." I was able to think on a significantly higher level than most, or so I thought. I was extremely logical and pragmatic. I was able to look at problems and issues with greater insight and clarity—it was this which enabled me to excel in school, and in general as a being on a path to enlightenment

Most importantly, I was able to include compassion and empathy in my logic.

As I was being sucked into Royce's deep well of fuckery, my feeling of self-worth was getting pulled right down with it. Like those choice few before him I had allowed this asshole into my head, and now he was deeply embedded in there like a prickly little weed. No matter how hard or how many times I tried to rip him from my mind, I couldn't dig out the entire root. He refused to give way; he kept coming back with more and more deeply entrenched and stronger roots.

And the voices in my head . . .

I was getting scared.

Chapter 11

PTSD

Mike Jagger, the Man With the Twisted Soul
Saturday, October 18, 1997

There was a gentle breeze running through the trees on this beautiful autumn afternoon. The sweet smell of the grass and falling leaves networked its way into my nostrils. Mike Jagger was over for the weekend. For the first time in a long while I was relaxed—the world was a good place to be in. Kat joined Mike and me out on our front porch, where we were enjoying a few beers. A cold beer, a greasy cigarette, and some meaningless conversation were all it took to make Mike happy.

Kat and I loved having Mike over for weekends and did so on a fairly regular basis.

The Internet fascinated Mike. He would spend hours looking things up.

It was about ten Sunday morning when I awoke. I had a slight hangover. The night before, just after dusk, we had moved in from the front porch and sat in the living room in front of the computer for hours. Kat had gone to bed shortly before midnight. Finally, around three o'clock, I too went to bed.

When I awoke, Kat lay by my side, still sleeping. I heard the mouse clicking away in the next room. I realized that Mike had not gone to bed at all.

I went into the front room where Mike sat. He was sitting there, eyes bloodshot, with a beer in his left hand and the mouse in his right. I looked at the computer screen.

I witnessed one of the most grotesque images I had ever seen.

Mike was looking at graphic images of human mutilation and suffering.

I was disgusted.

I asked Mike to exit from the website he was on. He ignored me. He was enjoying this. "Enjoying" may not be the correct term—he was being drawn into the grotesqueness. It was as if he *needed* to see these images. The Internet was just becoming popular in households back then, and Mike's only access to these images was at our house.

I asked him how he found this site. He said he had done a search for dead bodies and just kept following links. Somehow, he had found some backdoor into the site.

Mike worked as an industrial cleaner for minimum wage. He began to explain to me exactly what part of his job entailed. "Sometimes we have to go and clean up after murders and suicides."

He lit up a cigarette and began to tell his story.

They had warned him.

Mike was instructed to put on a white plastic bodysuit over his clothing. The suit included booties to cover his work boots.

They entered the house. A strong smell hung in the air. It smelled of rotting meat, sour and dense. The smell permeated Mike's clothing, cloying within his nostrils. His stomach churned as he realized where he was. This was the scene of a murder or suicide. Butterflies began floating in his stomach and his curiosity began to rise.

He was directed into a small bedroom. The pungent stench was stronger. He could smell shit too. The first thing he noticed was the blood splatter across the wall. The patterns mesmerized him. It reminded him of the splash paintings he had done as a child in kindergarten.

He imagined a variety of sick and twisted scenarios that may have led to this mess.

Mike was brought back to reality when a pail filled with hot sudsy water was thrust before him. It was not Mike's job to figure out what had happened. His job was to make it look as though it had never happened.

He kept his enthusiasm to himself.

The bittersweet smell of death came crashing into his nostrils again. He reached inside the pail and found a sponge. He began to wipe the blood from wall.

I watched his jaw tighten and his mouth form a slight "O." Mike blew a smoke ring in the air. He clicked on the next link. His eyes continued to widen in anticipation of every link.

"Turn this shit off, Mike," I demanded as the next image began downloading.

Mike turned without looking at me and stood up. He walked right by me. My eyes were glued to the computer screen. A woman's face, or what was left of it, appeared on the screen. In the distance I heard the *psst* sound of a beer bottle being opened. I moved to the computer and quickly closed the image. I proceeded to log off the Internet.

Mike came back in the room. "What did you do that for?" he demanded.

I looked at my friend. Poor Mike. What else had he seen? What was he not telling me? I could tell that the image of the blood-spattered room was both haunting and appealing to him. But there was something that he was not telling me. Something dark. Something that had aroused the goriest of fantasies within him. I looked at the printer beside the computer. There was a stack over half an inch thick of printouts. I reached over and began to look at the pictures. I have to admit that there was a macabre curiosity in my mind as I looked through the pictures. They were of dead bodies. Mutilated. Maimed. Twisted. Disfigured. Men and women. On every sheet.

All dead.

"What are you going to do with these?" I asked.

"Frame them and put them up in my apartment."

Usually when he was over, Mike printed off numerous explicit porn images to jerk off to. This was a major change in his curiosity. I wondered if my friend intended to masturbate to these images like he did the nudes.

I was dumbfounded. A wave of panicky paranoia hit me.

They know what you're looking at. They will be coming for you.

Those images. How disgusting.

Would I have to rat Mike out?

He's the freak, not me. He's the one who's haunted, not me.

The voices in my head were as active as ever.

You're overreacting. Mike did nothing illegal. You are not in any trouble.

I crawled back into bed and curled up into a ball beside my wife.

Please, my dear Kat, wake up! I need to hear your soothing voice. You'll make everything okay. I know you will.

The next thing I knew I was squinting to see the red numbers on my alarm clock. It was just after noon. I didn't know what time my troubled mind had finally put itself to rest. And then, like a bolt of lightning, those images struck my mind.

Oh my God—*Mike!*

I'd left him alone again. I rushed out into the living room. Mike was not there.

Where was he?

I ran downstairs. Thank God! He had crashed on the couch. I ran back upstairs into the living room. I went to log on to the Internet. I needed to prove to myself there was nothing wrong.

A message came sprawling across the screen: "Enter your password."

I entered my password. The same message came back up. I swear, it was a little bigger this time: "Enter your password."

My panic and paranoia were justified.

They have already hacked into my computer. They're checking me out.

I tried to reenter my password a dozen times. Each time I typed a little more carefully. Maybe I had mistyped part of the code. Still, it would not let me on. The password prompt became the width of the entire screen:

"ENTER YOUR PASSWORD."

I wanted to go wake up Kat. She'd make everything better.

Maybe Mike had inadvertently changed my password. I went to wake him up to see what he had done. He wasn't computer literate; he probably changed the password and didn't even know it.

It was Sunday afternoon around twelve-thirty and I was completely freaking out.

Mike groaned as I awakened him. I prompted him with a dozen questions. No, he did not change my password. When I was finally convinced, I went back upstairs.

Surely the Internet connection was fucked up. I shut down the computer and restarted it.

The same thing came up:

"ENTER YOUR PASSWORD."

I paced back and forth between the computer room and my bedroom, smoking cigarette after cigarette. The ashtray was overflowing with a clutter of small smoldering cigarette butts. That's the last thing I needed, a fire. I took the ashtray to the kitchen and dumped it into the dish-laden sink. I turned on the water until the smoke stopped. I lit another cigarette and went back to my bedroom. I stood there looking at my wife—she was just waking up herself.

Maybe the server had gone down. This has nothing to do with me.

Hours later I went back to bed and just kept telling myself everything was going to be okay.

Kat hadn't even rolled over since I had initially left our bed.

Days later I had finally convinced myself that the authorities were not out to get me. My computer had let me onto the Internet later that night after I had dropped Mike off at his home. No police had showed up at my door. Still, I had an uneasy feeling in the pit of my stomach. I told my wife about the incident, and she chuckled. She told me that I had overreacted. Mike was maybe a gore hound, but he had done nothing that thousands if not millions of other people hadn't done. It was just plain morbid curiosity.

She told me that she would talk with Mike the next time he was over.

This entire experience of paranoia at this level of intensity was a first for me.

Goodbye to She Who Was the Keeper of the Secret Key
Friday, October 31, 1997

"You are going places," she whispered in my ear as she tightly hugged me.

Her name was Cassie Andrews. She was the executive administrative assistant to the CEO/owner Wilson Van Horne. If anything was going on at the top level of the company, Cassie knew all about it. She worked hard for her money and she was paid *very* well for her ability to keep vital company and personal information secret.

Wilson Van Horne had announced his retirement in late September. His son Rick was the heir to the throne, but Wilson knew that his son wasn't mature enough for the job. So he hired on a new CEO and assigned Rick the position of VP of Technology months earlier, where he believed Rick could do the least amount of damage.

It was Cassie's last day of work. She was retiring. She was only fifty-five. She and her husband had never had children and had always wanted to travel around the world. On this her final day, the office staff held a little drop-in luncheon for anyone who wanted to say goodbye. I made it to the party just as they were wrapping things up.

As soon as she saw me, she ran to me and hugged me tightly.

"I was hoping that you would come!" she said.

Kat had worked with her and flat-out disliked her. According to Kat, Cassie was too focused on appearances and putting on a professional front rather than the quality of work that was being done.

I had always liked Cassie. From the moment I met her when I'd first started at W.V.H. Steel she'd been very friendly and made me feel like a part of the company family. When opportunity presented, we would always smile at each other and say hello.

I looked around the room—only a handful of our coworkers were still present. They were all looking at me with indescribable looks of awe.

You are going places.

The VP of Technology
Early November 1997

He was the heir to the throne, the one who would one day lead this empire to greatness beyond imagination. His was the coveted position: the vice president of technology.

He was Rick Van Horne, the son of the great Wilson Van Horne.

He was an asshole. Plain and simple.

Rick also seemed to be the kind of guy who would be a howl to go drinking and partying with. When we spoke he almost always made me laugh. A time or two he tried to be stern with me and it took all I had to stifle a chuckle. I wasn't careless though; I may have pushed a few boundaries but I knew that he could and would terminate me if he were so inclined.

Rick loved to play little head games, especially with humorless posers like Royce. Rick had more money than anyone would ever need, yet he would nickel and dime anyone out of anything. If not out of greed, then just because he could.

I felt bad for Royce. Not just because he was being harassed by Rick, but because he didn't know how to process Rick's nonsense. One minute Rick was being a pompous ass and joking around, the next he was being serious.

I felt even worse for Royce, because for such a brilliant man who had himself been abused, he was unable to rise above the bullying and fearmongering mentality. I expected him to be even more compassionate to others. Rather, he lowered himself to treat others in the same manner as lowbrow characters like Rick.

I thought quite highly of Royce and he knew it, yet rather than fulfill his promise to mentor me with my education and career path, he chose to abuse that trust and use it to tear me down.

It was at this point that I formally concluded that, despite his top-notch education and his numerous accomplishments, Royce was not as evolved as his initial impression suggested.

He was a wannabe.

He was my boss.

He scared the shit out of me.

I Sacrificed My Freedom for Peace
Mid-November 1997

I finally reached the point with Royce where I requested of him that if I was doing something he disapproved of he was to let me know immediately. I believed that it would be best for my mental well-being if he could respect me enough to calmly discuss issues at the onset, rather than follow his usual routine of letting things fester and suddenly blow up.

Deep down I knew that I was wasting my breath.

In response to my request, Royce created a "virtual rule book" just for me—it was a work in progress. This both troubled me and frightened me; I was left with no recourse. I had no way to address my grievances because I believed that everyone was on his side. I had chosen not to get involved in corporate politics. Royce quickly showed me that, because I was apolitical, I was without a safety net if and when things got messy, and it would be very easy for me to slip between the cracks.

His rules gradually started to become unreasonable and unfair, some even outright illegal.

One morning, Royce called me to his office. He objected to me bringing in coffee and a muffin to work. He told me that "professionals eat their breakfast at home before going to work." If it continued, he was going to dock me an hour's pay.

I must have missed the memo stating that one.

He told me that if I came into work without my long hair tied back, I would be sent home for the day without pay. I thought of all the women who worked in the company—they were not required to tie back their hair.

Wasn't that sexual discrimination?

He objected to me showing up at work with damp hair even if it was tied back. I figured that he was jealous that, unlike him with his balding crown, I had enough hair to be damp and tie back. Still, I was alerted, as Royce claimed that this too was an offense that would result in an unpaid day off.

I wondered, was I also supposed to dry my hair after I showered following a trial?

It was not long before I had to keep my tattoos completely covered at all times. Very few of us were tattooed back then, but one or two of my coworkers in the TTD also had them. I was quite bothered by the fact that I had to keep mine covered while the others didn't.

Royce went on to explain that "engineers did not get tattoos."

I told him to wait and see. *He did not like hearing that.*

I was beyond frustrated with this recent onslaught of nonsensical rules that were coming from out of nowhere. I realized that I had given Royce the key to my free will, and that, as much as it hurt, it was my decision and I now had to deal with the fallout. Sadly, Royce abused this power. Instead of alleviating my emotional pain, he intensified it.

As the company was growing, so was the number of new hires it was bringing in. The R&D team, including the students, was moved into a mobile trailer just outside of the main production plant. A new research/technical facility was being constructed to house all the corporate staff, including a mini-plant for the TTD to run trials.

Royce had his own office again. He spent most of his time in front of his laptop behind closed doors.

Shane and I were in back-to-back cubicles again. Never appeased, Royce started expressing disapproval when I asked Shane for technical or personal assistance and/or guidance. On more than a few occasions, Royce requested that I come to him when I had any questions, no matter what the topic.

When I did approach Royce, I found that he rarely had the time for me. He would give me the sense that I was bothering if not irritating him.

It was simply easier for me to see Shane; he was more knowledgeable and more approachable than Royce. I realized that I was turning into quite the judge; nonetheless, I quickly realized that Royce may have been harboring feelings of jealousy toward Shane.

The Letter
Late November 1997

Not so long ago, Royce had shared one of his deepest and most disturbing and personal memories with me: that he had it in him to kill. He could and would pull the trigger if he had to.

Had he made it all up? Was he trying to frighten and intimidate me? Was he trying to tell me that he wouldn't hold back and destroy me if he felt cornered or threatened?

What if this was all in my mind?

I decided to appeal to his humane and empathetic senses, so I wrote him a letter.

Royce,

I've never acknowledged this to anyone. For a while now I have suffered from ongoing bouts of increasing anxiety and paranoia. I've always kept those thoughts to myself—I thought of them as the product of an overactive imagination. I know how many people see me. They think I'm some intellectual weirdo or a strange savant. Maybe I am a bit of both. It's even been suggested that I was on the autism spectrum. If I ever told anyone some of the thoughts that really occupied my mind, I know everyone would look at me with shock and awe.

I leaned forward, face glued to the computer screen, and read my words. The anxiety I felt from sharing these words with anyone—just from putting them on the screen—made my skin crawl. I put my finger over the delete key, but then decided to continue.

I have never even told my wife about these thoughts.
All I know for sure is that I am suffering.
There's almost always at least one conversation going on in my head. I'm often arguing with myself, but it's only in my head. When it started I assumed that it was my conscience guiding me, and that everyone had to live with it. I don't know how I am able to hold down a conversation while managing my thoughts. But I manage. In fact, I'm doing it right now.
You told me that you had it within you to kill.
I'm telling you that I'm frightened because so do I.

I sat back in my chair and read what I had just typed. Could I trust Royce with this personal information? I was no longer dealing with the Royce I'd known in the past. Things were much different now. If Royce showed this letter to anyone else I could lose my job—and possibly even be charged for issuing a death threat. I wondered if that was his purpose in telling me his story in the first place.

I was no longer a kid without obligations. I had much at stake: I was financially bound to Kat, to our future family, and to my custody lawsuit for my son Rusty.

If Kat was here I would be discussing these things with her. I know with certainty that she is my confidante. I could not fathom her turning on me. That would have been the end of me.

I thought that maybe I should stop typing and wait until she got back from an overnight business trip the next day. I didn't think I could wait. I decided to e-mail her.

I leaned back to the keyboard and scrolled up to the top and changed "*Royce*" to "*Kat.*"

I removed the part about killing at the end.

I began typing more:

There's other shit too. At times, I've convinced myself that our home has been bugged by work. They sense my dissonance and are looking for reasons to entrap us to shove us out of the company before we can call them out on the bullshit. Kat, we can see through the window dressings that they have used to distract everyone from the truth.

I know things. Things that I once swore to never repeat, and I have no intention of ever going against my word, that is all I have left. But what if I had been lied to? What if these secrets were thoughts that had been purposefully implanted into my brain as a ruse to keep me preoccupied from seeing the truth that was in front of me?

These are not things that I just think about, these are things that I experience and feel. I've always been able to rationalize what's going through my mind . . . until recently.

Please Kat, help me.

This was all true.

I sat back and read what I had just written. It hit me like an atomic blast: I had just reached a defining moment in my life. I had just admitted that I had lost control of my mind.

I started to panic. I looked up mental illness and my symptoms on the Internet. I searched for paranoia, anxiety, and depression, and some other odd feelings and symptoms that I had been experiencing, such as delusional thoughts and voices. Several mental illnesses were listed, but schizophrenia stood out the most.

As I read on, I became convinced that I had schizophrenia.

I had seen so many movies and TV shows depicting schizophrenics as murderous maniacs who wore aluminum foil helmets and talked to themselves—this was not me. Yet when I thought about it, I *had* been having violent urges for some time: homicidal ideations about Royce. And in the past, I would entertain vivid thoughts of ending others who offended me. As always, I had dismissed those thoughts, thinking of them as "normal."

Kat called me on the phone immediately. It was approximately eleven-thirty a.m. I answered but refused to speak of these issues while at work—I knew that my work phone had been bugged.

I didn't want to risk being overheard by anyone in the office, so we agreed that I would leave work for lunch and call her back from the safety of our home, although I already questioned our safety there too.

I decided that I couldn't keep this to myself for a second longer, damn the consequences.

Once home I called Kat, finally telling her what I was going through.

She was clearly distraught, but she maintained a supportive tone. She told me that she had no idea that I was suffering—she thought my behavior was just a little of my eccentricity. She reminded me that I wasn't a doctor, but she insisted I call one. I realized that at different periods in my adult life I'd let my paranoia and anxiety get the best of me. Often, I would make up excuses to avoid social gatherings. Kat suffered from extreme anxiety as well, so she never pushed the issue. But what I was experiencing right now, this was the worst it had ever been.

I felt a little better for having finally shared my pain.

Through my entire life I had been bullied and teased. By the older kids, by the cool kids, by the smart kids, and by those in authoritative positions, like Sid and now Royce at work. I thought I'd learned to cope with bullies and difficult personalities. I thought I'd grown stronger. I thought that I was an adult, a real man.

I realized that I had e-mailed my message to her from a company computer. I started to freak out. The IT team would be crawling all over my computer while I was at home disclosing the details of my insanity to my wife.

I returned to work after talking with Kat, but only long enough to clear out my computer of any and all evidence of my message. I knew that from the moment I started typing they could track me down if it came down to it.

That night I went to bed but I couldn't sleep. The next day I didn't want to leave my bed. Not wanting to draw any unnecessary attention to myself, I dragged my miserable ass in to work.

Dr. Linda Gantt
Thursday, November 27, 1997

With a crack in my voice, I asked Royce if I could borrow his office to make a personal call. I didn't want my coworkers, especially Royce, eavesdropping. He was purposefully hesitant, but ultimately let me have my privacy.

I called my family doctor, Dr. Gantt.

I was shaking from my very inner core. Royce, and work in general, had me feeling so worthless and useless, and I was falling for his psychological campaign against me. I believed that I deserved this misery.

Dr. Gantt had been my family physician for only a few years.

The doctor's secretary, Erin, tended to be short and off-putting, but when I told her that I had been seeing, hearing, and spending my mind's time in la-la land, she was wonderful. She assured me that many people had similar issues and that I would be just fine. She had me in to see Dr. Gantt the next day.

Dr. Gantt was not a pretty woman, and her true personality hid behind a thick cloak of professionalism. She was an excellent practitioner. When I told her what was happening she promptly acted—but not alarmingly—to keep me calm. She said it sounded like schizophrenia, but that she wasn't trained to diagnose mental illnesses. She gave me a prescription for risperidone, a common antipsychotic. She had me return the next week, this time with Kat.

She also told me that if I had any issues before then to call her back immediately, or if I started really losing it to check into the hospital.

Kat had little idea of what was going on with me up to this point. Kat was very bright—she had interacted with me when I went on my scientific rants about this and that, and she could follow my philosophies and theories, which were logical and sound. She had always chalked it up to my "creative genius." On the other hand, I had hidden the occurrence of the wildly adventurous voices and the ongoing arguments from her.

As the doctor had promised, she had sent out referrals for psychiatrists, but she alerted us that it could take some time to hook me up with one. She showed me the letter she had scripted. Dr. Gantt was known for her promptness and keen observation of visit lengths, but she went overtime with us. She asked me how I was feeling, and she spent a great deal of her time speaking with Kat to ensure that she understood what was going on. She told us that the risperidone alone would not cure me. Because most of my symptoms were anxiety-based she also put me on clonazepam, an anti-anxiety narcotic to help me mellow out. The meds barely helped take the edge off, but I felt as though I was trudging through mud all day.

No one at work knew what I was going through. I knew of the stigma that can be associated with mental illness, and I knew that Royce would jump at the opportunity to mess with my already fucked-up head. I also knew that my mental health status could be used against me in my lawsuit against the O'Reillys for custody of Rusty.

It was late November. I had planned my second sabbatical from work in the upcoming January to accelerate the completion of my engineering degree. Dr. Gantt wanted me to take a leave of absence from work immediately. However, I was scared to death that if I took medical leave it could mess up my upcoming scholastic leave. Additionally, it made me feel like I had some tiny bit of empowerment over Royce—I would show him that I could take his shit for another month.

I should have taken the early leave when it was offered.

Before leaving for the holidays and my next academic sabbatical, despite Royce's assholistic behavior, I forced myself for one last time to put on a big smile and shake his hand in thanks. The clammy, fishlike hand that met mine made me want to slap him. He showed no emotion, good or bad, he was just sallow and sullen as always.

He didn't even wish me luck.

The Real Man
Christmas and the New Year, 1997/'98

After the third month into her pregnancy, Kat and I started to share our joyous news with everyone. It was Christmas—we couldn't have hoped for a better gift to share with our friends and family. It was such a happy time. Despite my declining mental health, everything was falling into place.

For that brief moment in time I felt as if I was a king.

In early January, around week fourteen of her pregnancy, Kat went to get an ultrasound. She came out of the testing room with her eyes filled with tears and a crazed look of terror. My heart sank. She had wanted this so badly. And that angel that had visited me a few short months ago *had* promised that my life was going to change. Kat was upset because the technician didn't say much other than that her doctor would contact her with the results within the next day or two.

I hugged Kat as tightly as I could, and I promised her that everything would work out perfectly. Deep down, I knew that she had miscarried.

The next day during class there was a knock on the classroom door. I somehow knew it was for me. The professor opened the door and the entire class heard a campus security officer ask to see me. Initially, I thought that someone had hit my car or something simple but inconvenient.

I stepped outside of the classroom and the officer handed me a note with Kat's supervisor's phone number and extension written on it, requesting that I call her as soon as I could. My first thought was that Kat had been in an accident of some sort.

But deep down I knew the truth.

I remember returning to the classroom and walking up to the prof, holding the letter in my shaking hand. With a sympathetic look, he excused me from the class.

My adrenaline was pumping like never before. I raced to my car and drove as fast as I reasonably could. While trying to weave between vehicles on the highway, I called Kat's supervisor. She didn't answer. I tried again, and still there was no answer. Finally, I called the front desk. With a little bit of prompting I convinced the receptionist to reveal what had happened. Kat *had* lost the baby. I was crushed, but all I could think about was how my Kat was. The receptionist told me that a work friend—the company nurse, Ann—had taken her home.

When I arrived home, Kat was in tears. Ann was with her awaiting my return. I went straight to Kat and hugged her. Kat was a frail little woman, only five one and 100 pounds. She had started to put on little weight, but she was still as delicate as a flower. She felt even smaller than usual.

"I . . . I am so sorry," she cried as she reached out and buried her head into my shoulder.

I squeezed her fragile frame even tighter and looked up to the ceiling hoping for some sage advice from a higher power as to what I should do or say.

"There is nothing to apologize for," I reassured her. That was all I could come up with.

She started sobbing even more. "I don't want you thinking that I'm a failure."

My heart broke.

"Never," I whispered into her ear. I pulled her in even closer to my chest.

"*Never.*"

Ann looked at us clinging to one another and began filling me in on the day's events. "From what I know, her doctor called her at work and plainly said that her baby was gone."

I felt Kat tremble in my arms as Ann spoke.

"Within seconds she started begging and bartering with the doctor—all she wanted was for her doctor to tell her everything was okay. That's when I arrived," Ann continued.

"Instead the doctor rushed from the phone." Ann had a look of disgust as she shared the doctor's lack of empathy. I felt angered as well. I would have expected that Kat's doctor would have called us in to her office to deliver the bad news in person. Instead, she left Kat to face this soul-crushing experience on her own.

"All anyone could hear was Kat's sobs. I had to pry the phone from her tear-soaked cheek," her friend finished.

I could *feel* the office halls being forever haunted with Kat's mournful moans, *no . . . no . . . no . . .* over and over.

As Ann was finishing the events with me, the phone rang. It was Kat's OBGYN. I spoke with her. "We should remove the . . . the fetus as soon as possible," she said.

I looked at Kat and calmly agreed. We scheduled the procedure for six o'clock.

That night was one of the most excruciating of my entire life. I knew Kat could physically handle the surgery, but it was the emotional part that chilled me to the bone.

I was in the exam room, sitting on a hard steel stool. My wife was lying upon an exam table. The stirrups were out and spread apart. The doctor asked my wife to put her feet in the ends of the stirrups.

She refused and began crying.

The doctor took a firm tone.

If you knew Kat, you'd know that is not usually the best way to deal with her. I continued holding her hand and trying to soothe her. The more the doctor prodded, the more resistant she became. She kept screaming, "You're not taking my baby away from me!"

I squeezed her hand as reassuringly as possible. She was flailing about on the table. Finally, the doctor had the nurse give her a sedative. I felt so horrible. I felt so afraid and powerless. I just wanted to run in any direction that would take me to where I couldn't remember why I was running in the first place.

But I knew my place. It was with my Kat.

That was what real men did.

Although on sabbatical, the next day I went to work to share with my team what had happened. They had already been made aware of what had occurred—the rumor mill was insane at the company. Within seconds of Kat getting the bad news the previous day, the story of our loss and her reaction started to spread.

As I trudged through the office, I received nothing but looks and words of sympathy. I knocked on Royce's open office door. He took his time, but after a few minutes he waved me in. I told him what had happened. He said nothing for a moment, and then he shrugged his shoulders and said that "it was probably for the best." He then turned his back to me.

I couldn't believe it, even if he did have it in for me.

It made me really want to see him suffer.

I wanted to put his father's revolver to his head and keep on pulling that trigger over and over until that magic chamber, the one that contained a bullet, fired, spreading his brains and skull all over.

Kat and I simply spent the rest of the week together mourning the loss of our little Peanut, as we had nicknamed it. I took the rest of the week off from my classes, and Kat called in sick as well. Except for Royce, no one questioned our grief—we received multitudes of sympathy.

Shortly after this experience, we both started to get seriously sick. I was becoming more and more delusional and paranoid having suffered through Royce's psychological campaign of terror; meanwhile, Kat became fixated on having a baby.

Kat never did get pregnant again.

Part IV
A Terrible Certainty

Chapter 12

I Live to Love and Love to Learn

Dr. Rose Edwin
January through April 1998

After having been seeing Dr. Gantt for a few months, my parents noticed that I was a little off. I was becoming even more of a recluse. They noticed that we weren't coming to visit them as frequently as we used to—they had to come to us. Plus, because of my meds I was putting on weight at a considerable rate. It would have been difficult to not see that something was going on. Kat and I discussed it and decided that it was time to let them know what was going on.

I asked my parents not to disclose to their friends until I was ready.

Both of our families were open and loving and let us know that they would be as accommodating as possible. It turned out much better than expected, and so we gave them the lowdown.

Mom told me over and over that she had seen it coming since my late teen years. I wasn't sure whether I agreed or not. I had always maintained the belief that I had just been a typical rebellious and withdrawn teen growing up. Mind you, that was one of the biggest aspects of psychosis or schizophrenia: it was not knowing or realizing that I was ill. The technical term was "anosognosia."

Kat's mother and Len were concerned but weren't sure how to react.

Everyone was equally concerned for Kat's mental health and the impact I was having on her.

I was fortunate. Dr. Gantt found me a psychiatrist within three months.

The first time I met Dr. Rose Edwin I had been on a small medicinal cocktail prescribed by Dr. Gantt. The side effects that I had been experiencing were brutal. Within a few short months I had gained over eighty pounds. My jeans no longer fit, and my belly was rock hard and spilling out from below my tees.

Dr. Edwin was not what I expected a psychiatrist to be. Honestly, I wasn't sure what to expect. From television and the movies, I had the impression that the psychiatrist was a doctor whose office housed a couch upon which the patient laid and proceeded to tell how their mommy fucked up their head, after which the shrink gained some brilliant insight into their problems and prescribed them drugs that would exorcise all of their demons.

In reality it was a very dry and clinical experience. She never revealed any emotion, be it empathy or even a slight smile. Kat and I sat across from her and I proceeded to answer numerous questions.

The first question she asked of me was if there was a history of mental illness in my family. I was unaware of any, but I knew that my dad was a little obsessive compulsive when it came to tidiness.

Next, she drilled me with questions such as: How was my general mood? Did I feel suicidal? Homicidal? What were the voices I heard saying? Did I hallucinate? How was my relationship with my wife? My parents? My friends?

She didn't ask questions about what may have caused my illness or how I felt physically; she focused on my emotional and mental instabilities. Was I anxious, depressed, or manic? Was I hearing voices, seeing things, or suffering from paranoia or delusional thinking? Her concern was my immediate state of mind.

Kat always joined me. We met Dr. Edwin at least once a week without fail.

Before and during each session, I was often deathly afraid of answering her questions honestly—I didn't want to be sent to the loony bin. I didn't want her to know just how deeply disturbing many of my thoughts were. My own mind was playing with me at every opportunity, and I didn't like it. I didn't want to look weak.

I know that most people talk to themselves when making a decision; for instance, weighing the pros and cons when making a large purchase. But my mind was filled with echoing emotions exploding back and forth at itself. I had begun to notice that I was having some slight difficulty concentrating on outside stimuli because I couldn't get my mind to shut up.

The peace I had from being away from the toxic work environment helped. For the entire four months away from work I didn't make any contact with any of my coworkers—except for stopping in following Kat's miscarriage—and they didn't try to contact me. At first, I had been a little concerned and anxious that I was going to one day receive a message that my job no longer existed. However, as I immersed myself in the academic world, I quickly felt the toxins from work just melt away.

The comfort I had while being in school was refreshing.

As Dr. Edwin and I began to understand each other, I came to trust and accept that she had my best interests in mind. Although I frequently thought otherwise, I knew I was sick and needed treatment, at least with anxiety and depression.

This brings up one critical concern: some individuals with serious mental health issues are not even aware that they have an issue. This was the anosognosia. This was what was happening to me: I was believing my own delusional thinking. My mind was feeding itself with its own poison.

Assuming that an individual is aware of their mental issue, the first point at which most people with an issue start to fall apart is that they refuse to admit that they need help, let alone open up and ask for it.

After all, mental and/or emotional health issues are a weakling's condition. It is especially so for men, but women are criticized for exhibiting anxiety or depression as well.

I realized that this was why Shane had shushed me when I revealed my deductions regarding Royce's mental/emotional health to him. If rumors surfaced that he had any kind of instability there could establish an automatic stigma associated with his name, whether the rumors were true or false, and that could be detrimental to his entire career and personal future.

For most of my years at W.V.H. Steel I had been told that I simply needed to "toughen up" or "thicken my skin," but no matter how I tried, I couldn't. That was not who I was. As a sensitive, empathetic man I couldn't ignore the pointless negativity and reckless politicking and backstabbing that I was observing and experiencing daily.

Although occasional attempts had been made to prove otherwise by coworkers, peers, and subordinates, I was not a liar, and I did not play games. It was beyond my comprehension as to how or why any individual would want to invite unnecessary grief upon themselves. But so many individuals did this exact thing. I came to the belief that these individuals were trying to drag others like me down into their misery; it was a result of their own insecurities, their own need to feel better about themselves, or to elevate their egos by making others feel less or worse than they do.

It's as the saying goes: misery loves company.

With that, I easily concluded that we all have the free will to opt out of spreading our misery, yet many of us most often do not. As Royce's actions showed, it is far easier to lash out at others than it is to work through our emotions. What we must be is cognizant of how our foul mood can turn into unretractable words and/or behaviors which can have a long-term damaging effect.

We *all* need some way to channel the negative energy that we encounter on a regular and unending basis. That's what hobbies are for. Some watch TV. Some collect things. Some talk it out with their friends or partners. Some use drugs or alcohol. A very rare few can remain positive and deflect most of all the negativity that is thrown their way.

And then there are those like me, the ones who run themselves ragged trying to fill all the cracks and holes in the dike to keep all the negativity from spilling out, trying to protect others from the lurking danger. Unfortunately, there is a limit to how many of these cracks and holes can be filled until eventually it all comes flooding out, drowning both the individual who had plugged the holes and those it was built to protect in the first place.

Anger is an emotion based on fear. Where there is fear there is no love. I'd made my share of blunders, but almost never with malicious intent. I say "almost" because I am only human, and despite my best efforts I did give in to my dark side on occasion. But when I did lash out, once I had regained control of my emotions I attempted to make amends almost immediately. I was always quick to apologize, sometimes even if I hadn't done anything wrong. I was the type who would apologize for apologizing. I am certain that this made some individuals believe that I was a doormat upon which they could wipe their shit-covered boots, and I must admit that there was some truth to that.

My only comfort is the hope, the belief, that there are those I may have offended in my life who will accept my extended hand and join me (and all others) on this journey on our tortuous paths to enlightenment.

As one of the sheep I generally wandered about, straying away from the shepherds and other sheep. I was on *my* path; I was slowly learning to not only trust my instincts, but also to act in accordance with them. I had been so wide-eyed and naive when I reached adulthood and joined the workforce that I trusted the "adults" who were in charge. I had constantly ignored the red flags as I basked in the glory of my surroundings.

All I really wanted was to belong and contribute to something greater than myself. That was why I worked so hard to be at the top in my field academically and professionally.

Sometimes it took me a while to consider and then reconsider how to approach an issue or problem. Unfortunately, in the fast-paced corporate environment that I was employed in, it was rare that time was given to consider all the elements of a problem. That was why so much time ended up being wasted when a team set out to solve a problem: the root cause of the problem wasn't addressed, rather a quick-fix or band-aid solution would be agreed upon. I cannot count how many times the light came on in my brain *after* the team had decided the best way to approaching a problem. And when I did add my opinion after the decision had been made, I was told I was working against the team.

School

I was finishing up my third level and beginning the fourth and final level of my engineering degree during this sabbatical.

I don't know how I pulled it off with all my meds and symptoms muddling me down as much as they were, yet the A's and A+'s kept rolling in.

Chapter 13

Life, Death, and Other Trivialities

As I was going through significant life changes due to my illness and recovery, I began to reflect on my purpose in life. This meant reassessing my core beliefs and philosophies. I found it quite cathartic to write out the ponderances and spiritual beliefs I was beginning to establish. The following are some examples of how I came to perceive the world around me, and how I attempted to regain some semblance of peace within myself.

It is a work in progress.

Father

God—Father—simply *is*.

I use the masculine noun and pronoun out of convenience. God may be male, female, or something completely inconceivable to many of us in the human plane of existence. God may even be a pantheon, if you so please.

Father has always been and always will be. I cannot prove it, and no one can disprove it. So I just accept it.

Father is all of us, and we are all Father.

I have my thoughts and opinions about Father as it pertains to religion and all the associated dogma, but it is not my function to sway anyone's belief system. I *do* believe that Father does not expect me to understand Him by dedicating my life to understanding Him; such is the calling of others, those who dedicate themselves to the research and study of religion and theology and other similar fields.

Father is the vast multiverse which extends beyond our grandest imagination, and He is the tiniest subatomic particle that we have yet to even conceive, that ever will be conceived. Father created everything out of nothing. Father is infinite.

With Father, there is only love. Father is the *only* source of absolute unconditional love.

Fear and Love

All that exists in humankind has come out of fear or love.

It is really that simple.

Fear is a natural *human* emotion given by Father.

A human is acting in a state of fear when he is emoting and/or experiencing feelings such as anxiety, anger, jealousy, sadness, depression, ignorance, defensiveness, hatred, etcetera. The reason for these fear-based feelings is complicated, yet also simple.

The foundation of fear is based upon the reality that we humans are filled with the need to deflect and distance ourselves from any unknown or unfamiliar circumstance, be it physical, intellectual, emotional, or spiritual.

Fear is driven by our desired state of self-preservation.

The innate goal of the person infected with fear is to escape or overcome it. However, when we deflect our fear, we release it upon others. Similarly, when we distance ourselves from it, we are making it someone else's problem, which is also a mode of spreading it. It is a virus. What we fail to realize is that by spreading fear, even when with do it with no intended malice, we are only indulging and adding to our own sense of fear.

It's a vicious circle.

The Self and the Soul

Each of us has a soul, which is an infinitesimally tiny piece of Father. Our soul is who we are when we are in our perfect state of love.

Some souls choose never to leave Father's realm. Other souls choose to reincarnate to human form millions of times. Our self is the human form that we take on when our soul decides to create a life experience; the self is what we know of ourselves: our physical, intellectual, mental, and spiritual consciousness.

Each incarnation of the soul to human form, the self, is different because of the free will given to humankind by Father.

Human life is a blank canvas. The self is the paintbrush that spreads the paint on the canvas, as chosen by our free will. Throughout our life, the self creates an experience. The experience is the culmination of each creation.

Before incarnation, the soul may arrange certain occurrences and opportunities; however, although many may argue otherwise, when the soul decides to incarnate itself, it yields a new creation to free will when the self comes to be.

Every human's destiny is a result of their choices as they create their experience.

I do believe that the soul learns from every experience that each self creates. There is a lesson which the self sets out to discover that will bring the soul closer to Father.

Enlightenment is achieved when the self and the soul resonate. It is an arduous journey.

Creating the Life Experience and Free Will

Father created humankind so that He may experience the infinite facets of life through us, whether we are amongst the greatest thinkers and/or philosophers or the frailest, most disabled, or even if we are the vilest of tyrants that the world has ever known.

He wants to experience the trials and tribulations of each of our lives. He wants to experience the happiness and joy that we feel. He wants to experience the sadness and emptiness that we feel. He wants to experience our anger and hatred. He wants to reside within each of us as we encounter all the twists and turns, and the ups and downs of our rollercoaster lives.

Once in human form, our sole purpose is to create a life experience. No two humans have ever or will ever have the exact same life experience, even if they share the same genes and are exposed to the exact same stimuli. Consider a case such as a pair of identical twins isolated, subjected to the same controlled circumstances and environment for their entire lifetime. They could possibly have differing thoughts and memories or differing personalities, even if only slightly distinct. One of the first key differences is that one of the twins would be born before the other, even if just by seconds.

We begin to create a new life experience from the moment of conception—when our mind becomes aware of its existence—until the moment we pass back into Father's realm of pure love. We create using our free will and the resulting decisions we make. Having free will means that we can do absolutely anything that we want to do. But for everything we do there are consequences. The consequences of our actions may be, and generally are, dictated by our fellow humans, whether right or wrong. Therefore, even if we make all the correct decisions we may still fail.

There have been many ups and downs, but I am thankful for this life experience which I have been creating. Father gave me the intellect to use logic and reasoning, and He gave me unfathomable freedom to make my own choices and decisions. He also gave me the wherewithal to be aware of the possible consequences of acting on my thoughts and words. Not everyone is afforded these luxuries.

He also gave me the power to forgive my transgressors, past and present.

I side with the axiom that the good, right, and just will always eventually be the winners.

Love will conquer all.

We may choose to judge ourselves. Others will certainly judge us. We always have the free will to ignore any judgment. Only Father does not judge. To Father there is no such thing as sin. Sin is a human concept; to Father there is no right or wrong.

Heaven and Hell

Energy cannot be created or destroyed. This is a fundamental law of physics. Therefore, there can be no such thing as divine intervention unto itself. Having said that, even I believe and have mentioned on a few occasions that there must have been an angel on my shoulder. So am I contradicting myself?

I believe that faith is a form of personal and emotional energy, and this positive energy can be harnessed and used to heal. When this positive energy is channeled, that is when divine intervention comes to be. It is therefore reasonable to conclude that there is power in prayer.

Similarly, there is no such a thing as Hell, because Father would not create a place that was not born of love. Negative energy is a result of fear. Like positive energy, negative energy can be concentrated and used to bring harm to others. Therefore, concepts such as the Devil and Hell are brought to fruition. It can be argued that free will, which is only given to humankind, is the source of all evil.

Others may ostracize us.

Others may shame us.

Others may jail us.

Others may even take our lives.

But we *always* have the free will to choose how we react to the words and actions of others.

The Prophets, Leaders, and Masters

Father has revealed to many that there were always prophets, leaders, and masters amongst us.

And there always will be.

The prophets are those whom Father speaks through. They are the ones who can read the writing on the walls. They can see the accidents before they happen. They are the empaths who can feel the suffering of millions, or that of just one in a million. They are the intuitive ones; they seem to know right from wrong, and love from fear.

By sharing Father's truths, the prophets can speak to those who are willing to listen, and they can awaken those who are called upon to lead and inspire. The prophets can see the countless paths that the shepherds throughout the universe are leading their flocks in.

Unfortunately, many of the shepherds are afraid of that which they cannot see, touch, or control. In other words, they lead by fear.

The prophets see this, but they are powerless to overcome the free will of these leaders.

The leaders must try to heed the words of the prophets while keeping their followers aligned and at peace, all while creating their own life experience. To be a good leader they must have a strong sense of integrity and faith in Father as advocated by the prophets.

Father has also warned against following false prophets. This can be extended to ill-intended leaders. Throughout history false prophets have been adorned and ill-intended leaders adored.

When a human is acting out of true unconditional love, they see the universe from a state of bliss. Their existence has been created to meet the perfection of Father. They are like gods, truly capable of healing and creating miracles.

They are what are known as the masters.

When a master is revealed, they espouse Father's truths and philosophies—not as religious zealots, but as true leaders. They do not endorse one religion over another. They speak of one love. One Father.

They would be recognized as a beacon to attract and guide the shepherds and sheep who were straying from their flocks. They would reveal the true pathway to enlightenment.

They would carry out their miracles with complete disregard to their own personal safety. Attempts would most certainly be made to discredit them—they would be shamed or jailed—but being masters, this would not stop them. They know only love. They have no need for hope, because in their mind everything is already in its perfect state. If they were to hope for something to happen, that would imply that they feared that something was lacking, and thus they would not be true masters.

One of the best-known masters was Jesus Christ. He led with love. He performed miracles, such as bringing Lazarus back from the dead. Turning water into wine. And then he accepted his fate upon the cross without begging or pleading for mercy, as most of us would. He was living in a constant state of love, and he died out of love. I'm not trying to push any religion or represent any faith. How you feel about the existence of Christ is your business; it is not my place to convince you of anything.

Chapter 14

You Can't Bring Me Down

A New Day to Stu Things Over and Barry the Hatchet
March 1998

With the new influx of students that would be filling the desks in the offices in May, Royce hired two individuals from the plant in March. He hired them early so that there wouldn't be a gap in knowledge as the new hires started.

The first hire was Stuart Hems. Stu was hired as a project coordinator. Most of his function would be to do the hands-on work and to coordinate the trials and experiments. Stu had been a lead hand in the plant. He was well regarded by both his supervisors and subordinates. I liked him.

The second new hire to the team was a young engineer, Barry Nichols. His function was to be a research engineer. Barry was a twenty-two-year-old kid fresh out of school. He reminded me a little of Sid Stanford and the other highbrow engineers. He was a nerdy little twat, and as it turned out I had no use for him.

Just When Things Were Looking Better
Late April 1998

The phone rang. It was about seven o'clock on a Thursday night.

It was Truman Kush. He had some good news, and he had some bad news.

The good news was that my weekly visits with Rusty had been going well.

He went on to inform me that Jenn was a complete mess—she was circling the drain. She was a full-out junkie and would disappear for days at a time. The O'Reillys had put her into rehab several times, but she kept running back to her crackhead ways. She had become a squatter on the streets, whoring herself out for a fix every time she started jonesing.

It had finally come to the point that Jenn was no longer allowed to have anything to do with Rusty unless overseen by the O'Reillys and a court-authorized social worker. The Prues had long ago taken full custody of Chucky. I wasn't in much contact with the Prues any longer, but I tried to get occasional updates on how Chucky was faring when I had the chance.

Although he wasn't even four yet, Rusty was extremely well spoken, insightful, and thoughtful. He and I had become well acquainted by this time. We had established a relationship, a little friendship. We had some little inside jokes that we shared with each other, and we had a little fist-bump handshake routine that was exclusive to us—no one else could use it.

I kept gently prodding him to call me "Daddy." I would say, "Daddy loves you," when we would part ways every visit. Eventually he began to say, "Me too."

This of course was a major step in our relationship. I suppose that I should have been happy with that at least; it had taken a couple of years to get him to express any emotion toward me at all.

Next came the bad news: Truman hadn't only called to tell me about Jenn's situation, he also had to discuss my mental health issues. I was still functioning as if there was nothing wrong. I was attending school now and planning on returning to full-time work in a week or two in May while still attending school on a part-time basis.

But I was under psychiatric care.

The O'Reillys' legal team had discovered a little bit regarding my psychiatric issues. They had also learned of Kat's emotional/mental issues. I shouldn't have been surprised: the O'Reillys' lawyers had investigators looking for dirt on us, just as Truman and his team did for us. These lawyers were worse than the assholes with their sneaky backstabbing politics back at W.V.H. Steel. And we were paying them to play these games. I despised the notion that so much bullshit had to be waded through just to get custody of my son.

Dr. Edwin had been adding and removing more and more medications, all at varying doses. This resulted in me being so dopey a lot of the time that some days I didn't know if I was coming or going.

But I pressed on, to the detriment of myself.

This was not good for our case.

Truman suggested that with my mental suitability in question, the O'Reilly case was stronger. His recommended solution was for my parents to sue for custody, as they were blood-related to Rusty. He told us that 99 percent of the time blood relations were granted custody above all others.

Rusty had only seen Kat and my parents through that window at the CAS during my regular visits. They had learned to love the boy from afar.

I've Been Knocking, but No One's Answering
Monday, May 4–Monday, May 11, 1998

It was a bright, sunny May morning. I had just finished my second sabbatical and was returning to work. I felt invigorated and ready to face the day and the team. Over the past months, I had really worked on improving my mindset in general, but especially toward Royce and the R&D team environment. I was going in with the attitude that this was an opportunity to start from scratch. As far as I was concerned, we were all starting with a clean slate.

To my chagrin, Shane was the only member of the team in the office that day. The rest, including the students, had gone off to a week-long steel convention. I played with my computer and muddled around a bit but spent most of the week doing nothing—Royce had left no instructions for me or Shane.

This made me a little paranoid.

The following Monday morning, Royce and the rest of the team returned.

There was no "welcome back," "good to see you," "how did it go?" or even a "hello."

I went to talk with Royce that afternoon once I thought that he'd had enough time to settle in. Royce had not seen or spoken with me for just shy of four months. Still, he rolled his eyes and thumped down his pencil when he saw that it was me who had knocked on his office door. He raised his hand up to his temple and looked down at his desk.

He looked up at me and sighed heavily. "Already?"

I started grasping at straws. What should I say? Hoping to appeal to his sense of compassion I decided to tell him about my mental/emotional health issues. Although I had never said anything to anyone but Shane, I knew that Royce had his own undisclosed mental health issues, so I thought that we would have something in common which would open the doors to friendship—or at least civility.

When I told him I was being treated for schizophrenia, his only words were, "I always thought you were delusional."

I was hurt beyond words.

To worsen matters, almost immediately upon my disclosing my illness to him he had let loose the shame and fearmongering associated with the illness. He shared my disclosure with the rest of the team, his peers, and Rick Van Horne.

Once Royce had put his own spin on the situation, no one would believe me or my side of the story. By having shared this I was instantly and permanently stigmatized. From that point on, I was "delusional." My every word or act was brought into question. Word spread throughout the company quite quickly.

I believed that he was determined to exploit my instabilities to take the focus from him and his erratic behavior, which was a result of his own ongoing mental struggles.

Royce had effectively weaponized my illness and turned it against me.

Shane was fair and reasonable about helping me deal with the myriad of moods, triggers, and symptoms that the workplace bullying and politicking had caused, but he had little to no direct experience with a mental illness like mine. No matter how hard I tried to explain what was happening with my mind, he couldn't quite grasp why I couldn't just let it go.

Chapter 15

The Never-Ending Lessons

Spectrums

I believe that all humans fall on innumerable spectrums in almost all characteristics and attributes.

Consider a basic color scale: one end approaches pure black, the combination of all colors. The other end approaches pure white, the complete absence of all color.

Differing color theories exist, but for this discussion I assume that everything in between the two extremes are combinations of black and white: shades of gray. As you move along the scale from black to white, the darkest shades of gray are closer to the pure black side. As you continue moving along the scale toward the pure white end, the grays become lighter shades until approaching pure white.

Statistical theory suggests that the most frequently witnessed shade on the scale is a gray which is equally black and white: a 50 percent makeup of black and a 50 percent makeup of white. More specifically, statistical theory indicates that two thirds of the shades will be neutral gray.

Black is often associated with evil—it absorbs all light. Similarly, white is often associated with good and purity—it rejects all color and represents enlightenment.

I apply the scale model to help explain the basic human condition. Please note that this theorem, when applied, excludes any and all variables such as race, pedigree, and other demographics. There are alternative mathematical/statistical models which could be used to describe humanity, but I'll not get into that.*

Common Sense – An Exceptional Fallacy

It doesn't take common sense to realize that common sense is a fallacy.

This should not be a surprising statement, although I am sure that to many it is. I say this not to offend, but to simply state a mathematical fact: the average person is average. Consider applying the spectrum theory: if at one end there is no logic, and at the other end there is absolute logic, 50 percent of people tend to have less than average logical capabilities, and 50 percent have above average capabilities. As per the statistical theory, two thirds of adults have moderate or average logistic capabilities: "common sense." Again, this theorem excludes any and all variables such as race, pedigree, and other demographics.

The problem is most of us don't want to be average, we want to be exceptional.

---

* For a much more in-depth mathematical understanding of this these theories, I recommend researching Normal, Bimodal, and Poisson distributions.

The way I see it, we are all exceptional in our own ways. There is something that separates each of us from the crowd—often several somethings. It is how we choose to apply our gifts or talents that counts, although, unfortunately, because of our free will it is not that simple. We, the sheep, are led by our shepherds whose free will directly impacts our own. The shepherds decide what is value-added and what is not. This tends to limit our creativity, and sooner or later we are forced to sell out.

Upon transitioning into adulthood, there is an expectation put on us by society that we have learned from our mistakes, and that we have built up an adequate tool kit that enables us to fit in and become contributors to our society. In other words, we are expected to have common sense.

As adults we are still expected to learn from our mistakes; after all, the purpose of life is to create a life experience. However, we compel ourselves to deny our misdoings because we are heavily scrutinized for making them in the first place.

As a species we need to appreciate and embrace one another for our gifts, instead of getting down in the mouth and/or jealous. We need to learn how to collaborate with one another rather than quarrel, or even worse, resorting to intimidation, hatred, and violence.

A healthy debate or conversation is an excellent tool for promoting collaboration and understanding different points of view. The key is to *actively* listen to one another, to engage in conversations rather than just spouting our own agendas or acting out on our emotions. And I mean *listen*, not just wait for our turn to speak again.

It's easier said than done. But when we do collaborate, great things can happen. I have experienced it, albeit rarely.

We all have the freedom to make choices that could lead us to experience happiness, although nothing in life is guaranteed. And although we will often make mistakes, at least we can then say we tried our best. This is how we learn, and there is nothing saying that we must quit trying even if at first we fall flat on our collaborative faces. Sometimes we may even need third or fourth or maybe *dozens* of chances before we succeed.

The truly successful individuals are the ones who do what they enjoy.

We must allow one another to develop and apply our skills.

We must allow one another to make mistakes.

We must consider and value one another's opinions.

We must hold ourselves accountable for our misdeeds.

It's just good old-fashioned common sense.

And therein lies the conundrum that our society lives with.

Am I Evil?

I am a good person. Or am I? I like to think that I am.

I used to believe that most people considered themselves to be good. However, applying the spectrum theory, this suggests that the average person is decent: they are equally good and bad.

But it is how they perceive themselves that matters.

For instance, did Adolf Hitler consider himself evil?

Hitler believed that ridding the world of the Jews (and other groups and cultures), advocating the Aryan race, and annexing the European countries would make for a better world. So, if he was acting to improve the Germans, wasn't he acting from a good place?

What about individuals like Charles Manson? He was evil—or was he? Was he evil or wildly crazed? There have been numerous other examples throughout history. When you consider the spectrum theory, 50 percent of humans tend to be on the side of evil.

I initially presumed that Royce was good.

But the math doesn't lie.

This reasoning clarified a lot of questions I was always asking. It always comes to the same conclusion: the average person is average. Royce and I were simply at different places on the innumerable human spectrums. Or could it be that I was just one of those people who pissed him off for no real reason? Is there a spectrum for that?

There is always going to be someone who will take offense to another's actions or words. There are those who would say black even though the truth is white.

Realizing this, I wondered how Royce felt about himself and his behavior at work.

Academia Versus the Corporate World

From those who never finished secondary school, or those who achieved advanced degrees from ivy league institutions, one of the primary issues facing young adults transitioning into the workforce is that they are at the mercy of potential employers' willingness to take a chance on them. And there is a great deal of competition at all levels.

Bringing on a new employee requires a significant investment from the employer; a great deal of time and resources must be invested in bringing them up to a requisite level of competence, and then more to retain them. Because of this, many employers prefer to hire employees who bring with them a certain amount of experience and/or knowledge.

As post-secondary graduating students seek entry into the workforce, this leaves the obvious and often-asked question: How can they gain experience in their field of study if the employers aren't willing to provide the opportunity to gain experience?

To answer this question, the employers look to the school systems to provide graduates with skills that are applicable from day one. This introduces another age-old question: How much influence should the corporate world have over academia?

The three-year community college diploma was specifically designed to give students hands-on skills with some solid practical theory, which lends to their desirability in the corporate world.

The purpose of the four-year university degree is to teach students how to approach ideas from a logical and analytical perspective. Students learn facts and theories/philosophies that may never be applied; however, in exploring such concepts the doors of opportunity swing open for those willing to pass through to further investigate new concepts.

I would be remiss if I was not to say that with education and experience there is a reasonable expectation of competence. As a technical professional it is expected that there is a minimal requisite understanding or ability to comprehend the logistics and/or technologies being used. Therefore, engineers get paid more than technologists and laborers because the bachelor's degree is a document representing a higher level of potential comprehension and thinking.

Thou Shalt Not Judge

Not one of us is in the position where we can judge another individual. We all have our own free will to craft out our own life experience. We may look upon a little crippled boy and pity him, but he is living his own life and does not ask for our pity; rather, he seeks to experience his own life on his own terms. We are incapable of knowing what his terms are, and frankly it is none of our business.

Yet, we all judge.

As my career proceeded, I realized that not only did I not belong in the corporate world, I did not want to be in it. I knew that I was in the throes of mental illness. It was interesting to wonder about whether my illness would have surfaced if I had taken the academic route. I came to believe I would have become emotionally unwell no matter where my career took me.

When all was said and done, whichever path I took, it was my path—fuck everyone and anyone who dared say otherwise.

War – Stones and Shields

Because no two people learn or interpret life lessons in the same way, our differences make us afraid of one another. We fear that which we do not understand. Rather than speak openly and honestly, we instinctually establish a need for shields and walls to protect us from one another.

In the face of potential adversity, we hasten to gather our shields and arm ourselves with whatever stones we can find. And then we anxiously wait. Eventually almost everyone will find themselves standing in a mob, each with their shields raised and stones ready to barrage the others.

"Let he who hath not sinned cast the first stone," Jesus said.

But we are fueled by fear.

We know that there are those sly few who will go on the offensive right off the bat. They are very astute and will immediately establish themselves as the dominants. They are the 1 percent that control the 99 percent. They choose to become manipulators, oppressors, and outright bullies. They will ultimately try to rule and dictate how the rest of us should behave. Some may come and go having left very little impact, others will shock humanity and live and die in infamy. Their sole purpose is to promote that sense of fear amongst the masses, often for their own personal amusement.

They will position themselves safely off to the side and start things by throwing a small handful of pebbles at one or two random persons' shields. And then another. And then another . . .

And then they will sit back and enjoy the show.

These are the Rick Van Hornes of the world.

Those struck by these first few harmless pebbles will in turn volley their stones in the direction of those they believed had initiated the skirmish. Once the stones start flying, very few individuals will hold back their arsenals.

These individuals will naturally coalesce into smaller groups. They will try to increase their power by grouping and regrouping by forming allegiances and alliances. There is strength in numbers.

These are the Royce Pincers, Milan Estebans, and Kyle Kerns of the world.

They may not even know who is throwing stones at them, but with some extreme prodding and a great deal of propaganda provided by those dominants, they are quick to launch their arsenals at whomever they believe are their adversaries. They will become preoccupied with developing arms and techniques to destroy those who have been identified as their foes, even though they don't even know who their true foes are. The dominants will manipulate these sheep to bend to their will. The sheep will follow.

This is the history of humanity.

And history has a habit of repeating.

And what of the enlightened?

I want to be one to offer my shield to another who has succumbed to the barrage of stones. But in my heart and soul I fear that I would not be able to do so; not so much out of the fear of being physically wounded or even killed, but out of knowing—*knowing*—that as soon as I take the place of the one I was protecting, they would take hold of my shield with one hand and wrap their fingers around the nearest stone and take aim at me.

I know. I have felt it. Those stones have smashed into my flesh and nearly broken me. Cruel words have lashed my mind until it bled tears no more. Now I live in fear of those people. Sadly, many of those people are the ones who would call themselves "friend."

Chapter 16

He Started Throwing Stones

Another Perfect Day
Tuesday, May 12, 1998 – Mid-Morning

The R&D team had been brainstorming ideas for a new processing project. Playing the Devil's advocate, I initiated a counterproposal, just to look at the problem from a completely different point of view. Mine was a minor but potential solution; it could open the doors to discovering new, more concrete solutions.

My idea went unheard—or so I thought. It was dismissed by the team as quickly as it had been spoken.

Later I was passing by Royce's office. He was working away on his computer, and almost without looking up, he waved his hand indicating that he wanted to see me. I stood in the doorway for about ten minutes while he finished writing up and sending out an e-mail. This was a powerplay that he frequently pulled: making me wait until he was done his "important" work, and I was always foolishly willing to indulge him in his little piece of self-righteousness.

Finally, he turned to me.

"Your ideas are"—he shrugged his shoulders—"meh at best."

I studied his appearance. He was just having an off day, or so I thought. His words smarted. I tried to maintain a composed and positive attitude. I was hoping for some pearls of wisdom or insight. My heart stilled as I waited for his next words.

The approach that the company had tried to burn into our minds was that "there are no bad ideas," especially during this initial spitballing phase of problem solving. All ideas were supposed to be recorded without judgment and then later analyzed and crossed out after consideration and discussion. This would require an ideal situation, a meeting of minds. However, I had learned that most people, myself included, tended by nature to judge and negate ideas rather than remaining open and writing them down.

This is the fundamental foundation upon which teamwork is established.

Someone had once told me the story of how the mouse used with computers came to be. While spitballing ideas on how to make personal computers more user-friendly, someone threw the idea of controlling the computer with a handheld device. The initial reaction was that it was a ridiculous suggestion. Flash forward a couple of years, and the mouse became a part of everyday life. I wasn't claiming that my idea would revolutionize the modern world like the mouse did, but there *was* some validity to it.

I shrugged off his comment, but then he did something that was to alter me for the rest of my life. He leaned forward in his chair, resting his elbows on the armrests, and looked me straight in the eye.

"You are just plain stupid."

I stood in front of him and let his words soak in.

I didn't know how to respond. I felt as if my spine had been simultaneously ripped out through my asshole and throat. I felt my body go limp. For a second, I honestly thought that I was going to black out. Just like Royce's cousin Cam so many years ago, he had just put a revolver to my head and pulled the trigger.

His words ruminated through my mind incessantly. I felt humiliated. Lost. Weak.

I wanted to die.

Without a word, I turned and went back to my cubicle and stared blankly at my computer screen, hoping it would offer some sage advice regarding how to deal with what had just happened.

My head was thundering blasts of ominous screams: *Stupid!*

I shifted some random papers around on my desk.

The next thing I knew, I was at home curled up in my bed like a fetus.

Fuck You, I Won't Do What You Tell Me
Tuesday, May 12, 1998 – Mid-afternoon

After a while I came out of the bedroom and headed straight to my computer. My fingers went to the keyboard, and I started to write out some positive affirmations to help overcome how I was feeling.

- I am not stupid!
- I am not a child any longer.
- I have a voice—I am free to use it.
- I am free to speak the truth—it is my obligation to speak it.
- My thoughts and beliefs are mine—I do not need anyone's approval.
- I am free to make my own decisions—be they popular or not—and I shall graciously accept the consequences knowing that Father is at my side.

- I will allow myself to make mistakes, and I will correct my behavior as I see necessary. However, I will not be arrogant and ignore feedback and guidance that will help prevent me from repeating my mistakes.
- For too long I have been a coward—I have too readily accepted the title "victim." No more!
- Fuck all the Royces in the world and all those who would seek to limit and discredit me. They will always be there—they always have been. They have figured out how to best me, but no longer.
- There are some significant life choices which I must make.
- They represent and rule by fear. In response I shall offer freedom and openly represent love. Even if they ostracize me and use my name as a curse, they are still using my name. The more hate they spew about me the more powerful I become.

What is the absolute worst that could happen to me for exposing and taking a stand against the fraudulent ways of our department, our company, our city, state, or country? Our entire socio-political framework?

I suppose that I could be publicly humiliated and crucified like Christ. Or I could be cast out of society to live with the other "failures" on the streets. Still, I would hope that my words would live on, bringing others to their path to enlightenment. I would become a martyr for the cause. Not that I want recognition, but I would be known by others for standing up for the little people, the ones whose happiness was being drained by the emotionless and disinterested rich and powerful.

Right now, instead of pitying myself, I should be rejoicing in this opportunity which Royce has provided me. I have not only succeeded in the face of adversity in the past, I have thrived. I just had my eyes closed to the potential which was within myself.

That night I quietly cried myself to sleep.

I didn't even tell Kat, let alone anyone else, for several days.

Those five little words were to haunt me evermore.

You.

Are.

Just.

Plain.

Stupid.

The subconscious voices were overpowering my conscious voice, creating a myriad of new conversations, some as beautiful as a rose in the hand of a virgin maiden, some as horrific as a pile of mutilated body parts piled upon one another. I couldn't sleep until I was exhausted beyond reason, and even then the voices continued arguing:

"You are stupid!" *You are a genius!*

"You are destined for nothing!" *You are destined for greatness!*

"You are a fraud!" *You are strong and true!*

"Everyone can see through you!" *You have nothing to hide!*

"You are delusional!" *You see the truth!*

"You are a little bitch. A princess. A snowflake!" *You are none of these things!*

"You are a madman!" Silence.

"Real men" brushed away their feelings like flakes of dandruff from their collars. They never showed any emotions. They didn't even entertain the idea of emoting. There was no place for feeling empathy or compassion; there was no place for showing vulnerability. This implied that as a real man, my ever-increasing anxiety, subsequent phobias, and depression were just something that must be ignored. Real men handled emotions by ignoring and suppressing them.

    Poor little me. Life sure is tough.

    But no one had ever said otherwise.

    So, I needed to get over it—to get over myself.

    To just let it go.

    And after all, what made me so special that I should be treated any differently?

    Although, it may seem that to some I wasn't a real man, I was man enough to say to those who looked down on me: "Fuck that notion."

    At least that was what I wanted to say.

Chapter 17

Salute the Flags

Outshined
Wednesday, May 13, 1998 – 12:30 a.m.

I couldn't sleep.

I had endured so much over the past four years and always managed to survive.

I had proven myself time and again.

But this time—*this time*—something in me snapped.

I wanted to show Royce that he couldn't bring me down. Every time he had raised the bar—as unnecessary as it may have been—I worked my ass off and met and exceeded his demands. But he rarely acknowledged my accomplishments. He was as determined to best me as I was determined to outshine him.

At long last I was starting to wear down.

This time I caved and called in sick the rest of the week. This was the first time that I had ever called in sick because of any mental/emotional health issue. I was playing hooky.

I just couldn't face anyone.

It stung as though I had just had the word STUPID freshly tattooed onto my forehead. I had to vent but it couldn't be to anyone at work. I was so embarrassed that I couldn't even bring myself to talk with Kat or my parents.

I felt as though even Father had abandoned me. I silently screamed at Him. I begged for Him to fill the emptiness that I felt. But I was so caught up in self-pity that I wasn't even listening back to hear if He was responding.

I had no one.

As I lay in my bed, I closed my eyes.

I stared out at the world in front of me. I was surrounded in a sea of red. A sea of red flags. They were everywhere. Each represented a situation, circumstance, or instinct that I had consciously, foolishly, dismissed and/or ignored.

Now I had no idea what my next step should be.

I had been sentenced to a life alone. Even Kat, bless her sweet soul, couldn't make me feel whole again. She had tried throughout; I couldn't burden her any further with my latest issue. I simply told her that I was feeling sick and a little depressed to justify to her why I wasn't going to work.

I feared I was leaving her untethered in this storm of despair.

I would tell her when she got home.

Carrots
Wednesday, May 13, 1998 – 5:30 a.m.

I was still wide awake.

I was lying on my bed staring at the ceiling. When I closed my eyes, I heard Father whispering to me.

He revealed three carrots before me. There was a golden carrot labeled "corporate" to my right, a golden carrot labeled "academia" to my left, and sitting between the two an enigmatic third carrot which was a weathered old piece of rusted iron with no label.

The golden carrots each promised potential financial success and even the possibility of fame and adoration. As I was learning, with the corporate option there is the promised risk of being discredited and/or blackballed. Such was my current position. But I had skills and a vast and vivid imagination, both of which I could apply at any company more open to accepting me.

There was a certainty that there would be politics and personal conflicts with the academic option as well. If I had learned nothing else over the past few years, it was that people are unpredictable.

I am a non-conformist by nature, not by choice.

And what exactly *is* success? Money? Power? Recognition? Plaques on the wall?

What about the satisfaction of helping others and sharing the feeling of happiness?

This unsavory-appearing rusted iron carrot choice promised a different form of success than the other two. It represented selflessness, insight. The high road. Pride and honor.

Hope. Peace. Integrity. Honesty. Justice. Freedom.

Love.

Yes, I wanted money—not more than I needed, but enough that I didn't need to worry about the well-being of my family.

Yes, I wanted power, but not more than I needed to help lead others to their path.

I wanted to promote peaceful change: political, religious, and personal. I wanted the masses to open their eyes and speak and act.

I wanted to be the unseen leader or the prophet who showed the paths to enlightenment to those who are willing to listen rather than have them wander aimlessly, from the shepherds who watch over the flocks to the sheep themselves.

Ultimately, I wanted happiness.

I *wanted* that rusted piece of iron.

But I was still trapped and dependent on the corporate world.

I was one with a questioning mind, built to use what I learned to see where there were new, uninvestigated questions. I was a student of life. The corporate world did not care about my questions or philosophies. They just wanted to see that piece of paper which proved that I had a requisite skillset that would/should enable me to satisfy the needs of the position that I was assigned.

They were only interested in the bottom line.

This is why the corporate world generally has little use for students of the arts. They deny the connection between the underlying skills that came with a four-year arts degree. The arts encourage the students to seek understanding by using critical thinking. It also gave the students insight into the human condition. Differing artforms offered differing skills—direct and indirect—that could be applied in the corporate world, if permitted.

Later that week, as I sat at home moping, I decided to reread my words. Although still feeling beaten and beleaguered, I also still felt that hint of excitement. I did deserve to be free of thought and action, just as Father had intended.

I realized that underneath all my pain there was an opportunity for me to better myself.

My path was becoming clearer.

I now understood that I had made a terrible mistake by joining the R&D team. I had ignored that first momentary gut feeling that something was awry in the interview, as I had ignored so many other instinctual hints that something was off. And now I was trapped and filled with regret. I had created this life experience.

I could attempt to forgive, but I couldn't forget.

And if I couldn't forget, I couldn't truly forgive.

Lamenting
Friday, May 15, 1998

It was the end of the week while I was playing hooky from work. Kat had gone to bed and I sat down in the basement with a twelve-pack of beer. My goal was to keep myself numb from the world and to get myself into a mindset of peace and tranquility. I hoped I could just forget for a while and regain a little of my dignity and self-esteem.

I kept repeating to myself: "I have to stand up for my rights. No one else is going to assert them for me."

As I sat drinking my beers and thinking, I recalled an experience that I'd had when I was about seven years old: two boys were fighting behind the school during the lunch hour. This wasn't unusual—I had seen it before but paid little or no attention. I had been bullied and in fights before, but by nature I had no use for violence. As I've said, I have difficulty processing anger, even though I certainly feel it.

It was winter, and there were huge white snowbanks and drifts around the corner of the school that had resulted from the gusting winter wind. When I came upon the scene the fight had been going on for only a few minutes. Like most fights in those days, the two boys were wrestling more than punching each other.

I had seen several schoolyard fights, but this time I took a moment to let what I was witnessing really sink in. What I observed from the crowd blew my mind. The crowd encircling the two pugilists were all chanting "Beef! Beef! Beef!" and hammering their fists into their opposing palms. There were at least twenty of these kids standing around and participating, all in a circle chanting and pounding their fists.

Curious, I made my way up to the front of the crowd.

I was quite disturbed to see my best friend, Trevor, participating in this barbaric group mindset. Trevor was one of the smart kids, and I thought he was intelligent enough to see through the mass hypnosis. I still remember Trevor's seven-year-old pink-cheeked face as clear as can be. His brown hair swayed in the chilled air with his fist slamming into his palm. His bright white buckteeth were bursting out from his chapped lips. His breath left his mouth in short puffs with every "Beef!"

I felt a little queasy as I watched my friend fall mesmerized under the spell of the crowd. The entire situation unnerved me. In an unprecedented act, I jumped into the fight and pulled the two warriors apart. The crowd started to boo me. By this time the teachers were coming out of the school and working their way through the crowd to break up the fight and disband the crowd. I walked away with a death threat from each of the fighters for stepping in. This scared the shit out of me and I was preoccupied with that fear for the remainder of the day, although nothing ever became of it.

I didn't, and don't, know why I stepped into that fight. Having been a victim of playground bullying, it was beyond ironic that I engaged at all.

More importantly, I will never forget the intensity of that school crowd and their mindless mantra, and how disappointed I was in my fellow students, especially Trevor, for acting as they did.

The mob mentality that the children had so easily become consumed with was no different than the corporate mentality at

W.V.H. Steel. I had difficulty comprehending how grown adults could behave the same as elementary-school kids. Good people were turning on one another in the name of empty wealth and power. Very few of us were able to see through the greed and corruption. I was especially dismayed by Royce's inability to be the hero that I had thought he would be. I had thought that he was smart enough to see through the crowd mentality.

It was all around me.

I was mentally suffering.

I was both a conscientious objector and a casualty of war.

And no one really cared.

No one.

A Flashback and a Sneak Peek Into the Future
Saturday, May 16, 1998

The real me was typically a trusting and kind person. I was sincere and tried to maintain a high degree of integrity. Some said I was too nice; I could never understand how someone could be too much of a good thing. I'm equally sure that others disagree, saying that I am a complete asshole. Sometimes I am.

It's all good. We're all entitled to our thoughts and opinions. All that I wanted was to experience happiness and love—no more fear.

Apparently, that didn't bode well with certain personalities. They seemed to catch a vibe from people like me, the sensitive and empathic, and for some reason that angered them. To those like Royce, these personal qualities were unfathomable. The concepts of absolute love and happiness were beyond their grasp and therefore they could never experience pure joy, they could only experience fear and envy.

Consequently, it was out of fear that they concluded I was a threat to their ways, to their basic set of personal principles. We—the pacifists and peacemakers—were regarded as easy marks to exploit and prey upon. We didn't fight back on their battlefields. We took in the pain and tried to morph the negative into positive energy. It wasn't easy. Often we were dragged down into the sludge and muck, turning us into the victims and sources of disparaging negativity which we had initially opposed.

But if there were those inspired by our martyrdom, it was worth it.

I now realized Royce had been setting me up from the beginning.

It began with Royce even before my interview in March 1997. Dare I say it began in 1989 when I took his course in my first go-round at my engineering degree. I had passed all my courses without really studying for them. I've been told time and again that this was because of my native intelligence. In Royce's course I scored a B+. This apparently soured Royce's palate—this was what had led to his "getting your education right the first time" comments. I think that he was jealous that I had pissed around and still surfaced to the top within the next few years.

Somehow, we were meant to meet.

And then I returned to school a few years later, and when I applied myself, I rocked it.

We were meant to meet again.

We were meant to cross paths, but the reasons why I could only fathom.

I believed that despite anyone's alleged concerns, Royce and Milan had been advised to hire me by someone powerful enough to put the fear into them. Once or twice, Royce had snorted that "someone high up the food chain" had spoken highly of me.

Whoever had planted me in Royce's domain did not interfere beyond that. Before I had even left for my sabbatical, I had been told by Dave Kerns and other leaders that I would most likely go to work for Milan Esteban when I returned. At that point no one at W.V.H. Steel had even heard of Dr. Royce Pincer. I thought of Dr. Dali El-Lim.

Upon joining the R&D team, it was up to me to sink or swim.

Royce had been presented with all my academic and experiential skills and told of my potential. He was given the freedom to groom me as he saw fit. Rather than continue to inspire and foster my skills, Royce's approach was to beat me down. He decided to break my will.

And he almost succeeded.

Part V

Ich Bin Ein Gott (I Am a God)

Chapter 18

King of the Castle

Playing Childish Games After the Week of Stupidity
Monday, May 18, 1998 through Sunday, May 24, 1998

I had called in sick for the remainder of the previous week. It was now early Monday morning. It was one a.m. and I was just crawling into bed.

Kat had been in bed since ten.

Trying not to disturb her, I gently lifted the blankets and climbed into bed with my back to hers. I was wired. I knew that I wouldn't fall asleep. I just lay there reminiscing—it was just hours shy of a week since having been called stupid.

The night before, I had finally let Kat know what had happened. She had noticed that I was more depressed and anxious than usual. I'm sure it wouldn't have been too difficult for anyone to notice. When I broke down and filled her in, Kat was disgusted with Royce's behavior and wanted to approach our team's HR rep, but I asked her to leave it alone. I wanted to deal with it on my own.

I checked the clock again. It was now two-thirty. Only an hour and a half had passed since I had last checked. I could already feel the sickness setting in. In six hours, I would be expected to be at my desk.

No, I would not be well enough for work the next day. All the grandeur of my thoughts was fluttering about in my stomach. I was learning about myself, and that excited me. I was also realizing that despite my growth over the years, I could never truly fit in with others (with some exceptions), and that sickened me.

I went into the bathroom and searched for a bottle of antacids and melatonin so that my stomach would settle and I could get a good sleep. I decided that the next day I might sleep in and call Dr. Gantt.

I didn't even set my alarm.

The red glow of my alarm clock stared at me all night. I stared right back until the sun began to rise and Kat's alarm went off.

I thought that if I could erase all the negative experiences—the people, the words, and the actions—that I could start with a clean slate. And then I realized that if I was granted a do-over, I wouldn't be anywhere ahead. I would have to relearn all that I wanted to purge.

It's like the saying, "I wish I knew what I know now when I was younger."

I didn't go to work that Monday.

Kat never asked why.

Work never called.

I didn't call the doctor either.

Hatred: The Very Notion Is Inconceivable
Early June 1998

I hated the very notion of hatred.

I wanted to feel pure seething hatred for Royce. But to me, to hate someone was the same as abolishing them from existence.

I did hate what he stood for, greed and power, especially at the expense of others.

I was so angry.

I liked to imagine the torment that I could exert on him. I wanted him to feel my innermost pain. I wanted to kick him in the balls with such force that they ruptured. I wanted him to live through the most torturous pain that I could imagine, and my sick mind knew no boundaries. Could I make Royce feel my sickness? I yearned for Royce to feel me creeping about inside his mind, slashing and ripping it apart as only I could. My lifetime of psychological wounds would become appended to his own.

Writhe slowly, you motherfucker. Live in fear and pain.

I knew that even if I could bring myself to kill him, he would remain very much alive within my mind. Furthermore, he would be lauded by the ignorant and impressionable masses as another victim of violence caused by a mentally ill person. I would only perpetuate the stigma that I already faced and fought to dispel.

But boy oh boy, did I ever delight in letting the notion of killing him linger on in my mind.

I knew that Father was not about revenge. Father was filling my head with thoughts of peace and forgiveness and love. He constantly brought back the memories from when Royce and I had been good friends. Father showed me that there was still a nagging little piece of compassion for Royce mingled within all my disturbing thoughts. And if there was just a nano-thought of hope, that meant that it could never be hatred that I was feeling. I just felt consumed with deep disapproval and disappointment.

I didn't know when, but I knew that someday it would be necessary to forgive him.

As usual, I cared.

I felt so low. I wondered, *Is this Royce, or is this another sign of my social failure?*

In retrospect, I realized that I often had difficulty keeping friends. That was not to say that I was without friends, although it often felt that I was alone. I just kept my circle of friends small and close. I knew that despite my weirdness I was likable, particularly once I'd reached my later teen and adult years.

It took me years before I realized that it wasn't healthy to surround myself with false friends, or to try to convince others to be my friend. I thought about how much time I had spent hoping to feel loved and appreciated only to be disappointed.

When a friendship or relationship didn't last, I was very hard on myself. I took it to heart, that either I was not good company or that I drew out the worst in others. I preferred to think that it was them not me, but I was too insecure to convince myself.

The voices in my head were flickering in and out of control. I was becoming completely caught up in a delusional state that caused me to exhibit paranoid thoughts and actions, but many of my delusions were completely logical.

Cashing Out
Mid-June 1998

Kat was the first of the two of us to start to really crack.

Like me, Kat had an extremely sensitive *self*—emotions like anger hit us harder than the average person.

When her parents finally split, her mother moved her boyfriend Len in the very day after her father left. Kat was only seventeen or eighteen and discovered that she was essentially parentless. Her parents never did divorce.

Kat cried a lot, as a child and as an adult.

Her father became a drunken recluse whom she never saw except on occasions when he needed money for his whiskey. He had been the janitor at a local school, but after twenty-five years he was fired for being drunk at work on multiple occasions.

He died of alcohol poisoning when he was only sixty-five.

I only met him once.

It was as if Kat was suddenly responsible for parenting her mother, who was out partying and carrying on with Len as if she was a twenty-one-year-old again. When Kat was coping with something, in a singsong voice her mother would often say, "Honey, listen to Len. He knows about these things."

Fortunately, Kat had a small group of friends she trusted.

She felt deeply betrayed by her mother.

She carried that resentment with her until the day her mother died.

Like me, Kat had a history of being abused at W.V.H. Steel.

She was extremely underemployed: over the past few years she had been bounced from department to department with promises of work in which she would be able to apply her practical and educational skills. Instead, she kept being slotted into lower-level clerical positions. Her typing speed was considered more important than her intellectual acuity.

At one point she was assigned a position in which she could have really thrived. This position was directly linked to her master's degree studies (by this time she was just past the halfway point). It was in the corporate education department, which fell under the corporate HR department. At long last she could spread her wings and fly.

She flew like Icarus.

Her new boss was a misogynistic asshole. He treated her like his personal assistant. He essentially made her his secretary. Her job was kept from developing educational courses to entering data and making accommodations for employees when they were traveling for training courses.

W.V.H. Steel was becoming so filled with an army of psychological warriors that a small but still significant number of employees were taking leaves of absence, and/or quitting or suing the company for wrongful dismissal and emotional distress.

Things were starting to spin out of control for Kat.

As much as she hated her job and being underemployed, she was ever vigilant. One day she approached her supervisor and showed him that she had found a huge gap in the data that her team was responsible for processing. She pointed out to him that this data was essential for an upcoming financial audit.

Her supervisor told her to ignore it.

Two weeks later, her supervisor called her into his office. They had failed the audit because of the missing data. Kat raised her eyebrows as if to say *I told you so.*

He wrote her up for not doing her job.

Kat was floored. Amongst all the bullshit mind games she had endured, she had never felt so betrayed. She had pointed this problem out to him and now she was being scapegoated. She was at a complete loss, with nowhere to turn because her supervisor was the HR corporate department leader.

From that point on, her reputation was sullied. She was essentially blackballed.

Later at a team meeting I told Royce what had happened to Kat. He grunted aloud that it was a bullshit decision. He never once said he could or would use his influence to save her job as he had done for others in the past. His concern was unconvincing. I sensed that he was trying to get at me through Kat. Maybe I was just being paranoid, but Royce had proven to me that it was not outside his purview to try to do more than bully and abuse me. The evil was within him, and I believed that he wanted to damage or outright destroy me.

Kat finally left W.V.H. Steel a couple of months after.

Like me, the abuse she had suffered left her self-confidence shaken to the core. She questioned her abilities and decided to downplay her skills and education. She picked up a permanent part-time job at the local Electron-X Depot, a small computer chain. The work was different than anything she had ever done before: she was a saleswoman.

It was not a professional job, and thus the requisite skillset and pay were minimal.

She continued working on her master's in education.

She was at the top of her class.

The Power Trip
Thursday, June 25, 1998

When I was on my first sabbatical, I had put together a seminar to present to my class for one of my courses. The topic that I chose was the one that I knew best: steel forging. Because of my experience I was able to add a great deal of information and detail to the presentation. But it was meant for the other students in the class, so I had to ensure that I explained the concepts clearly and accurately.

Although I considered myself a terrible public speaker, my presentation was a huge success.

As one of the leaders of the TTD, Milan Esteban was tasked with introducing the engineers and management at a new startup facility in Germany to the processes and key concepts that were involved in our manufacturing environment.

Somehow Milan heard about my school presentation. He asked me to finesse it and use it to show the new staff our company's overall production and processing methods. He also requested that I join him and one of our senior-level salesmen to go to Germany to personally deliver the presentation. I knew that this was a significant opportunity to advance my career as a professional in the engineering field and within the company.

This was the type of opportunity I had been waiting for since I had started at W.V.H. Steel.

Royce had never said anything to me directly about this presentation. However, I had overheard him recommend me to Milan for this project. I also heard him say that I was perhaps the best writer in the company. Based upon our working history, I was a little bewildered by his positive assessment of my skills.

I *knew* that he couldn't be entirely evil.

But then when I thought about it, I realized that he had always thrown in a little good with the bad. I think that was why I was so quick to question myself. A little positive reinforcement combined with some well-placed reprimands made for the perfect combination to drive me to chasing my tail.

As the day of the trip approached, my anxiety became insurmountable. I pictured myself stuttering and stumbling over my every word in front of thirty-plus professionals, all engineers and managers. The more I thought about it, the worse my anxieties became. I had been able to do it in school, but back then I didn't have any conceivable way of backing out. I either did the presentation or I failed.

I grew so anxious that all I could think about was how terrible it would be to go through with this presentation. I knew my stuff, but all I could think of was my being ridiculed and laughed at. I knew that there would be questions that I couldn't answer, even though there was only a handful of individuals who knew the details as well as I did.

I called Milan and backed out with only two days' notice. Milan simply told me that it was fine.

I believed that if I told Milan the truth, that my reason was due to my extreme anxiety, he would not have understood and that he would have been disappointed in me. So instead I decided that I would tell him I had an exam at school and would not be able to make the trip.

This decision was not easily made. I realized that I was trading one anxiety-riddled situation for another. I chose the one that I felt would be the easiest to live with. I felt that I could live with Milan's disappointment easier than I could live with making a fool of myself.

I instantly knew that I had just tanked my career.

The truth was that there *was* an exam scheduled, but the professor had agreed to allow me to write it when I returned from my business trip.

Not five minutes after bailing on the trip, Royce came to my cubicle and expressed his displeasure. He told me that despite his best intuition he had recommended me to Milan. As much as I looked bad, I had made him look bad as well.

Deep down, I had a feeling that he had contacted my professor and learned that I had lied.

I felt ashamed of myself for giving in to my illness.

This was happening a lot.

Maybe too much.

Chapter 19

Hello Me, It's Me Again

Bi-Polarized
Early July 1998

Royce sniped once again as I was working on a problem.

I thought that this issue had been addressed long ago. Finally, I was so fed up with questioning myself at Royce's hands that I mustered up the courage to have a knock-down, drag-out face to face with him regarding my schooling and how it was fitting in with my work. I went to his office. He was alone.

He leaned back into his chair and raised his legs to the table. The chair tilted too far back and he fell ass over teakettle. I put on a concerned face, but inside I was laughing my ass off.

Sweet ironic justice!

I jumped up from my seat. "Are you okay?"

He refused to take my hand to help him up; in fact he pushed it away. He fumbled up to the table for stability and started slowly pulling himself up. His face was so red that it was glowing. The table tilted toward him under his weight. Papers went flying in all directions as he fell back on his ass again.

Inside, I was giggling like an infant playing peek-a-boo for the first time. I don't know if I smiled outwardly. I was pretty sure that I'd maintained my composure. Once upon his feet, he crouched over and brushed himself off. He swayed a little. He ran his pasty white fingers through the thin blond hairs combed over the top of his bald head. He placed his palms on his brown corduroy slacks and breathed deeply for a minute or two.

I picked up his chair for him. With a whoop, he gulped down a breath of air as he stood up and sat back down, insisting that he was fine. His cheeks were still splotched pink with embarrassment and from the physical exertion—his power play had ended in folly. He was not smiling. Not that I expected he would be.

Based upon his demeanor and embarrassment over what had just happened, I realized that we were not going to be discussing my schooling or career that day, at least not in any objective manner. Royce did not like to be embarrassed or appear as if he wasn't in control. As tempting as it was, I decided that I would keep his little foible a secret.

I leaned back in my chair.

I looked at his bowed head. This was not a great man to be respected and feared. This was a pathetic little man to be pitied.

I could see it in his eyes: he was charging himself up to fight with all his strength to convince me how he was omniscient and omnipotent. I realized that he was digging deep inside to the bottom of his seemingly bottomless bag of tricks, searching to bring out my weakness. He knew that despite all that had happened in the past, deep down I still cared.

And then, as if hit by a bolt of lightning, I had a huge epiphany.

I realized that he resented me for being true to myself—the long hair, the beard, the tattoos. He didn't approve of my unconventional approach to work and problem solving; he only understood the archetype of how a corporate engineer/professional should act and look.

And right then I knew for certain that I occupied a space within his consciousness, just as he did mine. I could see it on his face as plain as day: mere intellectual envy wasn't the source of his inner need to dominate and belittle me, as I'd initially thought; rather, it outright enraged him that I had yet to reach my prime, while his was in the past. He saw that I could exceed and surpass him, mentally, academically, and physically.

No one could know this truth. He now needed to work even harder to keep me under his thumb. He needed to extinguish the spark that kept me going. He needed me dead—at least metaphorically.

I also realized that while I was scared shitless of him, he was just as afraid of me.

He started prattling on when, for the first time, I stood up to him.

I rose and excused myself.

I left his office while he was in the middle of a sentence about my incompetence.

I didn't look back.

I was scared shitless, but I never heard anything more about it.

I had been correct: Royce had bipolar disorder.

I secretly felt like celebrating. Or just sighing aloud in satisfaction. I wanted to tell Shane "I told you so." But I realized that any reaction short of feigned pity would have been in poor taste.

Royce had finally admitted to Milan that he suffered from emotional/mental health issues. He then chose to disclose his illness to the team. With Milan's support came the support of the other major players, such as Kyle Kerns. Human resources made specific accommodations for him, including decreased work hours. Royce had set up a sympathetic safety net in which he could securely fall if he lost his balance on the tightwire of company politics.

Now his outlandish behavior was excused by almost everyone.

I was pissed. I had not been afforded the same degree of sympathy or empathy, and I wasn't an asshole. In fact, I had experienced quite the opposite upon disclosing to Royce.

But I had to admit that Royce had tacitly warned me.

By being apolitical I had no safety net and I had fallen through the cracks.

Royce's peers didn't see what we his underlings saw, and if/when they did, they defended him.

"Oh, he can't help it."

"He has an illness."

"Poor guy, he just needs good moral support and patience."

Royce coped by actively seeking compassion and support from the team when he was in a depressive state. I believed that he thrived on the attention. I also believed that he had the right to emote as he saw fit. Everyone had the right to their emotions, including me.

My way of coping with my emotional issues was to try to hide them. I feigned numerous smiles. I tried to compensate by acting silly and using my wit. I forced myself into putting up an extroverted facade.

I couldn't understand why Royce was allowed to mope about when he was in a downswing. This made me feel even worse than I already did. Why were his leaders and peers—even Rick Van Horne—supportive and understanding to his cause? And when he was manic, they were quick to excuse his behavior because he had an illness? But for some reason they did not extend their proverbial hands out to me. It couldn't be just because I didn't play politics, could it? Were my colleagues and coworkers that shallow?

I felt as if I didn't even exist.

Even though well-intended individuals such as Shane were actively becoming more aware of the implications and symptoms of depression, anxiety, and other emotional health issues, I picked up on their desperation—they genuinely wanted to help me. What I discovered was that most people were never satisfied until they were convinced that they had helped. The truth was that they could not help; the best they could do was listen without judgment.

But I could not let them continue to believe that they had not helped.

So I learned to put on the most convincing fake smile for them.

They were supposed to be the big three, the up-and-comers, the future of the company. Kyle Kerns. Milan Esteban. Dr. Royce Pincer.

However, status in the boys' club, the final rung on the ladder, depended on a VP of Technology position at the company. I was acutely aware that there was a connection between me and this corporate and/or academic club. And I believed that they knew it and subtly opposed it.

The reason was that I really didn't give a shit. And I think that this pissed them off.

Even when I broke, there was still a fragment of myself left intact.

They could take my life, but short of that they could never take my free will.

Maybe that was the secret. Maybe that was the thing the big boys were looking for: I was different. I was unconventional. I was genuine. I was the real thing.

I knew that I had created my own experience and opportunities. Was it manifest destiny that I had been given the privilege of working with the R&D team with minds like Shane's? Why was it that I was able to earn the respect of some of the greatest scientific minds in academia at the university? Was Father shining a special light on me?

No.

I had worked hard and created my own opportunities.

My only failure, which led to my ultimate downfall, was that I didn't have enough faith in myself to trust my intuition and I let others influence me.

At the risk of sounding arrogant, there was only one man, a university professor, I had ever felt intimidated by, intellectually speaking. I had a difficult time speaking with him. His very presence sent shudders down my spine.

I wondered how I would feel if he worked for me.

Would I have the stones to promote him above me? Or would I do as had been done to me? Would I attempt to discredit him to keep the spotlight on myself? I knew that I was a loving individual, at least as much as I could be. So yes, I believe that I could have put him ahead of me. I had done it with Macy McBride. And to be honest, I did have my moments of jealousy when she succeeded, but when all was said and done I was proud of her and the incredible experience she created for herself. And she was ever gracious, which made it all worth it.

The Dropout
Late July 1998

I was attending three lectures for my class every week. With transportation time, I was absent for six hours per week. True to my word, I made up for these hours by working late.

A job-related statistics workshop was coming up. Both Barry Nichols and I expressed interest. Royce denied me, stating that I was studying a "very difficult subject," and that I wouldn't be able to handle the added stress. I told Royce that the subject was not difficult, and I was confident that I could easily earn an A+.

He maintained that I would be overburdened. I thought that if we traded roles that maybe he would have been overloaded, but I knew that I would be fine, and I knew that bothered him.

And then it finally happened.

I remember quite vividly being in the washroom relieving my bladder when Royce sauntered up to the urinal beside me, whipped out his impotent little dick, and told me that our team's HR rep would shit if she knew about how much time I was missing because of my schooling. I was hit with a wave of guilt. Rather than defend myself, I went into freeze mode and acknowledged his concern that my schooling was interfering with work.

"It ends now," he stated as he left my side.

Royce seemed to always know which buttons to press to elicit my greatest emotional response and self-deprecating thoughts. Now he was hitting me below the belt. He had brought out my Kryptonite—he knew that I loved my schooling.

I recalled one day early on when Shane had warned me that as I came closer to completing my degree it would be increasingly difficult for me to stay on track with my schooling. At the time I had dismissed it; Royce and I had a written and spoken understanding.

Royce was a reasonable man—wasn't he?

It was too late in the semester to simply drop the current university course which I was enrolled in; in fact, it was at the point that if I did not complete the course I would receive a failing grade by default. I called the professor, my old friend Dr. Leo Wilder, and he suggested we meet face to face to discuss my predicament.

He had to get permission from the dean of engineering to allow me to drop the course, because of the timing. He explained my case to the dean, who gave me permission to drop the course without penalty.

That was the last time I was ever on the university campus. I was forced to drop out of school.

On a side note, Barry was granted permission to attend the statistics workshop.

He failed miserably.

Dr. Edwin had me on a cocktail of meds for my depression, anxiety, and psychotic symptoms. The meds still needed to be severely tweaked—I was emotionally and mentally nowhere near 100 percent my old self.

School had been my safe haven.

But school was no longer an option. Royce had made sure of that with his guilting and threats of reporting me to HR.

Chapter 20

The Real Thing

Merry Friggin' Birthday
Sunday, August 9, 1998

Rusty had just turned four that previous Wednesday.

Four years old and I was still battling in court for my basic rights to see my son.

I wanted to take him out to the park, where the grass was green and the trees swished in the breeze. Perhaps we could make a kite and run along the beach strip with the kite tugging high above us. I wanted to take him out to the country where there was fresh air and water. I wanted to take him out for an afternoon in the sun to a lake and watch him catch his first fish, just as I remembered having done with my dad.

But those were just dreams.

Maybe someday . . .

A man could only hope.

I had bought him a little electric racetrack with a loop-de-loop like I'd been given by my parents when I was a child. I couldn't wait to see the look on his face when he saw it. I was in the meeting room at the CAS. I decided to take it upon myself to set up the racing-car kit.

Once the kit was assembled, I gave it a try to ensure it would work properly.

It worked!

I had a strange feeling—something was off. I looked up at the clock. It was three-thirty p.m. The O'Reillys were half an hour late. I looked back to the window and saw Kat, Ellyn, and my parents arguing with the visitation officer.

I was confused. Where was my son?

I started to grow paranoid and then I was overcome with panic—Rusty wasn't coming.

Please Father, let my son be safe and well.

I left the visiting room to see what was going on.

Mom was in tears. Dad was holding her by the shoulders. He was visibly upset as well.

I feared the worst. The panicky feeling had only just begun to fade when I'd left the room. It now came around full force. Kat was holding some papers and saying something to the guard. When she saw me she handed them over.

The O'Reillys had won temporary custody in the court case. I had just been denied my parental rights to see Rusty because I had been labeled mentally unstable. I knew this was just a glitch, because as per Truman we were mounting a case in which my parents would be named as the custodians.

Still, it was a major disappointment.

I knew that there was no reasoning with the guard; he was just doing his job. I tried to settle my family down, and suggested we leave and take a little bit of time to rethink our position. I also suggested we call my lawyer so that he could do some damage control, and hopefully get the court's decision reversed as soon as possible.

I packed up the racing-car set and brought it back home with me.

Maybe next time this would all be sorted out and I could see my Rusty.

Hammerhead
Tuesday, September 8, 1998

Every summer the plants had a two-week shutdown. When I worked in the plant, the shutdown was my busiest time: that was when the big projects could be completed. Now being in corporate I was expected to take two weeks off—without pay, or by using vacation time.

I talked it over with Kat and decided to just take the two-week hit and be stress-free.

It was a much-needed break, definitely worth two weeks' pay.

It was the first Monday back after the summer shutdown, the day after Labor Day. The company had started to hemorrhage money since expanding into foreign countries and adopting new technical/processing methods. When management first announced their brave new venture I had foreseen this happening, but I was no one worthy of being listened to.

From what I had been told, Milan Esteban was the primary leader pushing for this new technology that the company had invested in. He had been listened to by senior management. He was a typical engineer with a very charismatic personality, but his attitude was like Sid Stanford's, although he wasn't quite as noticeably narcissistic. I think he thought it was somewhat endearing that I was more intelligent than the average bear and that I was surpassing the expectations of most. I was not an expert in these new technologies, but I did do my homework, as I'm sure Milan had.

Again, it was not for me to speak out of turn, so I dutifully kept my mouth shut. Royce had taught me to know my place.

I Have a Bad Case of . . . Uhhh?
Monday, September 21, 1998–Friday, September 25, 1998

In my years with the company, with a few part-days peppered in, I had only missed four weeks of work.

Now, only two weeks after the summer shutdown, I called in, reporting that I was feverish and had the flu. I took the entire week off. I was not sick with the flu as I claimed. I was sick with anxiety, depression, and paranoia, which were all being magnified by Royce and associated with the toxicity of the workplace in general.

According to some of the other team members, Barry Nichols had the audacity to state how nice it must be to take a week off from work. I was also told that the team stuck by me and admonished him for his comment. Through Royce, the team had been made aware of my mental illness, but they didn't connect that it was the reason for my missing work. I was convinced that if they did know they would turn on me.

While at home "sick" that entire week in mid-September, I constantly agonized over Royce and work every second of every day. I feared that I was going to receive a phone call. I feared that I would be caught playing hooky.

Most people don't seem to understand when you can't go out because you are depressed or anxious, whether to work or socially, especially if there is someone or something triggering these emotions. If you are sick with a virus or infection, they understand. They will even insist that you go home and rest to get your strength back, as well as to keep from spreading the disease.

But if you feel like there is a load of emotional pain in your gut and all you want is for that burden to be lifted, well, they question that. I can't count how many times I was told to cheer up, or to just let it go.

Throughout the week I found myself ruminating on Royce and his ongoing abuse, rendering me unable to sleep. When I did sleep, I had horrific nightmares of him menacing me at work. I would awaken covered in sweat with my heart pounding in my throat. Soon I was also having warped visions of my coworkers laughing and pointing at me.

They kept screaming that I was a weakling. A loser. A betrayer. A fraud. Their voices coalesced into one loud monstrosity of noise that ripped and tore its way back and forth between each side of my skull.

I was "stupid."

I was in a constant state of anxiety when it came to work, whether I was there or not.

I started to think that taking the week off was perhaps more damaging to my mental state than it would have been if I'd been at work. Every second was spent worrying about what everyone else was thinking about me, and what I would say if and when confronted about being away. Even I didn't consider my mental health issues a legitimate reason for missing work. In my mind it seemed to always bounce back to that macho thick-skin metaphor.

Still, I could not get out of bed and get dressed.

Kat was very supportive of me, having been experiencing her own share of issues.

I'd read that something like 20–25 percent of adults will experience some form of mental illness at some point in their lives. This meant that 75–80 percent of adults will never experience any form of mental illness. This translated into the fact that most adults will never be able to understand these invisible illnesses that we suffer from, and therefore they would never be able to truly sympathize, let alone empathize. Try as they may, they would never truly understand why those who suffer cannot "just get over it."

I Have a Another Bad Case of . . . Uhhh?
Monday, October 5–Friday, October 16, 1998

It was seven o'clock Monday morning, early October. I had barely slept a wink that night.

Was that a tickle in my throat? Was my temperature rising? Was my skin flushed? I must have been getting sick. I felt dizzy. I could not even stand up. I felt so ill.

I had to call in sick to work. I just could not do it anymore.

I could not face Royce, or any of my coworkers. I would rather be sick than deal with them.

Kat was still lying next to me, just waking up. "How do I look?" I asked her.

She knew what I needed to hear. "You had best stay in bed today."

"Will you call in for me?" I sheepishly asked her. I was scared to death to speak with anyone at work.

Of course she would.

She called in sick for me every day through the remainder of the week.

I was so distraught with worry about when I was going to receive a call from Royce in which he would challenge my absence from work. Fortunately, Kat spoke with him and our team's HR rep and assured them that I was indeed sick. She further offered to bring in a doctor's note to confirm that I was legitimately sick.

They believed her and did not request a note.

So there I sat in my bed wearing nothing but the same crusty pair of underpants, smoking cigarettes in front of the television for the second week in two months. In both cases I reported having a fever and a case of the flu.

The next week came and I still wasn't up for work, but I realized that if I took more time HR would definitely require a doctor's note. I was convinced that if I brought in a note stating I was suffering from depression and anxiety and other symptoms as a result of constant harassment from my supervisor, I would be fired.

I was at an impasse.

What if I wasn't mentally ill? What if this was all in my head? Wouldn't that be a sickness unto itself? Yes, indeed it would be. I needed help. But I did not want to seek any help at work. And I hated going to see the doctors all the time. I convinced myself that I just needed to stay away from Royce. If I could stay in my warm and safe bed with my cigarettes and TV, he could not harm me.

But what if he called?

I knew that he was plotting against me. He was plotting to end my career, if not my life.

I knew that was an irrational thought, but as much as I questioned it, I believed it.

Yup! I was sick.

At this point I still hadn't been formally diagnosed by Dr. Edwin, although I was being treated for schizophrenia.

This was my third week calling in sick within about eight or nine weeks since the summer shutdown in September. I knew that they wouldn't buy my flu excuse any longer.

I would still maintain that I had the flu anyway.

I didn't have to go to work that day. I may not have to go in the day after either. Or the day after that. I hoped that this ailment would last all week. What a pleasure that would be. I could put up with the workplace bullshit next week. It would be worth it—another entire week away. If HR wanted a doctor's note, I would just use some of my vacation time. Or I knew that Dr. Gantt would write me a note—she was still trying to convince me to get away from the work environment as it was. My coworkers and supervisors knew that I was mentally ill, but I could not allow them to know that I was succumbing to it. I had to show them I was a strong man.

I felt my forehead again. Yes, I had a fever. I could barely open my eyes. The sunlight burned my eyes through the curtains. It was hot in there, yet I felt so dreadfully cold.

"Please Father, release me from my agony," I begged.

I was ready to die. It was such a dark place that I was in.

Wait!

Was that a lump I felt under my armpit?

Yes! Please Father, let it be cancer.

If I had cancer, they would surely not expect me to go to work. While sitting in bed, I could feel the cancer cells metastasizing. The cancer was growing and spreading.

I liked this sickly feeling much better than I liked the feelings I experienced at work.

If I was lucky enough to have cancer, then I might be able to escape work for several months. "Dearest Father, *please* let me have cancer."

But I knew that I was only trying to fool myself. I wasn't fortunate enough to have cancer.

So what about the next day? Was I just digging a hole from which I wouldn't be able to crawl out? The more time I missed from work, the more attention I was bringing to myself. And what of all the whispers that there would be?

I couldn't let that concern me. I would have to let tomorrow take care of itself.

I was very afraid. I was trembling. I wanted to explain myself to someone, someone who would empathize with me. The closest individual who might listen would be Shane. But by now I sensed that he too was growing tired of my tales of woe and complaining. The only person who could understand my illness was someone who had experienced it or had studied it.

Royce would have been the most likely choice. He understood the multitude of emotions. The ups. The downs. The hurt and the pain. The feeling of being isolated. The feeling of shifty eyes and hushed condemnations.

But I knew where I stood with him.

I needed someone to help me get answers. Why had I been experiencing these feelings?

When I wondered about it, I asked myself, Did I really want answers? Could it be possible that I liked the drama?

I reasoned that if I did enjoy this nonsense, I wouldn't be in the emotional state that I was in. Or would I? Was this all a delusional hallucination? Was it even possible that Royce was a figment of my imagination?

Perhaps I had not even been born into this world. Perhaps I was somewhere in the future, or the past, having a dream. A terrible unholy dream. But if I had been dreaming all of this, I would had to have existed.

I think therefore I am.

These were questions that the doctors were not addressing.

After having missed so much work, Dr. Edwin set me up with a psychologist/counselor I had started seeing after work on a regular basis. This allowed me to open up and express how I was feeling without being judged. She was able to draw out my demons and give me a few tools to deal with the workplace atmosphere.

She was great, open and honest, and although I knew it was her job to listen I really believed that she cared.

More recently, I had begun to understand that I had given Royce too much credit, or perhaps more accurately I hadn't given myself enough.

Royce was clever and crafty, but so was I—if not more so.

Unfortunately, this new insight left me with the same conundrum as my previous breakthroughs had: I needed to turn around how I perceived myself. I needed to completely believe in myself. I needed to completely have faith in myself. I needed to stop allowing others to infiltrate and influence me away from my own thoughts and ideas. I needed to learn to trust and act on my instincts.

I needed to be me.

I needed to stop needing.

I knew that I was intelligent. I knew that I could be strong. I knew that I could see the good in the world. I knew that no matter how grim things looked, good always triumphed over evil in the end, even though it often came at a great cost. I knew that for every answer there were hundreds of further questions, and that for those hundreds of questions each had a hundred more.

I also knew that I was a human, not a machine. I couldn't simply change overnight from who I was into who I wanted to be. And I had to be careful about what I wished for—did I want to be someone or something else?

There had been so many before me, those who had risen from the bottom to the top.

How could I go from being a broken man to a leader who others would have faith in and follow away from their safe comfortable lives? How could I know for sure that my thoughts and ideas were right and just, that they were in alignment with all that is good, when others shared the same passion for their opposing thoughts?

What was it about me that allowed me to believe that others should trust and follow?

It was love.

I had created this life through a series of events and choices, all made of free will. Plus, I held a unique and vast assortment of skills that I had attained and learned through exposure, experience, and application.

I realized that I could use the written word to help others.

Maybe I could let just one person know that they're not alone in dealing with a situation or set of circumstances. Maybe I could help build up just one person's self-esteem. Maybe I could help restore just one person's sense of free will, or help them make a choice that is healthier for their state of being. Maybe I could inspire just one person to become a better or happier person. Maybe I could even help lead just one person toward their path to enlightenment.

I had the potential.

XXX
Mid-November 1998

The entire TTD was beginning to collapse in on itself.

There were even whispers throughout the division of unionizing.

I realized that several people over the years had become tired of my endless "complaining," as Royce had once put it. I didn't do it to stir up trouble; I did it to try to get answers—to understand others and improve myself.

One day, Royce had been in a peculiarly friendly mood and invited me to his office. I was far beyond hesitant, for obvious reasons. We got chatting and it almost felt like the old days. His dark eyes seemed to have a jaunty glint, and his sagging Augie Doggie jowls were not drooping as much. He acknowledged that I was struggling and that I needed help. He told me that he had been talking with Milan Esteban, and that Milan suggested I be encouraged to google "XXX," hit the enter key and walk away from my computer. As soon as all the pornography started to download, the IT team would be all over me, and it would be all over for me. But according to Royce that was a *good* thing; I would get a huge severance, at the minimum up to two years' full pay plus benefits and bonuses. I had to admit that one thing that was going well for me under Royce's leadership was my salary.

According to Royce, another engineer at a sister plant had recently done the "XXX enter" and he had never been happier. He had been granted two years of full salary, full benefits and bonuses, plus a positive reference, just as I was being promised.

For some reason this didn't bode well with me. I believed that downloading porn at work would compromise my integrity. I didn't believe that Royce was looking out for my best interests; I felt as if he was trying to welcome me out the door.

That week I spoke with my psych counselor about taking a leave from work, as Dr. Gantt had been suggesting. We had met weekly for four or five sessions by this point. I spoke with her about Royce's suggestion of sabotaging my job by uploading porn. Her face stretched into a small grin and she casually eased back in her chair.

She proceeded to inform me that they didn't have to give me a dime if I was fired with cause.

And there it was! I now had proof that Royce, my once great friend and hero, was trying to screw me over.

Ding-Dong, the Bitch Is Gone
Wednesday November 25, 1998

On the last Wednesday of November, Milan sent out an e-mail to the team letting us know that Royce was taking an indefinite leave for personal reasons. I felt the weight being lifted from many with an instantaneous sigh of relief rising from each team member when they read the message.

Even though Royce was on leave, I was still deathly afraid of the workplace and my coworkers. I was ever paranoid—I could feel them looking at me. Looking through me.

On the last Monday of November, I called in sick again. That was the fourth week in as many months. I knew that the heads would be shaking, but I just could not deal with the workplace and with all the politics and plain old bullshit.

All those questions.

All those whisperings and sly looks.

With no one else I deemed trustworthy, I called Shane that afternoon to determine if Royce was too sick to show up to work that week and he assured me that he was—he had only been away for a few days. He also confirmed with me that many of the other team members had started to question *my* absence from work.

Even with Royce now out of the picture I was barely keeping my head above water, and now my paranoia was being justified.

Taking a Hit for the Team
Tuesday, December 1, 1998

Against my base instincts, I cautiously went in to work on the Tuesday morning. I really did feel physically sick, but the symptoms were all derived from my sick brain. I was afraid to be seen by anyone. I was afraid to be spoken to by anyone. I was terrified that I was going to be called out on my shenanigans.

I had fallen victim to the same machismo attitude as so many others before me had—only weaklings needed more than the occasional mental health day.

As I entered the main office, I saw that Royce's office lights were on.

I was ready to turn around and bolt. I consciously made the decision to move forward. I held back my panic as best as I could. I slowly approached my cubicle, which was right in front of his office, and then I saw him.

He looked over at me as I tried to skulk past him.

He addressed me with no malice that I could sense, and asked, "How are you feeling?"

"Actually, I still feel pretty shitty," I told him. "I feel both sick to my stomach and feverish. How are *you* doing?"

"I feel great! It feels great to be back so soon," he said enthusiastically.

I smiled awkwardly. I couldn't leave his presence fast enough. I went to the opposite end of the building and hid for over an hour until I worked up the courage to tell our admin assistant that I was going home for the remainder of the day.

Reading Minds
Wednesday, December 2, 1998 – 10:25 a.m.

The next day I called Shane from home to see if Royce had shown up again.

He assured me that he had not.

I had noticed that my short-term memory was about as dense as an old dried-up sponge. My sense of self-direction and initiative had dropped to below zero some time ago. It was due to my illness, and my meds. I felt that I wasn't being fair to my coworkers. I was standing around with my hands in my pockets, like a clay man waiting to be molded into a new shape.

That day Stu Hems, our team's project leader, freaked out on me for not reading the minds of the team. His exact words were that I needed "to anticipate and exceed the needs of the team." The last thing I wanted to do was be a burden to the team.

Afterward, in the locker room, Barry asked me what was wrong with Stu. I told him, and as I was speaking Stu walked in and shouted at me that I was twisting his words. He was outraged.

During lunch hour I approached Stu and laid it out flat to him.

"As you know, I'm heavily medicated and have some serious health issues," I cautiously said—I did not want to anger him any more than I already had. Anger frightened me.

"That's no excuse," he retorted.

I slowly shook my head with frustration and looked down at my hands, trying to figure out how to get my message through to him. How could I explain schizophrenia, or whatever mental illness it was that I had, to a man who knew very little, if anything at all, about it?

"I'm not trying to make excuses, I'm trying to tell you how it is. I'm in no condition to foresee and react to the needs of the team," I responded.

His face was red with rage. I couldn't explain any further; I could read his thoughts from his face. He had no comprehension of my illness, nor the limitations it put on me. All that he could grasp was that my meds made me physically slower and weaker—he understood the visible symptoms.

I didn't hold back. I tried to explain my illness and the effects of the meds on me in a clinical way. That didn't work. I then tried to explain it in layman's terms. That didn't work either.

Finally, I tried a different approach: "How can *you* help me?"

His eyes burned through mine. He remained silent but his aura was crimson: screaming rage. And then he finally said, "I am too livid to talk about it."

I pleaded with him, "I'm not capable of what you are expecting from me. Please, let me work with you to fix this."

Finally, his mouth opened and the bile burst forth. "Get the fuck out of my sight. You're making me sick."

I knew that Stu and the rest of the team were aware of my illness, but only enough to know that I was delusional, and that was in great part thanks to Royce and his big mouth. There had been no education or explanation to them regarding my illness, or Royce's for that matter.

I sincerely wanted to work things out with Stu, but by this time I was realizing that things had started to go too far to ever gain back his trust and respect. I was feeling that his reaction was really a statement on behalf of the entire team.

Even though just being at work gave me the heebie-jeebies, I had convinced myself that with Royce out of the picture I would no longer be as anxious or depressed in the work environment.

I was wrong.

That was the last time I ever spoke with Stu Hems.

As far as I knew, Royce would still be away for a long time for his health issues. I whispered a prayer to Father that Royce find solace in this time of pain. I know that many would call me a sucker or a doormat for having pity on Royce after all the shit he had put me through, but to me it was the right thing to do. Note that despite my earlier thinking, I was not forgiving him or dismissing his behavior in any way. I wasn't there yet.

After my ordeal with Stu, I escaped to the cafeteria and then to my cubicle. I was sitting down in front of my computer sipping on a coffee and eating a blueberry muffin. Stu had crushed my spirit, but I just had to keep plodding along.

I was suffering from an unending panic attack. My heart was thundering in my chest. My lungs seemed incapable of holding air. I was drowning. To divert my attention I started reading my e-mail. I saw a message from Royce. It was addressed to me personally from his home e-mail account. As if I should have been surprised—he just couldn't leave me alone.

This was too much.

I threw up a little bit of coffee and muffin into my mouth.

Without ever reading his message, I turned off my computer and went to find Shane.

With that I gave up.

Royce had won.

To Infinity and Beyond . . .
Wednesday, December 2, 1998 – 1:45 p.m.

It was in early December when I left W.V.H. Steel Inc. and went on long-term sick leave due to mental/emotional health reasons. I had spoken with Shane at work the previous day and bared my soul to him. He was a good man; he didn't look down on me or berate me in any way. He just sat and listened. I told Shane that if I wasn't present the next day it was because my psychiatrist had granted me sick leave.

Kat completely commiserated with me. She had witnessed my decline, and she supported my strategy to take leave from work to collect my thoughts and rebuild my confidence.

If Dr. Edwin objected to giving me leave that afternoon, I was going to kill myself. I couldn't survive another day.

Kat and I entered Dr. Edwin's office and I described what was going on within my head. Her first words were: "You need a week away from work." Inside I was dancing a little jig, but it was short-lived; not because of anything she said or did, just by my immediate realization that this leave had a lifespan.

I remembered the weeks, days, and minutes leading up to my leave. Royce himself had taken medical leave because of his own mental health issues. I was later told that he had made appearances on and off over the first two or three months, but he, like me, was unwanted. I felt bad for him, because I knew how much it hurt to have an emotional sickness.

As always, I cared.

Chapter 21

Yield to Oncoming Traffic

Less Than Zero

Every day I had begged Father for leadership and to show me my way back to my path.

For weeks I had heard nothing from Him. I was teetering on the edge of losing my sanity for good. The world would be better without me. I wasn't going to hurt myself, but I certainly felt like it. Dr. Edwin called this "suicidal ideation."

And then, just as I was about to give up, I heard Him:

I have provided you with all that you need. It is for you to determine how to use your proficiencies. Believe in me and I will take you to places beyond your wildest dreams. I am Peace. I am Hope. I am Love. I am you and you are me.

I wondered if I had heard Father, or if I had just heard yet another voice.

Perhaps Kat was the angel I prayed for. That which I sought had been beside me for so long that I had overlooked it. Had I not called her my angel? Certainly, on numerous occasions. And perhaps I was her angel. We were leading and creating with each other through this tortuous path called life. Our life experiences were intertwined.

I would give my life for Kat.

And I knew that she would give hers for me.

We shared true love.

I asked Kat what I should do about Royce, and she was speechless. She too had experienced hell at the hands of the corporate world. We both sought the same answers to our questions, the same resolution. We were two peas in a pod. Perhaps it was our mutual misery and determination to overcome it that drew us together.

From day one of our relationship, Kat and I were both unknowingly starting to get ill.

The Transparent Sheep

Throughout my life I had been exposed to numerous sheep, all with differing levels of influence, experience, and intellect, many brimming with a blind faith that their posturing and intermingling with one flock over another would align them with that which they perceived to be the winning team.

It was very common for these sheep to run themselves ragged, flip-flopping between every new "winning" idea, all because they were unable or unwilling to collaborate or think a problem through and come up with their own ideas and conclusions.

Like everyone else, I had often fallen victim to this game of needlessly chasing my own tail. However, as I evolved I learned to effectively apply my critical-thinking skills. I tried to listen for the facts and rule out the fiction.

This is where the application of the "teamwork" concept, if adhered to properly, should work to come up with the most effective and efficient solution. The team composed of members representing different backgrounds and insights will come up with the best solution, be it temporary or permanent.

Next, the "educationism" concept comes into the picture. Generally speaking, the education of an individual is equated with expertise and intellect; however, this is not always the reality. The most educated are often the most revered, although experience, with or without education, is also fundamental in the team construct.

Finally, the "charismatic leader" concept comes into play: by definition, the individual with the most personable affect is the one who is often the most readily followed. The role of the leader is to bring the ideas of the team together and to propose the best possible solution to a defined problem.

Unfortunately, as humans we seem unable to collaborate effectively most of the time. Egos and personalities disrupt the decision-making process. Therefore, the sheep tend to jump from flock to flock, from idea to idea, and we are left at the mercy of the leader's decision. Ultimately, the autocratic system is called upon to reach conclusions and is the most effective.

The entire game is played in the name of success. And success, the prize for winning the game, is usually equated with monetary income and/or power. To me this success is both vapid and hypocritical. There is no true happiness or joy derived from being on the winning team if no real commitment has been applied. Simply stating that one had agreed with the final solution is too easy.

It is too easy to blend in with the largest flock of sheep, to go along with the crowd.

Yet it happens every day.

Coming up with the best possible final solution to a problem is the true challenge. And that final solution may not be the correct or absolute answer, but isn't it better to remain focused and consistent, to align with the most logical and probable? I believe it is. Only the strongest of individuals can go against the grain to truly enjoy satisfaction or success. And if—*when*—they fail, they learn from their mistakes, even though they are often subjugated by the "winners."

The hardest part for me was the shame I was made to feel when I was wrong or made a mistake. I took it personally. But that was who I was.

Ignition – Gaslighting

There were always going to be Royces in my world. I quite possibly had Royces I didn't even know existed. In my relationships, be they personal, professional, or other, the Royces were the bullies, the naysayers, the saboteurs. But unlike the bullies of my childhood years, these Royces were wise enough to know that direct physical violence was not an option. Jennifer Albright was a Royce, as was Sidney Stanford.

It all made sense after I did some research. An old concept recently resurrected called "gaslighting" popped up, and suddenly it all clicked.

Gaslighting is a systematic method of emotional/mental manipulation used for psychological intimidation or even all-out warfare. Basically, it is a highly effective bullying and/or conditioning technique in which a targeted individual is led into questioning their thoughts, ideas, and/or positions on an idea, concept, or action; this is accomplished by using a variety of inconsistent and misleading statements, responses, and actions. The gaslighter's endgame is to bring their victims to an emotional or mental state filled with self-doubt and confusion. The effects can go as far as causing a mental breakdown in the victim and leaving them questioning reality itself.

It is a very dangerous game.

One of the key skills of the talented gaslighter is knowing when and where to place a lie or chain of lies into their victim's mind. By lying, they establish a sense of unbalance in their intended's mind; this makes their victim slowly begin to question when their tormentor is being truthful or spinning another dandy. Essentially, they cause the victim to question right from wrong, truth from lie. By keeping their target on their toes, they can lead their victim into believing whatever they want.

Often, they start out using little snippets and snide comments against their victims. These deprecating comments usually crescendo in intensity as the gaslighter becomes more effective and the target weakens. If they are in the position to do so, they will attack that which their victim holds most precious. Often, the gaslighter conspires to isolate their victim from their peers and/or colleagues. The goal of the gaslighter is to get their prey to come back to them more and more. By establishing this, the victim comes to have a reliance on their tormentor; the victim becomes convinced that the gaslighter is on their side. But then they will plant another lie, putting the victim off kilter once again.

Sometimes the gaslighter's lies are those of omission: they spoke the words, the words were heard, but they then deny saying them. Ultimately, the victims begin to question themselves. "Did I really hear that? Was that just my imagination? Am I going crazy?"

Another trick from the gaslighter's handbook is that they will incite their victims to chase their own tails in search of the so-called truth. They will make their victims question their values or doubt their very integrity. They will ultimately accuse their victim of doing the wrong which they, the gaslighter, has done, even though their prey is innocent.

When I first learned of this bullying technique, the first image that appeared in my mind's eye was that of Royce's self-righteous yet sullen visage. This simple definition explained all my woes.

Royce was indeed brilliant—I felt that I was a complete fool.

As Royce had once so boldly stated, I was "just plain stupid."

How could I have fallen for such a blatantly obvious scheme? I knew that I was a very trusting individual by nature, but I thought that I was at least smart enough to see through this kind of crap. I did some further research and was relieved to see that even the most logical and/or emotionally savvy of people could fall victim to this dangerous and damaging form of manipulation.

I realized that everyone in our department had been a victim of Royce's gaslighting to varying degrees. I also came to the realization that Royce was something of a narcissist.

I equally recognized the characteristics of the gaslighter in Sid Stanfield. Like Royce, his narcissistic ways kept me convinced that he had my best interests in mind. He kept me caring about him, all the while screwing me over with my peers and other managers, such as Milan Esteban.

But Royce, it was as if he'd studied it, like he wrote the book on gaslighting.

The more I researched it, the clearer it became.

When I took a step backward and took a critical look at my relationship with Royce, I realized that I had been playing the role of the subservient, the mental slave. He had been slowly stripping me of all my dignity and even some of my basic human rights. His technique was so refined that he positioned me into agreeing and requesting that I be his victim.

And I kept letting him.

I didn't even have freedom of speech. When someone had found their way into his bad books, he would forbid me from speaking with them, even if it was only a conversation between friends.

All I had was fear.

I had no love for myself.

That was not how it was supposed to be.

Only a small handful of people saw the actual inner truth that was me. These people were my true family and friends. They embraced me for who I was, and because I was who I was. Simply put, that was the answer to my quandary:

I was who I was.

I could not let others change me. Take me as I am or do not take me at all.

I should not be who I am not.

I should not be expected to be who I am not.

Only I could change me, and that change should be for the betterment of me, not others.

At the time, I was suffering from extreme delusions of grandeur and persecution.

I started to actively consider the possibility that God was my real Father. I believed it was completely possible that I was a master, a son of God.

But how? I had sinned. Father's son would not sin or give in to temptation.

Or would he?

Christ, like me, was human. He had free will like everyone else. I had always begged Father for forgiveness when I sinned, whether my sin was on purpose or out of ignorance. Maybe that was enough.

I prayed to Father for guidance.

He was a patient God.

He reminded me that all was already within my reach. I just needed to trust and love myself. I needed to open my heart and mind to my soul. I was a piece of Father and I had use of my free will to create a life experience in any way I saw fit.

The secret that Father revealed to me was twofold.

The first secret was that I had to accept my own imperfections, rather than look for and blame these imperfections on others. I had to learn to love myself and to stop depending on others for validation. I had always tried so hard to please everyone else that I had literally gone mad. Of course, I did realize that there was much more to my emotional/mental issues than just trying to be a people-pleaser. My illness was organic and would still have manifested in some form or another in this or any alternate universe or dimension.

I had learned to accept and understand what Dr. Edwin had told me: I was responsible for my own actions. This statement meant that I was not allowed to use my illness as an excuse to do wrong to myself or others. If I acted out on any irrational/delusional thoughts I would be held accountable. When I had homicidal or suicidal thoughts it was my responsibility to notify my doctors and counselors before I acted out. Therefore, if I acted on my emotions it was my choice. Like every human being, I suffered from free will.

And with that realization, I had to accept that there would be consequences to my actions.

The second secret was that I had to embrace my fears. I had to become more self-aware. I had been an emotionally driven child, and I was still emotionally driven as an adult. I had always feared negativity and the plethora of emotions that came along with it, especially anger, whether it was directed at me or not. It didn't matter whether the negativity was displeasure or disappointment or outright hatred., I felt it and I took it upon myself to make sense of it. I realized that this was quite arrogant—who the hell was I to take it upon myself to cleanse humankind of its woes? Still, in my sick mind I believed that it was my burden to carry.

The world weighed heavily on my shoulders. It had become too much for me to carry.

This had turned me from an idealist into a cynic.

Schizophrenia
Thursday, December 3, 1998

Dr. Edwin formally diagnosed me with schizophrenia. She had to write it on the paperwork that I had to give to HR at work.

It was now formal and official.

I felt a mixture of emotions. On one hand, I was relieved. Now that my illness had been defined, it could be specifically addressed. On the other hand, I was now a statistic and open to the spectrum of stigma associated with the illness.

Dr. Edwin wrote me a note granting me leave for one week.

Misery
Friday, December 4, 1998

The first morning of my leave, I got up and called our admin assistant and Milan Esteban. Neither answered their phones, so I left each a brief message letting them know that I was taking the next week off for medical reasons.

At about ten a.m., Shane called me. Apparently both Milan and our admin assistant were absent that morning. I felt bad that I hadn't called Shane as well, but how was I to know that he wouldn't get the message?

Later that day Milan called me and told me to keep in touch with Shane. He didn't sound very sympathetic like he had when Royce called him. But at least he wasn't dismissive.

At last I could breathe as a free man, even if it was just for a temporary amount of time.

I was on leave from work.

And despite all my previous reservations, it felt great.

I knew that Royce wasn't the cause of all my misery, but it was easiest to put the blame on him. In retrospect, he had only been but a minor blip in my life, but the intensity of his blip was substantial. When I thought deeply on it and discussed it with Father, I realized that I had to be judicious. I had to consider the possibility that I should hold myself responsible for my misery. After all, regardless of the huge mistake that it had been, it was me who had invited Royce into my life—into my mind—and so it must be my responsibility to root him out.

The thought of returning to work was overwhelming, but I thought that after just a week or two I would be fine. But when I returned, things had to be different, whether Royce was back or not.

I thought that perhaps I should attempt to alter my actions and behavior. I could alter how I was perceived. I could become an actor and play the role of a lifetime. I had the intellectual chops to pull it off. I could be that cookie-cutter professional that was so revered by the likes of Dr. Royce Pincer and Milan Esteban.

Droll. Emotionless. Arrogant.

A yes-man.

A Barry Nichols, for example.

The most important questions were: Did I want to change me? And if so, to what end?

During the week away, rather than improving I was becoming less and less stable. One week away from work just hadn't cut it. I was delusional and emotionally handicapped. I was heavily medicated, but all that did was make me feel like a zombie all day.

I went back to see Dr. Edwin again the following week. Her concern was clearly obvious. She wrote a letter granting me a month away from work this time. I still couldn't bring myself to deliver the letter to HR. Kat once again had my back. I couldn't bear being on that piece of land. To me it was like a cemetery on a full-moon night: all the ghouls and ghosts from the past were coming out to torment the late-night visitors. I knew that by now the rumor mill would be hard at work.

Still, over the next month I grew sicker and sicker.

Finally, Dr. Edwin decided to grant me an indefinite leave. Again, I had to get Kat to drop the letter off. Ironically, she still bore the wounds from her experience at W.V.H. Steel. She understood that I couldn't return. She felt the same, yet she put herself in this awkward position for me.

Talk about love.

I was fortunate that the company had a disability benefit. With this benefit I was able to collect a pension rather than go on government-funded disability.

Kat later told me that she had spoken with the R&D team's HR rep about Royce's abuse. The response she received was that our rep was aware of Royce's antics and the impact it was having on individuals like me, but that Royce was sick as well and therefore he could not be held accountable.

I later learned that this was not even a legal position. In fact, I later learned that most of Royce's threats and bullying were not just morally reprehensible, they were outright illegal.

We all thought that being removed from the toxic work environment for a while would allow me to heal and lead to a better, healthier headspace for me.

We were proved wrong.

I had a significantly deeper hole to sink into before I would hit rock bottom.

I was at home, lying on our couch in the basement, sick and tired of feeling sick and tired. And just like that, my thoughts took on a voice of their own and exploded:

This has been a long time in coming.

Fuck with me, will you?

I will teach you what it means to fuck with someone. Not simple little mind-fucking bouts; I will show you real power. Your judgment day has arrived. I am the Lord. I am Christ. I am God's son. You will pay for your crimes against humanity. You will pay for your sins against Father. You will pay for your sins against me.

Those glassy brown bespectacled eyes. Looking at me. Looking at me with contempt. Looking at me without mercy. Looking at me for mercy.

Looking.

Your shiny bald head. Reflecting the light from above. Reflecting my image. That head—it should be battered. It should be lacerated. Blood should flow. You should feel the pain that Father has felt in watching you.

You not only should. You will.

I tried my best. I brought my best to the table. I put my best foot forward. I tried. I succeeded. But you turned my success into failure.

You will die with my cock up your bloody hemorrhoidal asshole. I will rape you until you beg me to stop. I will make you eat your own shit. And then I will cut off your genitals and shove them up your ass. I will make you enjoy it. You will enjoy it, or you will suffer more.

I'll strike you hard across the face. Over and over.

No one is going to be there to stop me. I will be exacting my revenge. The pain that you triggered in me emotionally shall be regurgitated and inverted onto you physically.

A heart-stopping crack as most of what were your front teeth will fly in shards toward the back of your throat. One of those shards, embedded in the bloodied meat of my fist, will come at you again and again, gleaming white enamel, gnashing into your nose. White lights will flash through your skull and be forced out by the thin rivulets of blood in waves of sobering pain.

"What the fuck?" those eyes will ask before they widen and watch the concrete floor approach.

I will strike you hard in the face again and again. I will feel your skull collapsing beneath the strength of my blows. Fractures. Lacerations. Contusions. Blood.

A lot of blood.

You will be on the ground, but I will not care. I will not yet be finished with you, you stinky little cunt. You attempted to strip me of my self-worth. You succeeded. You have left only the base animal in my soul.

Fuck my pacifist beliefs. I shall strip you of your skin.

A thin pool of blood will form a halo around your head from which one of those ugly eyes will dangle, staring. Questioning. Those eyes will remain implanted in my mind forever.

I have stripped you. I am raping you. I am getting off on the violence.

I have a knife. I am holding it to your genitals as my cock tears your asshole.

You are whimpering. Like a little baby, you cry. You cry for your mother. I will fuck and mutilate her in front of you. No! I will make you fuck and mutilate her. You are my bitch.

I think I am going to take my knife and peel your skin off. First, I shall flay the flesh from your extremities, your hands and your feet. Then your genitals. I will laugh as you cry. You are a sinner. They have believed your stories. They too are to be judged and punished accordingly. It shall be done in Father's name. For I am the Son of God.

I cut into your skin with my blade. Right under your balls where your scrotum connects, I will slice. You will howl. I will pull your head back by the thin hair on the back of your head. With a gruesome grunt, I will ram my cock as far up your bleeding asshole as it will go. I feel your flesh yielding under my force.

I pull my shit-covered cock from your asshole. The knife will still be digging into the flesh between your balls. I will see the blood running between your legs. You will be pissing. You will be pissing all over the floor. You will be crying. I will feel no mercy for you, you merciless son of a bitch.

I force you down on all fours. There is blood everywhere. The blood is good. You shall be bathed in the blood. But not the blood of Father. You shall be baptized in your own blood. I will be performing the ceremony. Thank you for this opportunity, Father in Heaven.

I pull the knife from behind your balls to your asshole. I watch with delight as the flesh yields. The fatty tissue spreads like a young girl's legs on prom night. I will tease your asshole with the knife. I will make little cuts and scrapes.

I loved you. Now, our roles have reversed; you are now one of my children. I am teaching you, my child, a lesson. You cannot go around treating people poorly. You cannot abuse people. You cannot break Father's law. But because you have free will, you have done all these things. You have committed these crimes.

It is with love that I insert the knife into your asshole and I twist it.

I once read that such a wound will kill a man. That it is perhaps the slowest way for a man to die by a blade. Judgment will come swiftly, as you are learning, but that does not mean that it is meted out swiftly. The punishment must suit the crime. You were a warlord. You are responsible for destroying the lives of people through your slavery to the dollar and the ensuing corporate slaughter.

See the dog.
See the dog lie.
See the dog howl.
See the dog beg.
See the man.
See the man begin to twitch.
See the man twitching on the floor die.
See the punisher cry.
Jesus wept
It's that easy.
A.
B.
C.

Sorry about your luck. It will never happen again. Trust me. And by the way, Fuck You.

I realized that I was filling up with hatred, that emotion I had always so vehemently despised. I wanted to make Royce suffer. I wanted him obliterated from reality. This was against my core values, but I was beginning to believe that I must act.

I was both frightened and excited about where my thoughts were taking me.

Part VI

Rock Bottom

Chapter 22

The Struggle Continues

The Battle Has Been Won, but the War Is Just Beginning
Mid-December 1998

I had simply stopped actively creating. I just sat around feeling sorry for myself and upset with how things had turned out with work. I was so busy blaming others, including Father, because I couldn't see or hear the truth. Or maybe more specifically, I refused to see or hear the truth. And therefore my ambition and initiative had become nothing. I felt like less than a rotting lump of shit.

I suppose that was my experience for that time, because deep inside I knew that my creativity was endless. So why had I so easily accepted this miserable fate? The truth was that I had let my dedication to the corporate machine, and more specifically to Royce, conquer me.

A tiny voice spoke up from an infinitesimal crevice in my mind: *Fuck that notion!*

I could not let myself be so easily defeated.

I was virtually free. The only influence that my tormentors at W.V.H. Steel had over me now was that which I allowed them. Sadly, my nerves were still exposed and raw. But I kept telling myself that I was recuperating. I was getting stronger. The doctors had often told me that to endure and survive the psychological terror while excelling in school made me a very strong person.

I was learning to take things one day at a time.

The journey to recovery would be long and arduous, but I had hope.

Leave Me the Fuck Alone . . . Please!
Thursday, January 7, 1999

One requirement for my sick leave was that I had to contact and update Shane every week for the first six months of my leave. Shane did not always call back, his reasoning being that he wanted me to relax and keep my mind away from all the shit that had helped bring me to this point. But every third or fourth week we would talk.

Ironically, when I first took leave the weeks when Shane and I didn't talk I would become just as anxious as when we did. Early on I had convinced myself that I would just need a few weeks, or maybe a couple of months, and I would be emotionally refreshed and reenergized and ready to face the music with a heroic return to work.

Instead of getting better whilst being away, my mental health continued to decline. I couldn't tell whether my deluded mind was exaggerating my memories or if they were real. My recollections had remained consistent all along, and when I had spoken with Shane he had never told me that I was overthinking or misremembering what had happened.

Fortunately, I was receiving full pay as per my workplace benefits. I would continue to make this amount for six months from the day I left, after which I would only receive a percentage of my full pay. With my declining mental health, I was becoming convinced that I would not be returning to work any time soon, possibly not even before my first six months were over. I was in no mental frame of mind to budget our household bills. Suffice it to say I was concerned about how we would manage with such a significant loss in income.

On the first Thursday back to work in the new year, Shane and I had our usual conversation. We discussed how our Christmas holidays had been. It was a nice fluffy little conversation, right up until Shane shared some unwelcomed news: Royce had returned to work again.

Apparently, Royce felt that he was well enough to work again, although Shane revealed that he had returned against his doctor's orders. My irrational mind became convinced that HR would use this as justification to either require me to go back to work or fire me.

I believed that if I returned to work for more than five minutes I would be terminated and lose my income, be it salary or disability. Prior to his leave, Royce had been actively trying to get rid of me for quite a while; he just didn't count on my determination to survive and innate ability to see through his attempts. I surmised that Royce had backing from his peers and supervisors with this plan.

By taking the indefinite sick leave I believed I had dodged a bullet.

Although the idea was unfounded, I was deathly afraid that I was going to be required to return to work.

There was no way that I could endure Royce's presence ever again.

As if on cue, Royce had the balls to call me at home that night. It had been well over a month since I'd had to deal with him and my nerves were still raw. His call was the last thing that I wanted or needed. I felt as though he was rubbing my face in his shit and then complimenting me on my appearance. I believed that the only reason he called was to show off to the rest of the team that he was a sincere and concerned leader, that he was trying to show that he had changed, or possibly that he had always been a "good guy" and that I was the one with the real issues.

As contradictory as it may sound, I was so overwhelmed with fear and angst upon hearing his voice that my mind somehow twisted itself into a knot until I was left feeling genuinely thankful that he had called. He was giving the gas just one more little light, one more mind-fuck, just to show who held the real power.

The conversation lasted about ten to fifteen minutes, although it seemed like a lifetime. I let him prattle on about how the workplace wasn't the same without me, and that everyone in the TTD was concerned for my well-being. I could feel his lack of sincerity.

I believed that he was arrogant enough to think that by reaching out to me he would tell others that he had been the bigger man and tried to tie up and put to rest any loose ends that existed between us, thus washing his hands of all of his misdoings.

After I hung up the phone I felt like killing myself.

I was so weak.

I had once again fortified whatever power it was that he had over me. I had reacted exactly the way he had wanted. I should have put him in his place. I should have made him feel as low as he had made me feel. Instead I told him that I was doing well, but it would be a few more weeks until I would feel ready to return. He made a little more chitchat, all lies and empty words. I could feel my blood pressure rise. I wanted to reach through the phone and tear out his throat. But throughout our conversation I remained calm and polite.

Even after all he had put me through, I still cared.

Go Home!
Thursday, January 28, 1999

The next time that I spoke with Shane, he informed me that Royce had only returned to work for an entire three days after the holidays. It was just enough time to stir up all the old bullshit and reopen healing wounds.

He hadn't even gone to work the day after he called me.

Although I had already experienced intense feelings of hatred toward Royce, learning of this had truly awakened the demons within me. I wasn't just thinking about it, I wanted revenge.

Repentless
February 1999

At times, my delusions had tended to be quite grandiose. For quite a while I had been coming up with some pretty high-in-the-sky scientific reasoning and theories. I expected perfection from myself. I felt that if I did not completely understand a topic or concept I didn't comprehend it at all. This thirst for understanding grew a thousand-fold back when I returned to school to complete my engineering degree.

But for every answer there were a hundred more questions.

In the corporate world, apart from R&D programs the questions that were affecting the bottom line were the only ones that were addressed. It was generally too costly to address the small questions.

As my mind had been blossoming in school, I had begun to embrace new and often near-inconceivable concepts. I went so far as to extend and apply scientific theories into human and psychological conditions. Intellectually, there was only one boundary that could hold me back.

It was people.

There was no logic behind people.

People were so multi-dimensional and complicated.

I'd had difficulty understanding the concept of people since I was a child.

No one else seemed interested, but I was driven to understand people. It was the curious armchair psychologist in me. I was perplexed with other individuals' motives and actions, especially when their behavior was irrational to me. If they continued to act erratically and it affected me, I would usually seek counsel from a neutral third party.

It took me a long time before I realized that I was searching for answers that only Father could give.

I was often dismissed for being too sensitive, yet I observed how a great number of people would get quite defensive, even offended, if their egos weren't stroked when they believed it was called for. It was extremely perplexing to witness how sensitive they would become when they disagreed with an accepted topic or concept.

It was then that I first realized that, despite what I was being told, it was okay to be a sensitive man. I may not have been one who resorted to anger, bullying, or violence when many would say it was called for, but when it came down to what mattered, I *was* a real man. Perhaps even more than others because I considered the human impact of my decision-making process.

I was a gentleman, not some boorish chest-thumping ape of a man.

When others were in a sensitive state, depending on the depth of their wounded ego their solution could be to anywhere from conceding defeat to further complaining, all the way up to outright sabotaging the success of the offensive concept or person.

That was not to suggest that those with differing opinions should give up or concede their position, it was how they behaved after their ideas or insights had gone unconsidered. Logic dictates that they should have a free exchange of thoughts and ideas. They should collaborate to find a better solution.

But as soon as feelings were brought to the table, everyone seemed to go squirrely.

When I first started out in the manufacturing/engineering field, I didn't realize that workplace politics existed, at least to the degree that I was experiencing, and later I couldn't understand why they needed to exist. It was like back when we were children on the playground—I couldn't grasp why some kids chose to bully the others. Why was there this urge to establish dominance?

There was no need to exploit the weaknesses of others. There was no need for gaslighting or any form of bullying, especially when it was done selfishly.

I used to love learning about math and science and sharing my findings.

Politics destroyed the manufacturing/engineering experience for me.

Over the Top
Early March 1999

To add to all our problems, late that winter I discovered eBay.

The thrill of winning an auction was absolutely sublime. I would see an item that I thought would be cool to own and I would put in my bid. And I would watch it. And the more I watched it, the more I needed to have it. As the bids poured in, I kept increasing mine to ensure I won. It came down to the gambling that I was addicted to. Yes, I bought things I wanted, but I would spend ridiculous amounts on them. I spent my money mostly on LPs. Most of the items I bought were collectors. I had a huge and valuable Metallica collection.

At first, I would spend up to $100 a day on a couple of items every few days. I was still receiving my full pay from W.V.H. Steel, as per their medical leave policy.

Before long I was spending around $1,000 per week.

I remember one day thinking I made enough in two weeks to afford to spend the money I was yet to receive. I spent nearly $2,000 within two or three days.

As I've said, the thrill of the auction was intoxicating, but winning was the cherry on top.

Pissed off at all my spending, for revenge and a good asskicking reality check, Kat showed up one afternoon with a brand-new computer, laser printer, and a digital camera. I knew that I was the last person who was in a position to speak up, but I freaked out. My own madness had caught up with me. Unfortunately, by this time I was out of control.

Kat returned the computer and printer. We kept the camera.

One would think that I had learned my lesson.

As time passed, Kat had watched me transform into a monster right in front of her. Her depression and anxiety were feeding from mine, and her condition was weakening. For her own health, her doctors were repeatedly telling her to leave me.

But still she persevered.

S.O.S.
Mid-March 1999

Kat was at her wit's end.

I was faithfully taking my meds. I wanted to feel better. I wanted to be better. But so far progress was minimal.

All I did was spend our money on eBay, watch television in my underwear, and smoke my cigarettes. I wasn't showering or bathing for long periods of time. My long hair was straggly and matted. I reeked of body odor. Kat had told me that I was getting so disgusting that she was going to start sleeping in one of the spare rooms if I didn't smarten up.

Sex was definitely off the table.

No matter how hard she tried, Kat couldn't motivate me to do anything.

I couldn't motivate myself.

Somewhere along the line some of my anxieties had morphed into outright phobias, which I later learned are not uncommon for people suffering with schizophrenia. I was extremely paranoid. I was deathly afraid of slipping in the bathtub, which was my main reason for not showering. I was also afraid of the soap and water itself: I believed it was a deadly chemical that would eat away at my flesh. I stopped brushing my teeth because I was afraid of gagging and choking to death.

With nowhere left to turn, Kat finally broke down and asked my parents for help, who arrived to help within an hour of receiving the call.

Kat and I owned a house which was about a forty-five-minute highway drive away from theirs in Pittsburgh.

I had avoided contact from almost everyone, including my parents, for a few months by this time. They were aware of my illness but had no idea what a shitstorm they were walking into. When they saw what was going on, they took quick action. Dad got me into the shower to clean up and I put on fresh underwear and shorts. Mom leaned me over the bathtub and washed my hair while Dad took the bed linens and put them in the wash.

Kat told my parents about my eBay activity. Mom wanted me to return all the items that I had purchased, but I refused. So the next step was to take away my credit cards to prevent me from spending any more on eBay.

That was no big deal to me. After Kat went to bed, I pulled out her credit card and was back online faster than a fly to a piece of shit. This new bout of spending lasted about a week; that was how long it took for them to find out what I was doing.

I had grown deathly afraid of being seen by anyone I knew, except for Kat and my parents, which was why I only left the bedroom to use the washroom. With my fear of being seen by others, I could no longer face the delivery man in the mornings. Plus, with my parents' intervention I was no longer going on the computer to use eBay, and finally the deliveries stopped coming.

I remember one evening my two grandmothers came over for dinner and I couldn't leave our bedroom out of fear that I would be seen by anyone other than Kat or my parents. I called out for Kat and she came into the room to see what I needed. She shielded me as I scooted across the five-foot space between the bedroom and bathroom so that I wouldn't be seen. She escorted me back as well.

There was no rational explanation for my behavior.

I overheard my grandmothers asking my parents and Kat why I wouldn't come out of our bedroom to visit with them. They simply didn't understand, although they were sympathetic. As they left, they both called out that they loved me. Through a tear-filled voice I replied that I loved them as well.

Coffee and Donuts
Late March 1999

At one point early that spring, I learned that an old friend who used to work at the Black Bass with me had moved into our neighborhood. He was a pothead. So naturally, when we reconnected I began habitually smoking pot again, just as I had when I was several years younger and living with Jennifer Albright. The pot helped a little with my anxiety and increased the influx of creative thoughts, but it also raised my paranoia through the roof.

Having only experimented with pot a little when she was younger, Kat freaked out when she discovered that I had begun using it on a regular basis. She kept me honest and insisted I tell Dr. Edwin about it.

Dr. Edwin reminded me a lot of my mom: she didn't fool around and she was as straight-laced and cautious as they came. I already knew what she was going to say about the weed.

Mom and Dad signed up for a group class to learn about schizophrenia, specifically the nature of the illness and how to deal with me and my irrational behavior. Mom also began attending my weekly meetings with Dr. Edwin with Kat and me. They wanted to help and understand to the best of their abilities.

After taking leave from work in December, my psych counselor had set me up with a daily therapy group that was to begin in April. Through the group, I was assigned a new counselor, Melissa.

As March turned to April, group therapy started. Every morning Dad was at my front door bright and early, wearing a big, bright smile, ready to take me out for coffee and then to group. My parents wanted to be a part of our lives. They wanted the best for Kat and me.

Slowly, my sick mind started to question their motives.

I attended the group for two or three weeks, but it was not for me. I discussed it with Mom and Dad, and with Melissa. My parents thought that I should see it through, but Melissa supported my decision to leave the group. The group was mainly for those who suffered from extreme depression and anxiety, which I admitted I did need help with, but my schizophrenic symptoms superseded the others at that time. I felt that I couldn't relate with anyone else in the group, although I was told that there was another group member with the same ailment I had.

After I left the group, Dad kept showing up every morning to go out for coffee and donuts.

I kept on seeing Melissa every week. My relationship with my dad had always been casual, although he had always tended to intimidate me when he would yell. We had shared a familial love but had never been close. So being on leave enabled Dad and me to start developing a good friendship with each other. With all the negativity surrounding me, this was one amazing thing that I would cherish forever.

Auf Wiedersehen
April 1999

I presumed that as far as Royce was concerned his hands were wiped clean of all the messes that he had created at work. Shane later informed me that over the first few months into the new year Royce would show up at work for a day or two, each time against his doctor's orders. All he would do was immerse himself in the workplace politics by sitting in his office and sending out e-mails. Royce behaved as if nothing had changed, although the team had moved on since his leave had begun. He was reopening long-closed doors. His unpredictable presence was being regarded by the team as selfish. He had no regard for the impact he was having; his sole purpose seemed to be to make himself look like a superman who wouldn't be defeated by his illness.

I could identify with that feeling. I did not want to be sick either, but I could not be so selfish as to try to overcome it at the expense of others.

So, as Royce was posturing himself as if he was stable, he was leaving the team and its members shattered and suffering, trying to rebuild under new leadership.

HR finally had to tell Royce that he couldn't keep up his off-and-on behavior. I wished I had been a fly on the wall when Royce was told that he was no longer welcome on W.V.H. Steel property without a doctor's signed note certifying that he was well enough to work.

As far as I knew, I would never have anything to do with Royce again.

Chapter 23

Good Times, Bad Times

Remembering the Beast
Early May 1999

I was lying in bed one mid-spring afternoon, smoking cigarette after cigarette, when I had a flashback of the look on Mom's face when she used to hit me with Dad's belt. I couldn't get the images of her whipping me out of my mine: the rabid froth of saliva at the sides of her mouth as she compelled me to beg for penance, bellowing at me to stop crying or I'd get it worse. It was that crazed look in her eyes that I was afraid of the most. All she had to do was look deep into my eyes and I knew . . .

I remembered standing naked in front of the bathroom mirror looking at the long, red, raised welts across my buttocks and rear thighs after the lashings.

I recalled the taste of the soap caked on the back of my teeth after I had first said the word "fuck" in front of her.

I started wondering about Dad—where was he when these punishments were doled out? Why didn't he stand up for me when Mom whipped me? Why didn't he say "enough"?

I began to wonder why my parents were being so supportive as Kat and I dissected and tried to make sense of our issues.

As I started questioning their motives, it started to make sense.

They were acting out of guilt.

The Perfect Shitstorm
Late May 1999

I was the perfect baby, as per Mom.

I was speaking words by six months and sentences by the time I was one year old.

I was potty trained by the time I was eighteen months old.

I was on a sleep schedule within the first month of my life: asleep in bed by seven p.m., awake at seven a.m., except for nighttime feedings. I slept through any commotion. I rarely cried or fussed.

Being the golden child, it was bred into me to always be on my best behavior. I became a people-pleaser; more to the point, I aimed to please the authoritative people in my life—any adult. If I acted out I was dutifully punished.

I did quite well in school.

I always said please, thank you, and sorry.

I didn't ask for much.

Usually, with a little prodding I confessed to my sins and misdeeds and tried to be genuinely committed to not repeating my errors, or making them in the first place. When whipped or grounded, I learned my lessons.

However, the lessons that I learned were not just about correcting certain behaviors. I learned to take my punishment as ordered, no matter how humiliating. Reading between the lines,

I learned additional lessons. Don't look to others for help; no one wants to get involved. Don't stick up for myself or the consequences would be more severe. I must take my punishment when it was called for. Never defend myself or cry or I would get it twice as bad. Furthermore, adults or authoritarians were never to be challenged—children were to be seen and not heard.

My sister Ellyn was treated quite differently than me when it came to discipline. She was rarely punished as extremely as I was. I remember her arguing with my parents about how I was their favorite. As a child and teen, she would declare that she hated living with them, and that she couldn't wait to be old enough to leave home.

In many cases I was punished because of something she had done or instigated.

If I was whipped, I was left nursing my wounds and begging for forgiveness and swearing that I would never repeat whatever evil deed I had done. If I was grounded, I dared not be a minute late, knowing that there would be a greater punishment awaiting me when I did get home.

The only time I can remember Ellyn getting into real shit was after she started dating Marshall Moore. They were both sixteen, and he had his driving license and complete access to his parents' car. It didn't take much imagination to know what they were up to every night. The problem with Marshall was that he had no respect for my parents or their rules. Marshall would intentionally keep Ellyn out past her curfew. Mom would lecture him and he would roll his eyes as she spoke.

My parents only grounded my sister from seeing Marshall. She still snuck out every night. She was never really punished, only threatened.

Ellyn's spirit was intact.

When she was spanked, there was no brutality—a bare hand on her clad bottom. If she was grounded, she would get away with not obeying the conditions as she was supposed to.

There was a clear double standard between the two of us.

When we were older and brought up some of Mom's actions, Mom claimed that we were remembering incorrectly. If it had just been me who recalled certain events, I would have been more open to believing that I was exaggerating or that my memories of the past were distorted. However, Ellyn usually had the exact same recollections.

All I could remember with certainty was that every time I expressed myself in any way that didn't align with Mom's values, or if I embarrassed her, it was time to be grounded or whipped. At the time, I had yet to realize that my sick mind was probably overexaggerating the frequency of abuse that I had endured, but the trauma had been significant enough to scar my psyche.

I was beginning to figure out how and why I had become so damaged and fragile.

I began to blame my parents for my illness. I became fixated. After all, schizophrenia is an emotional illness, so in my mind it must have been brought on by long-buried emotions. I temporarily stopped to consider that it was also an organic/physical disease, but as far as I was concerned at that time I was sick because my parents had broken my spirit.

I was out of my mind.

I was broken.

Mommy was the one who broke me.

And Daddy did nothing to curb her behavior.

That was why I had been torn and shredded by people in the corporate/manufacturing world. I didn't have the correct tools in my kit to enable me to successfully deal with that which I never fathomed possible by adults. I was bullied as much as I was because it made people like Sid Stanford and Dr. Royce Pincer feel powerful. I think that they recognized me as an easy mark. When bullied, I did as I had been taught: I tried to please my abuser to avoid their wrath. And when I realized I was being mistreated, I set out to find an adult to help me. It was a hard lesson for me when I learned that my supervisors were not like my parents.

I was supposed to be the adult.

My memories and thoughts were mounting. I discussed my thoughts and feelings with Kat.

I knew that corporal punishment was still a commonly accepted practice when I was a kid. I also knew that the majority of those from my generation and generations before who were punished in similar ways were dismissive of it. They believed they learned their lessons and became good adults and parents because of it.

I woefully tried to explain what I was feeling to Kat until I had cried my eyes dry. These feelings of betrayal and torment kept building up until I submitted to a voice in my head that had started screaming for revenge against my parents. With Kat's assent, I e-mailed Mom and insisted that she tell me why she had done all those terrible things to me. I wanted to know why Dad hadn't stepped in. I wanted her to atone for her role in bringing me to this emotional low point. As for Dad, I couldn't remember him usually being around in my younger years; probably because he worked shifts at the steel mill. I did recall him dissociating from the situation when he *was* around.

Mom's answer was that things weren't as bad or brutal as I was recalling. Maybe they weren't, but my pain was very real. I had arrived at this conclusion and only Mom and Dad could explain it away. I became hellbent on punishing my parents to the best of my ability. I wanted them to feel what it was like to be betrayed by the ones you looked up to the most. When Mom phoned us to respond, we refused to answer.

I e-mailed her, requesting that they not try to contact me or Kat again until she was willing to admit the truth. In turn, she told me that they were still seeking professional assistance from their counselor in their group, but she couldn't respond to my request.

I bawled like a baby for hours.

For days.

I basically told her that they could fuck off until they were willing to face me and tell me the truth about why she had pushed me so hard.

I told her the only way I would talk to her was via e-mail.

Mom begged me to let her back into my life. Kat stood strong with me. Mom kept telling me she couldn't respond—their counselor told them not to feed my delusions. I called her out on it. She had done these things; I just wanted to know why.

Deep down, I didn't like pushing my parents away. They had been so good to us since my illness progressed. But I felt that I had to do this. I had to hear from Mom, the original bully. What and why? And what of Dad?

I believed that if I could understand why Mom had bullied me, I could understand why I was so insecure and felt easily victimized by so many others.

I was still seeing my counselor, Melissa, and brought her up to speed on what was going on. I knew I was breaking Mom's heart by keeping her out of our lives. I couldn't understand why she wouldn't simply answer my questions.

After about a month of weekly meetings, Melissa asked me if I wanted a relationship with my parents. Of course I did! After some lengthy discussion, she agreed to see my parents and mediate between us. First Mom and Dad would meet with her and then the next day Kat and I would see her.

After our meetings, Melissa explained to me that the advice my parents had been given was the same she would have given them. Under most conditions I wasn't one to hold a grudge, but that didn't necessarily mean I was quick to forgive, and certainly not to forget, but I liked to keep my karma as clean as I could. As upset as I was with my parents, I didn't want the misery to continue. I simply wanted answers and accountability.

That night after my session with Melissa, I called Mom. We talked about my memories, and specifically why she was unwilling to answer my questions. She cried during the entire conversation.

We agreed to have them over for dinner the next evening. When they arrived, they both stood in the doorway. Mom was crying; Dad looked a little misty as well. I could see the dark tear-sodden circles around Mom's eyes. We all apologized and hugged.

"This is the best decision you could have made," Mom said, weeping as I hugged her.

It was a difficult conversation, but eventually Mom told me that the counselor they were seeing had strongly advised them against giving in to my demands, whether they were real or distorted. Their counselor advised that if they gave in to my delusions it could make matters worse. It would cement my thinking and could harbor permanent discord. Additionally, they were told to never lie to someone with schizophrenia, as it would permanently destroy every iota of trust and therefore any chance of reestablishing a relationship with them.

So although we never really addressed the truth that was fueling my memories, Melissa had given me her professional opinion, and after some discussion Kat and I felt that there was no good that could come from further arguing about what had happened over twenty-five years before then. I was still haunted by these memories—they would always be a part of me—but I agreed that we had to move on.

I wished that I could have the same conversation with Royce.

Just Let It Go
Early June 1999

Individuals like Dr. Shane Wulf, who were empathetic and caring individuals by nature, had a heightened patience and accommodating nature. But even good men like Shane had their limits. While I was on leave, Shane told me that during one of his short-lived stints back at work from his leave, Royce had apologized to the team for his past behavior. I made the point that Royce had never apologized to me. Shane simply could not grasp my point, and I think that ultimately we both became frustrated. I could sense it in his voice—he had nothing more to offer.

I wanted to just get over it.

I wanted to forgive and forget.

I wanted to just let it go.

Because I was unable to do as I wanted, I remained connected to work. To Royce.

I feared that I had lost a friend in Shane because I couldn't just let it go.

Even as I write this passage, I feel the anxiety and I am reliving those experiences.

Chapter 24

The Gift

A Little Light Reading
Mid-June 1999

I'd read that in some cultures, schizophrenia was considered a gift and was celebrated.

In my culture it was a highly stigmatized and misunderstood illness.

However, I did see the beauty in the madness. Having schizophrenia had brought out all kinds of heightened cerebral activity. If the sick mind's activity could be harnessed it could be a great source of creativity and insight into wherever the mind wandered. I came to believe that this was in part the reason I could grasp and manipulate so many of the complex theories and concepts that I had studied in school.

However, this creativity came at a dangerously high price. The creativity did not stop once mapped out, calculated, or written down on paper. It would start to snowball into more voices and delusions, each of which created a unique new universe for the brain to explore. However, these multiple delusions also made my sick brain evermore paranoid.

I started having difficulty separating reality from what was perceived versus what really was. Basically, I could no longer distinguish between reality and my delusional world.

Having heightened creativity was not always as wonderous as it may have sounded. For all the brightly sparkling insights, my mind also created dark elements and thoughts of horrific images and notions, such as how I was beginning to plot against Royce.

Such had been the case with my longtime friend Mike Jagger when he had downloaded all those grimacing images of dead and mutilated bodies. My creative thoughts came in the form of paranoid delusions, leaving me convinced for quite a long time that I was under some form of surveillance, be it by work, government, or worse.

I'd also read that only about one third of those who suffered from mental health issues ever admitted to their illnesses. Simply using the terms "sufferers" and "illnesses" alone hints that these individuals were sick and therefore lesser in some way than the rest of the population. It is akin to a cancer patient: they suffer from an illness and are therefore labeled victims of that illness.

I would think that this would make for a more empathetic society.

I believe that education is key. People need to understand that a person dealing with a mental illness is suffering, just as a victim of any physical ailment.

Sadly, we all want to be perceived as being stronger and smarter than we are. We want to hide our truths, our flaws and mistakes. This is the source of any stigma.

It makes no sense to me.

The current mental health issues that are being targeted for de-stigmatization are the less feared and more common ailments, such as anxiety and depression. This is not meant to dismiss these illnesses; they are very serious and can be quite ominous to treat.

I surmise that almost everyone has experienced anxiety at some point in their lives. Anxiety asking for a first date. Anxiety when starting a new job. Anxiety over buying a car or house. Anxiety is the butterflies that you feel in your stomach as you dare yourself to press forward into the unknown while creating a new life experience.

Similarly, I would go so far as to state that almost everyone has suffered from depression. Depression from ending a relationship with your girlfriend/boyfriend. Depression from getting let go from a job. Depression due to the death of a parent or friend. It's the weighty sadness that you feel in your head and the emptiness you feel in your stomach.

Now, try to imagine those feelings magnified one thousand times. Try to step into the shoes of someone with the inability to overcome these devastating sensations. The feeling of being crippled and caged. The feeling of being unable to move forward. The feeling that despite your best intentions, you are unable to get up in the morning for work. Unable to do anything but attempt to put on a convincing smile for your friends and family. You'll do whatever you need just to get through the day.

That is mental illness.

Next, try to imagine sharing your feelings of desperation with your friends, family, or coworkers—if you are bold enough to face the potential damning stigma. The last thing you want is to be labeled. And unless they have experienced something similar, and they themselves are willing to open up, you'll get the same old rhetoric from them. "You're just in a temporary funk. It's not as bad as you think. You're overreacting. It will pass soon enough. Tomorrow is a new day. You'll have forgotten about it by then. Face your fears and you will overcome them."

Just let it go.

That is what others may and most likely will say to you. And that will often reinforce and possibly exaggerate your mental health issues by introducing self-doubt and a feeling of isolation. This may dissuade you from seeking help, as it did me. In general, others are not trying to slough you off, they just don't know what to do. You still may not consider yourself to have an illness or health issue. You'll remain in denial. You're left to believe that you should be able to handle these feelings. Right?

Welcome to your nightmare: you have been stigmatized.

And it can get worse. Eventually, you'll start to feel like there is no hope. Even though you may have hinted at your issues, your friends and family, not being able to comprehend, may slowly drift away. They may consider you to be a downer, or a complainer. Soon, they won't have time to listen to you reiterating your woes. Meanwhile, your mind has become consumed with negativity. You may start to feel that perhaps you are not expressing yourself adequately. You may start to believe that you're sounding weak and whiny—you may even be told that you are. So you bury it deeper inside of you and trudge on as always, hoping that it will just go away.

Let me tell you, it will never just go away.

You are in pain. Deep emotional pain. It starts to consume you. You try to rationalize it, but you cannot. You may feel a myriad of emotions, one at a time or all at once. You may feel stupid. You may feel angry. You may feel sad. You may feel weak. You may feel unworthy. You may even think that you're getting kicked in the ass by karma if your slate isn't clean.

And then the fallout starts to really kick you in the ass. You don't want to go out with your partner or friends, or you may be able to put on a happy mask and go out anyway, but it's a mask, which by definition means it is meant to cover up the reality.

You may self-medicate with booze or drugs. Or self-harm. Or harm others.

And then there's the workplace. You're dragging your ass. Your mind is constantly wandering—you're having difficulties concentrating on the most basic of tasks. Your coworkers and/or supervisors are starting to complain. You have likely tried to hide your issues. And sometimes, even though you've tried to explain your situation, you see they either don't understand or they don't care.

After all, it's not their job to make you feel safe and/or happy.

You're being paid to carry out certain tasks, not to solve your personal problems.

If you're fortunate enough to have access to professional help, and you are brave enough to seek it, you may start to see light at the end of the tunnel. Eventually you'll probably be prescribed some antidepressant medication by a doctor, and hopefully you'll finally start to feel better.

Not everyone with anxiety and/or depression may go through everything that I have just described. Some people are able to just shrug it off. Some can plaster on a false smile and suffer silently, hiding it until they just accept it as a part of them. Some people can face their fears and walk out on the other side feeling whole again.

But I have yet to meet anyone like that.

One Step Closer to the Edge
Late June 1999

As my mental instabilities escalated—and believe me they escalated exponentially before I was able to even think about taking my life back—I started to wonder if I was making it all up to get out of working for a living. I was so afraid of being called a liar or being outed as a faker that I started trying to justify my thoughts more and more.

This was the key to the delusional and paranoid components of my illness: the saner I tried to be, the less sane I became. I failed to see that the more rational I convinced myself to be, the less rational I was being.

I was afraid to move from the bedroom. I watched a little nineteen-inch TV that sat upon a dresser in front of our bed. Other than that, all I did was smoke cigarettes all day. Frequently—sometimes more than once in an hour—I would call Kat at work, crying my eyes out for no apparent reason. She came home to be with me every time.

That past January, Kat had finished her master's degree in education while continuing to work at the Electron-X depot. She had excelled in school just as I had. She maintained an A average. This, plus her time away from the crap at W.V.H. Steel, enabled her to regain her confidence—she started applying for jobs in her field again.

A few months after she finished her master's she began a new job as a teacher for a private college. She had finally found something that made her happy and that paid her what she was worth. We had been married just shy of three years.

Logically, I understood that it was unacceptable for me to call her every half hour like when she was at Electron-X—she had warned me that it could cost her the job. But for the first several weeks into her new job I couldn't control myself. I was used to having her come home to comfort me. She was forced to insist that I refrain from calling her at work.

The last thing I wanted was to be the reason she was terminated from her dream job.

I can't explain how the depression weighed on me. My gut felt like I had swallowed a giant mass of I don't know what. I wanted to rip it out from my stomach. My skin felt as if it were just hanging from my body from all the extra weight that I had gained. I even had stretch marks on my stomach and arms. I was suffering from real deep-seated depression, not the kind that could be fixed with a little bit of sympathy or empathy. Even the antidepressants that Dr. Edwin had prescribed for me weren't helping.

Clickety-Clack Zip-Ding
Early July 1999

I have always been a writer and a creator.

The purpose of life is to create; this creation is the life experience.

I can remember being five years old, barely old enough to put pencil to paper, and writing little stories to pass time and amuse myself. Throughout my childhood and adolescence I received prizes and rewards for best story in the class, or whatever. When I was eight or nine I was into the band Kiss, so I started writing stories about the makeup-laden quartet coming to my house. We would hang out and go on wild adventures. I can still remember some of those stories as if I had written them yesterday.

I have always been a history buff. In middle school I was particularly fascinated, if not obsessed, by the Vietnam War. I couldn't watch enough movies such as *Apocalypse Now*, *The Deer Hunter*, and *Uncommon Valor*. My favorite was *First Blood*.

The "leave no man behind" paradigm resonated with me. Every actor was going back to Vietnam to save the POWs. It was everywhere. It was the early '80s and the Vietnam War veterans were finally getting a little respect and recognition for their sacrifices.

As a young empath I couldn't help but sympathize with the prisoners of war. I couldn't imagine how it must have felt to be trapped and spending years hoping for release from captivity. I wrote a series of stories about a young draftee who suffered through the war, zooming in on how he dealt with his personal war—the physical and psychological.

In high school I wrote stories about how I would get revenge on those who bullied me.

It was an extensive list.

Heavy metal was in its formative years. I recall being barely fourteen years old and seeing the band Venom's video for their song "Bloodlust" on the TV—this was when music videos were still in their infancy. I was instantly hooked. I was introduced to bands such as Metallica and Slayer years before they became familiar to the masses. This new type of music was dark and edgy, unlike anything before.

My mother became convinced that I became a different person after listening to this music. She swore that I withdrew into myself and was a gloomier and darker person. I wasn't the sweet-natured little boy she had raised. Naturally, I disagreed. I believed that I was growing into the person I was meant to be. The more vehement she became, the more I opposed and argued with her, thus proving her point. She ended up banning me from listening to this music. Of course, I still bought the records and listened to them; I was just careful to ensure that she was not around when I did.

In addition to buying records, when I was fourteen I saved up my money from my paper route and bought my first typewriter.

When I was about fifteen, I wrote a short story about a group of kids in a high school. The gist of this story was that this fat kid farted, and it was so vile that the school had to be evacuated and the armed forces were brought in to quarantine the area.

Everyone who read it laughed themselves to tears, even Mom, who didn't care for that kind of toilet humor. She still applauds the stories I wrote as being like "that John Belushi guy" from one of the greatest comedic movies ever: *Animal House*.

When I was sixteen, I wrote a very graphic story about killing my family and all who mocked me as they burned all my precious vinyl in the backyard. To be honest, I'm surprised that my English teacher never voiced any concern about the violence in my stories. Instead he praised me for my prose.

In retrospect, I think that as far back as then I was starting to develop emotional/mental issues.

Mom insists it was then.

After Jennifer Albright and I split, I started writing some truly dark and violent, if not outright disturbing, short pieces.

From my mid-twenties on, my writing became a way to vent my personal issues, such as those about work and my personal struggles. Although a great deal of it was fictional, it was very cathartic. I liked delving deep into my mind and seeing what I was capable of creating and combining it with experiences that I had endured.

Je Suis l'Artiste!
Mid-July 1999

I considered—and in fact somewhat arrogantly declared—myself to be an *artiste*.

To me, math, science, and engineering were not just about theories and calculations, they were about taking a notion or observation and molding it into something more meaningful. Mathematics was a language unto itself—the stories that numbers could tell! I wanted everyone to see the vibrant, colorful thoughts that were dancing about in my mind.

I managed to convince myself that I could mathematically rationalize the meaning of life, the universe, and Father. It could be said that I deluded myself into believing in these rationalizations, but even when lucid my logic stayed true, although not conclusive.

Kat was seemingly captivated by my sense of logic. Equally, I was enthralled by her aptitude and ability to follow my mathematical/scientific reasoning, especially because she had no technical training or background.

I don't know if she knew or believed it, but she was equally as intelligent as I was; she just applied herself in different ways. I know I didn't tell her often enough.

My thoughts and hypotheses were established from within my own mind. Before leaving the Church, I had already began exploring alternative philosophies just by spending time with my eyes closed. As I matured into an adult, my thoughts became more fluid. They snaked their way through the boundaries of science and humanity. I began to believe my own thoughts and then built up some highly subjective theories that ended with me being a higher power intended for great things. When delusional, I thought that I was perhaps an angel, a prophet, or a master for Father. I mentally mapped out and positioned all the people in my life—everyone I knew had a role, a specific place that fit into the future, if not the final days.

When all was said and done, it was my duty to lead the sheep away from their shepherds and toward enlightenment.

Chapter 25

He Shall Kill

Visiting Hours
Late July 1999

I had been consumed with it for months. At some point within almost every hour of every day since I had left work I was devoured by thoughts about Royce; specifically, how to end his life. I had studied and stalked him. I knew his routine, probably better than he did.

I had done my due diligence over the previous few months.

While on sick leave, Royce had taken on a volunteer job at a private college, teaching engineering grad students how to perform high-end mathematical calculations. He worked from nine a.m. to five p.m. every Monday, Tuesday, and Friday.

I had quickly learned his work hours and the details of such things as his commute time to and from work—I had inconspicuously followed him several times. On a few occasions, I had slept in my car parked down the street to watch over his daily comings and goings. The summer air was a little chilly at times, so I was sure to bring my heavy hoodie and I got the spare blankets out from the trunk of my car when necessary.

I knew where he lived. I had been there several times when we had first been friends.

I knew what time he went to bed and at what time he rose. I had staked out his moves.

I knew his car. He had been driving the same rusty old Ford sedan for as long as I'd known him.

I knew what days he stopped to fill up on gas: Mondays and Thursdays.

On several occasions I let myself into his home while he was away at work. That enabled me to take stock of his habits. I could see which utensils he had used to prepare his meals. He was very predictable.

I knew at what time he ate.

There was one little issue I had to work through: I had no idea how exactly he spent his nights and weekends. Further investigation was warranted.

If Royce was to die, I would still need to get even deeper inside his head, deeper than I had ever been. I needed to know every detail of his life, everything from what he was reading to what time he took a shit.

And so that is what I did for the next several weeks:

Monday June 7, 1999
- Arrived at work at 9:03 a.m.
- Had a sandwich with a Coke for lunch at 12:22 p.m.
- Left work at 4:58 p.m.
- Took 45 minutes to arrive home.
- Turned off all lights at 11:01 p.m.

Tuesday June 8, 1999
- Arrived at work at 8:46 a.m.
- Had a sandwich with a Coke for lunch at 12:17 p.m.
- Left work at 5:11 p.m.
- Took 47 minutes to arrive home.
- Turned off all lights at 11:09 p.m.

On Wednesdays and Thursdays, he did not volunteer. He did his grocery shopping and ran errands. Sometimes he went to the university library and would spend hours in the stacks. He would treat himself to lunch at the local deli. There was no routine that he followed on these days when he was not volunteering. I knew that those would not be good days to "visit" him.

The Friday of that first week was just the same as the Monday and Tuesday.

After a few weeks of carefully studying his routines, I had satisfactorily established that he was a creature of habit, so I slept in my car on the Monday night. After he left for work and stopped to get gas, I approached his home. I remained as vigilant as possible—several of his neighbors were elderly and had known me from earlier years, and because of my unique appearance I wasn't hard to miss. I studied their habits as well.

I peeked into the living room window. He still had that small TV and books stacked throughout. I cautiously gathered his key from his mailbox and entered the apartment. I perused his book collection—there was nothing of interest to me. Same with his music collection, which mostly contained old LPs from the '60s and '70s. Nothing in his apartment had changed since the last time I had been in it a couple of years ago.

I went into his bedroom and opened the closet doors. It was filled with cardigan sweaters and $12.99 slacks from Walmart. He had a small tie rack. There were only three ties: one black clip-on and two pre-tied blue and gray striped. At the end of the closet was an ironing board and a steam-pressing iron. There were five white collared long-sleeved dress shirts which had recently been pressed. And finally, there was a little space where he kept his shoes. There were three pairs, all made of fine Tuscan leather.

I stepped into the closet. The doors were made of an imitation oak pressboard, with slats facing downward. I pulled the hinged doors closed and crouched down. I could see the bottom of his bed and night table. His dresser couldn't be seen from this angle. I stood up again, contemplating—could I stay in hiding for an entire evening? Could I sneak out in the middle of the night and go unheard?

I decided that I could.

As I sat inside his closet, I imagined myself brooding over him as he slept, just looking at his closed eyes and his balding scalp. I could see the outline of his pajamaed body under his sheets. I could see myself caressing his soggy sullen face with a small revolver. Would he awaken to the touch of the cold steel? And if he did, could I pull the trigger? I knew that if our roles were reversed, he could. He had told me so. When would I pull the trigger? I wanted him to suffer. But no, a gun would be too noisy—and too easy.

I could slice him up. Just one quick swipe of a blade across his throat. But that too would be messy. There would be blood all over the room. Blood all over me. It would be hard to hide any evidence. And what of his suffering? Again, his screams for mercy would carry through the walls into his neighbors' ears.

I could strangle him with one of his ties. Or with my bare hands. I could see myself bringing him to the edge of death with his throat in my hands and then repeatedly bringing him back. But even that could get noisy.

I could poison him. But should I do it with a fast-acting poison, or should I draw things out with a poison that had to accumulate within his system? The problem with this option was that I wouldn't get to see him suffer. And that was unacceptable.

I could grind up some glass and mix it in with his peanut butter or jelly. He wouldn't even know what was happening, his organs would simply be shredded by teeny glass molecules and he would bleed from the inside out.

I was acutely aware of the insanity that others would see in my thoughts. They would not be able to comprehend my logic. They would blame my actions on my illness, because that was the simplest way they could explain them away. But it was so clear to me what had to be done. One day they would understand and be thankful. Evil beings like Royce had to be stopped. It was all for the betterment of mankind.

One of the greatest ordeals that I faced over the past few weeks was explaining my late nights to Kat. I couldn't lie to her; that would be contrary to my beliefs. However, I realized that she wouldn't understand my thought process with any more clarity than anyone else.

After a great deal of consideration, I finally came up with a plan.

I decided that I would stick a ball of his socks in his mouth and duct-tape them in place. That would mute any noise he made. And then I would torture him by cutting him in non-lethal locations. Finally, when I could see his will to live escaping, I would castrate him, just as he had psychologically done to me. Then I would slowly slice his throat. But to minimize the mess, I would need a change of clothes. I would use a towel to hold the knife as it leisurely slipped across his neck. This would reduce the cast-off and spurting blood.

There! I had a plan. I used the rest of the week to work out the details and I readied myself to put my plan into action the following week.

On Monday the twenty-first of June I parked farther up the block than usual and wore a light hoodie to avoid being recognized. I waited until 11:35 p.m. Most of the neighborhood lights were off. This sleepy little town was shutting down for the night. No more late-night dogwalkers. No more late-night strollers or joggers.

Around one a.m. I got out of my car, put on a Toronto Blue Jays cap, and tightened my hoodie around my face. I looked left and right—one last check for witnesses. I crossed the street and walked up to Royce's home. The inside lights were out. I had practiced my approach from the outside numerous times over the past weeks. I knew that there were no cameras or motion-sensing lights. I had leather gloves on. I peeked through his bedroom window.

As predicted, he was asleep.

I went around to the mailbox, where I knew he kept the key to his front entrance.

I quietly let myself in.

I helped myself to a beer from his fridge.

The moon was full, making it easy for me to see where I was moving and when I needed to maneuver. I reached his bedroom door and looked in at the sleeping old man. For a moment I thought he looked peaceful sleeping on his side. I slowly approached him and withdrew the knife I had brought from home.

I hovered the knife over his cheek. I stood there for a millennium, just thinking of how sweet my revenge, my justice, was going to be. He barely stirred.

But that was not the night he was intended to die.

I eventually let myself out when his alarm clock read 3:00 a.m. I returned to my car and drove home.

My wife was asleep on the couch in the basement when I got in. I could hear her gently snoring. The TV was still on. I went down and pulled a blanket over her and gave her a kiss on the forehead. She sleepily asked what I was doing. As I had been doing over the past few weeks, I made up some stupid excuse, went upstairs, undressed and crawled into bed.

The next morning, Kat was visibly concerned about my nighttime absences over those past few weeks. I knew I was doing Father's work, so I bluntly told her what I had been doing. I shall never forget the look of horror on her face.

Never.

"You have to tell Dr. Edwin!" She stood up, knocking her coffee over. "I can't take this. Please, for me, tell Dr. Edwin," she pleaded.

I told her that Dr. Edwin would have me locked up if she knew that my homicidal ideation had become an active homicidal plan. She said she had to tell my mom. This was some serious shit. I tried to reason with her, to convince her that it was my duty to rid the world of Royce. It was my calling. Father himself had whispered it in my ear.

She would have none of it, no matter how I tried to justify it.

I typically took Kat—and now Mom—with me when we went to see Dr. Edwin. She did this at my request, because I could see myself crumbling. And as much as I disliked it, Kat kept me honest.

I convinced her to let me leave out the stalking and invading when discussing it with Mom, and when we next met with Dr. Edwin. I had committed actual crimes and I would at the very least be hospitalized for an unknown period of time, or worse, I could be put into jail. I also knew that if the doctor became aware that I was a credible threat to a person, she was ethically required to notify the police and my intended target. That would put Royce in the winner's circle once again. I couldn't have that.

I had no idea what was going through Kat's head. She was probably scared shitless. I swore that I would no longer engage in any criminal activities. I guess I was pretty convincing, because I somehow managed to get her to finally agree to my stipulations.

She insisted that I tell the doctor that I'd been having homicidal ideations, but we didn't specify that my murderous thoughts were about Royce. I assured Kat there would be no repercussions for her or me, because I had gotten away with my crimes.

As expected, Dr. Edwin instantly told me to check myself into the hospital. She said if I wouldn't go voluntarily she would have to send for the police. And she was quick to add that once the police were involved I would be entered into the system, which she warned was something I did not want.

My parents were deeply involved with helping Kat deal with me. Mom had been with us at Dr. Edwin's. I remember returning home from Dr. Edwin's that day. Kat and Mom knew what had to be done—Dr. Edwin had insisted that I be hospitalized because of my homicidal ideation. After leaving the doctor's office I tried to bargain my way out of going to the hospital. I promised never to act on my thoughts. I pleaded. But Mom and Kat weren't going to let me off the hook. They both insisted that they would call the police if I wouldn't go voluntarily.

The one falsehood that they believed was that I would remain in the hospital until my medications could be fine-tuned. They didn't understand that the sole purpose of being admitted to the hospital was that I was to be incarcerated in the psych ward for a seventy-two-hour observation, or until the staff psychiatrist deemed me as a non-threat to myself or anyone else.

I was afraid of Dr. Edwin, because I knew she meant what she said, and so I agreed to go for observation. I explained to the doctor that I'd been having thoughts of murdering the source of my illness, my former supervisor. Dr. Edwin was alarmed, but we had discussed Royce's ill-treatment of me on several occasions, including my homicidal thoughts toward him. I reassured her that I was not presently a danger to myself or anyone else.

Kat never did tell Mom or Dr. Edwin that I had stalked and entered Royce's dwelling.

Reluctantly, I packed my knapsack. I made sure to remember my Motörhead CD collection for my stay. I procrastinated as much as possible. Finally, after I had dallied as long as I could, I gave in.

Royce never learned of my nocturnal visit.

I wish I had killed Royce when I'd had the chance.

One Flew Over the Cuckoo's Nest
June 22–June 25, 1999

I didn't know what to expect once at the hospital. I first thought of the film *One Flew Over the Cuckoo's Nest* with Randle McMurphy, the pretend insane man, and his ongoing struggle with the shrewd oppressor, Nurse Ratched. I was deathly afraid of being indefinitely committed, and/or being permanently stigmatized and thus making my thoughts and opinions questionable if not outright ignored from then on, as had happened in the movie.

I then realized that what I had done to Royce was not only alarming, but irrational.

I remembered when I had first arrived at the hospital. Usually there would be a two- to eight-hour wait to see a physician, but this time they had me in a psych ward almost immediately. The nurse began drilling me with questions regarding my frame of mind. I remember thinking that I was smarter than her and that I could hoodwink my way out of this. I agreed that yes, I'd had a psychotic break, but I was fine now.

Long story short, it turns out that I was not so smart after all. She asked me if I wanted to voluntarily admit myself, or if I was going to have to be forced.

I was pissed off. Why was no one listening to me? I was fine. I wasn't a threat to Royce—that was just me joking around. It was all a joke! As far as anyone but Kat knew, I had never been anywhere near him.

They interviewed Kat. She was honest and told my parents and the hospital staff that I had stayed out overnight a few times. But she stayed true to me and her word: she didn't tell anyone about my intrusion into Royce's home.

"Well?" prompted the nurse.

I agreed to be admitted.

I had a private room. It was painted dull beige. The door had no locks on it, and the rule was that the door must always remain open at least a crack.

I reached into my knapsack and pulled out my CD Walkman and headphones and started listening to Motörhead—the almighty Lemmy Kilmister was singing over some amazing guitar, bass, and drum work. I laid back on my tiny bed and closed my eyes. Maybe I could get some rest while I was there.

Father had once told me that a handful of masters, prophets, and leaders were always present, and throughout history they had always been. Two modern examples were Mahatma Gandhi and Nelson Mandela. They had suffered at the hands of their fellow man but did so with grace and dignity. They did not fear the truth, nor did they fear speaking it.

Like many, I also believed that George Carlin was something of a modern-day prophet—he spoke the truth but he got the point across by guising it as humor. He did it with such eloquence that he sounded like an average guy making some average observations. However, if you really listened to his message there was nothing funny about it.

I was a prophet. Perhaps a leader. A shepherd to guide the sheep. But I couldn't let the doctors or nurses know—I would be locked up for much longer than a seventy-two-hour stint in the psych ward. I had already been diagnosed with schizophrenia; this meant that whatever I said or did could be attributed to my illness. And honestly, as much as I felt this way I couldn't be certain that I wasn't deluding myself. I knew that the media and sheep would more readily accept the idea that I was delusional, rather than seeing the reasoning and message that I was trying to spread.

My first day in the psych ward went okay. Upon arrival, the staff nurses made me give them my Zippo lighter. I handed it over, not even having to ask why—it was taken for fear that I would try to burn the place down. Although I had no such intentions, I could see their reasoning. On the bright side, at the time that I was incarcerated it was still legal to have smoking areas in the hospitals.

On the first night I tried to be a shadow. I had to use the bathroom, which was down the hall to the left, about halfway to the smoke room. I slinked my way down the hallway. There was a community TV room just outside of my door. Several of the other inmates were settled around the TV.

I heard giggling and laughing.

"I guess he's scared of us," one young lady cackled.

Shit! Now I had to acknowledge them. I turned shyly and said hello as I rushed down to the washroom. The anxiety-inducing stress of interacting with even such a small group of strange people led me to the smoke room. After a couple of smokes I could relax and return to my bedroom. And so that is what I did.

The next two and a half days I spent smoking, playing billiards, swimming, and playing euchre with the staff and other inmates. The nurses and most of the patients were very open and even blunt when asking about me as a person, my thoughts, or about my illness.

As I got to know them, I realized that most of the people in the psych ward were normal, like me. They all had a story to tell—they had a host of anxiety, depression, and suicidal, homicidal, and psychotic thoughts. I didn't tell anyone anything more than that I'd had a psychotic break. They didn't share much more than the basics either.

There was one kid in particular. He scared the shit out of me, literally. I was in the bathroom stall when I heard a screaming and wailing coming from a few stalls down. I finished my business and walked by the stall this poor kid was in. He couldn't have been more than sixteen or seventeen years old. He had his pants and underwear off and his T-shirt pulled up to his midsection. He was covered in his own shit, rocking back and forth screeching at the top of his lungs. I asked him if he was okay, but I may as well have not been there. To this day I get spooked when I think of that kid—I couldn't imagine being that delusional and out of touch with reality.

On my third night I was anticipating the visit from the staff psychiatrist the next morning. I knew that I had cooled down quite a bit—I still wanted Royce dead but I wasn't going to do it. I couldn't rationalize taking his life; as much damage as he had done, he hadn't done enough to deserve being obliterated from existence.

The only way that I could justify taking his life was if he attempted to take mine.

I was perplexed by how all these strangers with whom I was temporarily cohabitating were so alike and yet so different in so many ways. None of them were potential murderers, not that I knew of. They all seemed like normal people, as I assumed I seemed to them.

I was so excited that I was being released the next day that I couldn't sleep. I just assumed I was being discharged because the seventy-two hours was up. When the nurse came around for bed check I told her I couldn't sleep. She asked why and I told her. She brought me a lorazepam and I was good for the night.

I saw the psychiatrist at nine-thirty a.m. He asked me the standard questions, which I answered correctly. Note that I say "correctly" instead of "truthfully."

He deemed me safe and no longer a risk to myself and others and released me. There was no need for any further follow-up, just to continue meeting with Dr. Edwin each week.

I called Kat and my parents to come pick me up.

My dad still came around every day, but as the summer progressed I didn't seem to be stabilizing. I was still feeling bouts of severe anxiety and paranoia, and couldn't shake the depression.

Tattoo Me

One of the nurses was particularly interested in my tattoos. Since I had taken leave from work, I'd had some extensive work done. She asked what they meant. I know that when you get tattooed like me you are putting yourself out there for comments, praise, and, back then, looks of disapproval, especially when you have as many as I do. I loved discussing the meaning of my tats to interested parties; at the same time, I never got used to the attention.

My tattoos all have some spiritual or personal meaning to me. My largest is a back piece that I had completed when I was about twenty-eight years old.

The first key meaning behind this collage was "forgiveness" and "the master."

The phrase "Forgive Them for They Know Not What They've Done" was a spin on the Biblical quote of Jesus in Luke 23:34: "Father, forgive them for they know not what they are doing." This phrase was meant to address the ignorance of the masses who cried out for Jesus's crucifixion, in particular the soldiers who gambled for Jesus's clothes. My spin was to forgive those like Sid Stanford and Royce Pincer who were incapable of knowing or disinterested in what impact their actions had on me.

The crucifix, depicting Christ hanging on the cross, is in the dead center of my back. The symbolism represents the master, Jesus Christ, who lived and died peacefully with no fear, only with Father's love. He was not afraid to die.

The second key representation of the tattoo is the four elements of nature. The element fire is represented by a fiery dragon. The element air is represented by an angel kneeling on a cloud. The element water is represented by the air angel pouring water into a vase held by a second angel. And the element earth is represented by two skulls.

It Takes One to Know One
Thursday, August 5, 1999

It was Rusty's fifth birthday.

In one month he was going to begin a long journey that would be filled with learning—he was starting Kindergarten. During our visits over the past years I had watched my son blossom. By the time he was four years old he could read quite adeptly. Instead of me reading to him, he would ask if I would bring him a book that he could read to me.

Like I had when I was young, he enjoyed reading superhero comic books.

He also had a pretty decent handle on his basic math skills; again, surprising for his age. Rusty used to enjoy showing me how well he could add and subtract. He liked it when I would bring a small bag of coins so that he could count my money, which became his upon being counted. And he even knew his times tables up to four times four.

When I would brag to my family about how bright my son was, Mom would tell me that I had hit these milestones at an early age as well. This excited me—I had so much that I wanted to share with him. I couldn't wait until he was old enough to talk politics, religion, and philosophies.

I couldn't wait until he reached the point at which he exceeded me and my abilities.

I also wanted him to learn how to avoid the mistakes I had made. I wanted to raise him to be a strong and sensitive man. But I needed to teach him how to maintain his confidence without being arrogant. I needed to teach him to be himself, not who someone else thought he should be. Not even me.

My greatest fear was that my schizophrenia was a hereditary condition.

Unfortunately, at this time our funds had dwindled. I had spent a significant amount of our savings and income on eBay. Additionally, my disability pension had been reduced from full pay to a fraction of my full pay after six months had passed.

Kat was making decent money but we had some unexpected expenses. We needed a new roof on the house, and we needed a new furnace and central air conditioning system. We couldn't afford Truman's counsel any longer.

There was also that everlasting label that Kat and I had pinned on our chests: we were "mentally ill." We were diligently focusing on healing ourselves and turning our lives around into something positive, but we just weren't there yet.

We had our furnace replaced by a friend of a friend, a fireman who installed furnaces etcetera as a second job. He outright refused to do the job unless my parents paid—he wouldn't take a check from Kat and me for fear that it would bounce.

I was both embarrassed and offended.

I was a total emotional mess. The only thing keeping Kat from being overwhelmed by her issues was that she was excelling in her teaching job. She was focusing on her career. For once she was putting herself first—so far in our relationship I had unintentionally taken center stage.

And now, even as much as I hated to admit it, I realized that I would not be a fit parent.

Once again I was forced to turn to my parents for assistance.

Because of my mental health issues, the O'Reillys' case was strengthened, so this time when we approached Truman Kush we had to change our strategy.

The O'Reillys had what seemed to be an unending source of wealth. My parents had enough to hold their own.

The O'Reillys had held custody of Rusty for most of his life. My parents had never even ruffled the thick thatch of red hair on the top of his head.

The O'Reillys were good people.

My parents were good people.

The O'Reillys believed that the DNA evidence was wrong. The DNA evidence proved that my parents and I were Rusty's blood relatives. Truman's angle for the lawsuit was still that my parents were seeking full custody.

Dr. Dennis O'Liam
Late August 1999

Dr. Edwin had done as much as she could, but I was still suffering. That was not to say that I hadn't improved. The voices had been somewhat quelled. But the delusional thinking and paranoia were still active. I was a far cry from being considered well.

She told us that there was one last option: a medication called clozapine. She explained that it could only be prescribed by special psychiatrists/clinics because it required rigorous attention and medical monitoring that went along with its use, and she was not authorized to prescribe it.

She referred me to a clinic in my parents' hometown, Pittsburgh.

I was immediately set up with an appointment to meet with Dr. Dennis O'Liam the following week.

Although we didn't yet know it, we were beginning a new chapter in our lives.

Having my parents back in our lives turned out to be a true blessing. We had been able to put our differences aside, permanently. I recall Mom one day telling us that she was talking with an acquaintance and she had mentioned our conflict. Her friend turned to her and asked, "Are you a Christian family?" to which she responded yes. He knowingly nodded and said that was the reason we had been able to patch up our differences—we understood love.

The day before I was scheduled to meet Dr. O'Liam, I was lying in bed with Kat. I was wide awake while she was deep asleep. I was mumbling about God knows what when I found it particularly important that she be awake and listening. I shook her. She yawned and exhaled deeply.

She didn't get it—I wanted her *immediate* attention.

I shook her again, this time with a little more force.

"What . . .?" she yawned. Her eyes opened for a moment. Her beautiful blue eyes.

"Listen to me!" I ordered.

At some point I had raised my fist. Her eyes fluttered open. When she saw my fist her eyes widened. "I'm awake," she said soberly.

I don't even remember what it was that was so important to say to her, but it was too late to take it back. She sat up. I looked at my fist and lowered it.

I could see the terror in her eyes. I instantaneously knew that I'd screwed up big time.

"Please don't tell my parents!" I begged.

"I have to," she stressed.

I was not a violent man by nature—quite the opposite, in fact. I couldn't believe that I had just threatened my wife, my soulmate. I wanted to take it back. I tried to downplay it. I tried to make out that

I was just kidding around. But I knew what had happened and that she was afraid of me.

I had just changed my relationship with my wife forever.

I was still in bed smoking my umpteenth cigarette of the day when Mom and Dad arrived. I begged Kat one more time. I overheard her tell them. Mom called Dr. Edwin, who of course insisted I be hospitalized.

I reluctantly got dressed and we went to the hospital, which I had been a guest at not so long ago. We waited about thirty minutes. Finally, Mom suggested we go to the hospital in Pittsburgh, which was where Dr. O'Liam's office was located.

When we arrived at the hospital I was feeling mentally and emotionally fine—a little ticked off that I had to be there, but fine. I was admitted into the psych ward. They took my keys and lighter for my and their protection, and left me, Mom, and Kat alone in a tiny green room with a single white bed. Dad was somewhere parking the car.

Finally, a doctor came in. I managed to convince him that I'd had a minor psychotic break but that I was no longer a danger to Kat or anyone, myself included. He was hesitant, but Mom backed me up and told him that I was going to see a new psychiatrist the next day.

I was released from the hospital after about two hours.

Kat was clearly alarmed and afraid.

I never raised a hand to anyone after that day.

The next day we went to see Dr. O'Liam, or so we thought. What it was in fact was an interview with two of his psychiatric nurses. My wife and mother had nothing but praise for me. When prompted, both even went so far as to refer to me as a genius, which I have often emphasized that I typically disliked, but it felt good this time. I sat silent. The nurses said that my illness tended to be common in highly intelligent people, especially logical people, because we can make comprehensive and sound connections that most people cannot.

I was sitting in a shrink's office being praised and flattered, all the while discussing my mental instability. It felt somewhat ironic to me.

As for my near-violent outburst, the nurses strongly recommended that Kat sleep in one of our spare bedrooms with the door locked. I assured everyone that I would never be remotely violent again, and that I wanted Kat beside me at night. I was told that I was too unstable for that.

A week later I met Dr. Dennis O'Liam for the first time. He appeared to be in his late fifties or early sixties. He was tall and thin with a bald crown, except for the hair around his ears, which was wild and curly. And he was one of the most non-clinical, friendly people I had encountered since I had been seeing so many doctors and counselors. He asked me questions about my hobbies, and other non-clinical activities. He seemed genuinely interested in me as a person, not just as another schizophrenic patient.

And when we did get clinical his demeanor did not change. He was so used to dealing with people with varying degrees of this illness that he was able to be completely sympathetic to both me and my family.

We discussed treatment options. The one with the most promise was the medication Dr. Edwin had mentioned: clozapine. It had been available in the psychiatric field for over twenty-five years but was not prescribed until at least two other antipsychotics had been tried. I was a perfect candidate to try it.

There was one addendum. I had to go for blood tests every week, because this medicine could result in a low white blood cell count, which could inhibit my immune system's effectiveness.

There were some potentially severe side effects with this new medicine, but Dr. O'Liam was confident that there would be no significant repercussions or interactions with my other meds.

I was ready to give it a try. I wanted to be as mentally healthy as I could be. I was willing to deal with any side effects if it meant that I could feel the peace of a silent and sound mind.

I started on the clozapine immediately, in addition to all of the other meds that Dr.'s Edwin and Gantt had me on. Dr. O'Liam tweaked my depression and anxiety meds.

Within two or three weeks the noise in my brain finally started to quiet down.

As I was recovering, I heard a tiny little voice coming to the forefront of my thoughts:

I want to create again.

Part VII

Children of the Damned

Chapter 26

A Self-Righteous Hypocrite

Mike the Damned – I
Friday, September 3, 1999

My phone was ringing. I turned over and looked at the alarm clock. It was about four in the morning. A wave of panic swept over me. No one calls at this time in the morning unless something bad has happened. My mind conjured images of my family, bloodied and battered, their corpses lying twisted in metal from a car crash, or worse, lying broken on hospital gurneys waiting to be identified.

I just knew that it was the authorities or Ellyn on the other end of this call.

I grew panicky. I tried to prepare for the worst. The adrenaline was heightening the sensations throughout my entire body as never before.

I quickly picked up the phone. "Hello?"

It was Mike Jagger.

Mike and I hadn't been in much contact over the past year, mostly because the sicker I had grown, the farther I had retreated within myself. But we still spoke every now and then, enough for me to fill him in on my life and for him to share that he too was having his share of mental issues.

It had been at least a month since the last time we had spoken.

I wasn't afraid to tell Mike of my ailments and thoughts, but Mike was more sensitive about being stigmatized than I was—he'd had learning disabilities in school, and as long as he could remember he had been teased because of it, so he wasn't going to open himself up to further ridicule again.

I couldn't remember the last time he had been over to visit with us.

He was panting heavily, and grunting, "I . . . I . . . I . . ."

My feelings of panic and distress quickly abated.

"What the hell are you doing calling me now?" I asked angrily.

There was a pause on the other end of the phone. The panting gradually subsided.

Then it occurred to me that Mike was possibly in trouble. "Are you okay?"

I heard maniacal laughter on the other end of the phone.

Mike was more than okay. He was in a state of bliss.

Flashback – The Party
Saturday, March 8, 1997

Mike and Royce knew of each other, mostly from what I had told each of them about the other. I had told Mike a great deal about Royce's psychological manipulation and abuse. For as long as I had worked at W.V.H. Steel, Mike had been openly disgusted by the way I had been treated. From his perspective, I had done everything right. He believed that I should be rewarded for my hard work and dedication to my schooling and job. What Mike saw in me was a good and honorable man. Mine should be a story of success. I think that Mike was upset because I had what it took to live the dream and I was being robbed of it.

The two men had briefly met once at a party in March of 1997 that Kat and I had thrown to celebrate my academic achievements after my first sabbatical, shortly after Royce had hired me. To the best of my knowledge, Mike and Royce hadn't even spoken to each other except to exchange brief pleasantries when I introduced them early in the evening. Their meeting had lasted all of three seconds, long enough for them to shake hands and mumble hello. Otherwise, they probably wouldn't know each other if collided walking down the street.

Royce had remained sober that night, sipping on the same diet ginger ale the entire time he was there. He seemed content to leave his seat to add ice cubes to his glass, but I swear he never once freshened up his drink. I don't think he even got up to use the washroom. Short of the obligatory introductions, he didn't really talk with anyone that night, except when Kat or I sat and chatted with him for a bit.

Royce had arrived around eight o'clock and he left around nine-thirty.

To be honest, I was a little surprised that he had shown up at all. Royce was a quiet man, and although I barely knew him at this point, I'd never have guessed that he could be antisocial or that he suffered from social anxiety. I think he had hoped there would be more work or science-related conversations. He was not a philosophical man like I was, but he did enjoy the occasional God discussion. Essentially, I believed that he was bored.

I tried to talk him out of leaving, but he claimed he wasn't feeling so well—his stomach was acting up. I sensed that he was also feeling a little out of place being amongst a crowd of younger twenty-somethings like us. I had a good buzz going and I was determined not to let Royce's mood destroy it. I walked him to his car and wished him a good night.

While the party was still going on downstairs, Mike disappeared and spent the rest of the evening by himself, playing on the computer upstairs. At one point I had gone upstairs and shared a joint with him. I tried to convince him to come back downstairs to join the party. At the time I had no idea what he was looking at, and after our last experience I didn't want to know. After his last dance with the macabre, we never said a word to Mike about the dead bodies—the topic was taboo. To my relief, the next morning he showed me a stack of pornographic pictures that he had printed off. He had spent most of the night gulping down beers and looking at porn.

Eventually Mike had come back downstairs, after most of our friends had left or crashed in one of the spare rooms. I was still up drinking and watching old episodes of *The Twilight Zone*. Mike was almost incoherent—he was wasted out of his tree. He had gotten so loaded that he ended up throwing up all over my basement bathroom. Most of it missed the toilet. It was clear that he had tried to clean it up, but he could barely stand up let alone effectively use a paper towel.

I was just glad he made it to the bathroom.

The next day I awoke around noon.

Kat never really complained about my drinking, except that I usually became rather pensive when I started to get loaded. And it wasn't the conversation per se, it was the time of night that I started getting chatty that she didn't like—it was usually well past her bedtime of ten o'clock.

Because we rarely had more than one or two friends over at a time, she didn't mind helping with the cleanup after the party. But make no mistake, she always made sure that I did my fair share of the work, hungover or not. And if I'd been drinking alone with her she didn't touch my mess.

The morning after the party, I put on my robe and went downstairs. Kat was already up and tidying—she was vacuuming the carpet. Mike was sprawled out face down across the couch. There were small chunks of puke clinging to his rather bushy goatee. I shook him and he moaned. Eventually he woke up. He sat up and, holding his belly, asked me for a cigarette. Kat had already emptied the ashtrays. She turned off the vacuum and handed him one. She proceeded to sit on the chair adjacent to the couch that Mike was sitting in.

I sat down beside Mike on the couch and looked at him.

"Man, you were fucked up last night," I stated.

Mike was running his hand through his goatee when he felt a crusty piece of puke. He picked at it and then asked me what had happened later in the evening.

I told him not to worry, that he hadn't done anything terrifically stupid, but I told him that he had to clean up my bathroom. He seemed somewhat relieved. Knowing Mike as I did, I knew that he was always concerned about having embarrassed himself, although this rarely kept him from getting wasted out of his gourd.

"I wanted to smash that Royce guy in the face," Mike said. Unlike me, Mike was not a pacifist. He didn't go looking for fights, but he could be quick to be use his fists when he was feeling challenged.

"Is that why you spent so long upstairs by yourself?" I asked.

"No," Mike responded. "I just felt like hanging out by myself."

That was typical of Mike. He had always been a loner, at least as long as I had known him. Mike had a few other friends, and like me he preferred to keep his circle small.

Kat and I kept prodding Mike to tell us what Royce had done to illicit such an attitude.

"He just seemed kind of . . . *off*, as if he was masking an inner evil."

Kat and I exchanged a look. We thought Royce was anything but evil.

If only we'd known.

In many ways Mike and I were a little eccentric, if not outright twisted. Although the dead bodies disturbed me, I did share Mike's morbid curiosity. It just happened that I was high and resultingly paranoid that night that he chose to explore the ghastly dark side of humanity. Although he had a criminal background, we shared the same sense of integrity and moral fiber. We had realized this early on in our friendship.

I think that is what bound us together so tightly.

Mike the Damned – II
Friday, September 3, 1999

Now it was four a.m. and here I was engaging Mike on the phone.

Maybe I had told Mike more than I thought regarding how I had been treated by Royce. I had also subtly revealed to him that I had stalked and entered Royce's home. Only Mike and Kat knew of the latter. They were the only two people who I felt were trustworthy enough to tell, and I was even a little hesitant about telling them.

Mike was a man of honor. When he said he would never repeat whatever was shared with him, he meant it. His father had been an asshole throughout his entire life, but Mike wore and openly displayed his badge of honor. He was very proud that he was not a rat, as he had established back when his dad had used him as a lookout several years back. In a world full of self-serving liars, he was a man of integrity. His word was his honor. Just as I had kept Royce's will to kill secret, even after his workplace abuse, I knew that my secret was safe with Mike.

Kat was also loyal to a fault, although she still expressed some serious reservations about not having told Dr. Edwin and Mom about my active homicidal planning. I believed that enough time had passed that she was no longer concerned—it had been over three months and I hadn't done anything alarming. At the very least, I could rely on the spousal privilege law so that she could not be compelled to testify against me.

But whatever Mike was currently doing sounded excessive and inconceivable.

Sometime after I had been on medical leave from work, Mike and I were talking on the phone when he proceeded to tell me how it was necessary that Royce be brought up on charges and punished for his entire campaign of psychological attacks against me.

Mike knew that any laws that Royce—and the company, for that matter—had broken would only end with a monetary settlement at best. They would never suffer the traumatizing pain and humiliation as I had. Mike knew that money alone wouldn't fix my sick mind; he believed that the only way I could move on was by knowing that Royce had suffered as I had. Royce needed to feel my pain in a way that he would not forget.

It was time for the professor to be taught a lesson.

A violent lesson.

Mike knew that I hadn't and couldn't do anything much more than I had done about exacting my revenge on Royce. It wasn't within me; it was beyond my creative thoughts. I had even surprised myself that I had gone as far as I had in the first place.

I was so messed up that I wouldn't—couldn't—even seek legal counsel. Later, I vaguely recalled my parents saying something about suing the company. But I had adopted the mindset that I would be best off letting karma take care of Royce. I did not want to be involved in any further criminal activity, especially such as that which Mike was suggesting.

I already deeply regretted what I had done, which was guaranteed to be a misdemeanor if not a felony. And that was over three months ago.

When I first told Mike of my plans back in June he had practically begged me to join in on the fun, as he put it. I had brought Mike along on one of my first brief stakeouts when I was observing Royce's daily activities. Because of this, it didn't take much effort for Mike to locate Royce on his own. Some of the details were hazy, but he decided to head there on his own anyway.

Before heading out, Mike had called Royce at the school at about three in the afternoon. As soon as Royce answered the call, Mike quickly hung up—he just wanted to ensure that Royce was not going to be home when he initiated his plan.

Again, through me Mike knew that there was little to no security at Royce's dwelling. To seem inconspicuous, Mike had bought some flowers with a card and pretended to be delivering them to Royce's house. Mike was no master thief or lock-picker, but he revealed that he'd had easy access into Royce's apartment.

I may have also let it slip about the hidden key in the mailbox.

Mike had placed the flowers just outside of Royce's front door.

I suddenly found myself wishing that I had never told Mike about any of my issues with Royce. I really wished I had never shared any details or included him in my stalking and intruding activities.

While I was speaking with Mike on the phone, it occurred to me that perhaps I had purposefully shared all of these little details with him because deep inside I wanted him to make Royce feel an equivalent pain to what I had suffered at his hands.

I began to think that in my heart that was exactly what I had wished for.

But now I felt terrible for thinking that way.

I felt sick about the entire period in my life in which I was involved with W.V.H. Steel. I wished it gone. I particularly regretted the entire period of my life which involved Royce, from the mixer at school that I had first seen him in 1989 all the way to the that night that he had last called me when I was on medical leave back in the first week of January.

I immediately sought atonement from Father for suggesting to Mike that I wanted him to avenge me, and for allowing myself to arrogantly think that I was above the notion of anger/hate and wanting to take revenge.

Mike had hidden in Royce's front hall closet for about an hour and a half before Royce arrived home. He had buried himself behind a long leather trench coat and a small variety of seasonal jackets. There were some shoes in the back of the closet. He crouched there motionless, just waiting for the right moment to spring forth. When he wasn't cleaning up after murders or suicides, Mike was doing demolition, reconstruction, and home repairs, among a variety of other labor-intensive jobs. He had gotten used to sitting or squatting in the same position for several hours at a time. He claimed to have barely moved during the time he awaited Royce's arrival.

Finally, he heard Royce jostling the flowers and retrieving his key from the mailbox.

As he entered his house, Royce read aloud the attached card, "Don't look up!"

At that moment Mike burst from the closet, bringing his fists down on his intended's face. He knocked off Royce's glasses.

Royce crumpled like a fallen leaf in autumn.

"Mike, you've got to be kidding!" I shouted into the phone as I sat up in my bed.

Mike was using his flip phone to call me. He was quickly whispering all the gory details of his misadventure. The phone was pressed so tightly against my ear that it was beginning to hurt. My thoughts went into hyperdrive. Fear gripped me.

As waves of paranoia swept over me, I couldn't even hear Mike over my thoughts.

Royce is dead.

Mike has killed him.

This is all my fault. I led Mike to this.

The police will find out that I am the only link between these two men.

Royce had been right, I am stupid.

How much more stupid could I have been? Why had I shared my thoughts with Mike?

I was guilty.

Damn you, Royce! You don't deserve to get the last a-ha! You should be the one who is going to be imprisoned. You should be jailed for your mental cruelty. For your lying and cheating. Your physical wounds will heal, my emotional wounds may never.

I raised myself farther up on the mattress, peering out the bedroom window in search of flashing cop car lights. There was nothing so far.

"I'm still here," Mike cackled.

I pressed the phone even more tightly to my now numbed ear. I heard a muffled moaning in the background.

That meant that Royce was still alive. But how alive I didn't know.

Mike told me that he had taken wire coat hangers and tied Royce's arms and legs to a wooden kitchen chair with them. Just as I had planned, he gagged Royce with a ball of socks and secured them with a scarf that he had found in Royce's bedroom. Royce had barely resisted; he was completely surprised by Mike's flower ruse. He was like a weak and feeble old man, even though he was barely fifty years old. From the first blow that Mike delivered, Royce had started bawling.

Mike proceeded to tell Royce that he was an instrument of God, and he was doing God's bidding. God was very upset with Royce. He explained how Royce had betrayed and destroyed so many lives, and how that enraged God.

When God was angry, it was Mike's duty to carry out vengeance.

"Get the hell out of there, Mike!" I shouted into the phone. "Untie him and leave, for God's sake!"

My brain wouldn't shut up:

They're going to trace your call, Mike.

They're coming for you.

They're coming for me.

I am doomed. I have committed the highest of sins—I am a murderer by proxy.

We still have a chance to minimize the damage done—just let Royce live!

I heard Mike's flip phone drop to the floor, followed by his shoes tapering away across the floor as he moved back to where Royce was seated. With crystal clarity I then heard him slap Royce across the face. He demanded that Royce admit to his sins of "faggotry and bullying." Royce sat there bound and gagged, crying and grunting into the gag.

His tears seemed to anger Mike even more.

I overheard Royce cry out as Mike removed the gag from his mouth. He struck Royce in the face again. As much as it sickened me, I had to admit that Royce's cries of woe put a wicked little smile on my face, if only for a moment.

"What do you want? Why are you doing this to me?" Royce whimpered.

Royce was tied into place, screaming and pleading with Mike for mercy.

Almost as I had pled for mercy from *his* abuse.

As I was listening, I realized that Royce hadn't linked Mike to me—at least not yet.

I could still overhear Mike and Royce over the phone. It was as if I was inside of Mike's head.

I could see it as clear as day within my mind. Mike stuffed the gag back into Royce's mouth. He tied the gag in place and pinched Royce's nose closed. Royce began to wriggle about, his lungs screaming for air. I could hear the legs of the chair he was tied to rattling back and forth against the floor. Mike persisted. He was enjoying this.

This is what it was all about: existing on the brink between life and death.

After a few more long seconds Mike let go of Royce's nose. Snot blew out as he exhaled. Mike repeated this near-suffocation torture over and over, until he finally grew tired of it.

And then I heard a loud whack as Mike struck him again.

Royce grew quiet.

I was relieved at last.

Mike began to preach against his "faggotry and bullying" again. He told Royce over and over that he was doing God's work.

Mike returned to his phone and filled the blanks in my imagination and confirmed what I had been picturing was happening. I was still panicking. I sat there as Mike described the entire multitude of atrocities to me in graphic detail.

They are coming for you.

I screamed into the phone, "Mike, *please* get out of there. Untie Royce and get the hell out of there!"

Mike told me that Royce was bleeding and bruised from having been struck so many times. His eyes were practically swollen shut. Mike described in detail how he had gone so far as to lick the caking blood from Royce's swelling facial wounds. He relished the coppery-salty taste. He had struck him one last time, square in the nose. I had heard it crack from afar. More snot and blood had come gushing out.

Mike had expressed his disgust to Royce.

I could overhear Royce in the background over Mike's panting. He was having difficulty breathing—the snot and blood were clogging his only breathing path. I could see the conglomerate of snot and blood spewing in and out with every breath that he took.

I sensed that he was barely conscious.

Mike dropped the phone once again. I could only hear Royce crying in the background.

I could never have been prepared for what Mike told me he had done next.

Mike had dropped his pants and boxers.

He jerked off onto Royce's face. His cum shot across Royce's bloodied forehead and into his teary swollen eyes. It ran down his nose and onto his gag. Mike then spat on him and noted how the cum, blood, and snot all intermingled into one grotesque glob of sludge.

"This is what you deserve, faggot."

Mike had said his piece. He was satisfied he had impressed his point on Royce.

Royce was no longer crying; at long last he was unconscious. I heard Mike strike his limp body one last time. I heard the chair tip over with this final strike. Royce's head made a damning slam as it landed against the floor.

I heard Mike's footsteps shuffling around as he drew nearer to his phone. He picked it up and stuffed it into his pocket. His sounds were muffled, but I clearly heard a door slam.

I called out to Mike but the line was now disconnected. After a minute I called Mike's phone number, but the phone only beeped and went to voicemail.

I didn't even know if Royce was alive or dead.

I wasn't sure at what point Kat had awakened during my dialog with Mike.

She hadn't said a word during the entire call, which had only lasted fifteen minutes in total, although it seemed to have lasted much longer. She simply turned toward me under the cover and put her hand on my thigh as I had sat up in the bed, yelling at Mike.

After Mike had run off leaving Royce in an unknown condition, she insisted we call the police. We discussed the potential repercussions and implications that Mike's activities could have on me. After a lengthy discussion I hesitantly agreed, but I stipulated that it had to be an anonymous call.

She agreed.

I tried to prepare for the worst.

Royce was found barely alive inside his home. Things like this didn't happen in sleepy little towns like this. It was big news; the local station covering the story stated that it was a miracle he'd survived. The only details that they mentioned were that he had been discovered lying on his side, tied to a chair, with a bloodied scarf and ball of socks beside him. He was nude. His nose was still gushing a steady stream of blood and snot. He was a bloody swollen mess. There were dried fluids on his face.

One fun fact that I had been made aware of by Mike was that he had crudely removed Royce's genitals, just as I had once fancied.

The police had discovered Royce lying unconscious in his home thanks to an anonymous tip. He was sent to the hospital in critical condition.

Mike Jagger was arrested ten days later.

At arraignment, he pled guilty to assault and battery and attempted murder. He admitted to the crimes and was sentenced to spend ten years in a federal prison, with eligibility for parole after seven.

His knuckles were still swollen, bloody, and cracked from the beating he had laid upon Royce.

I Would Do Anything for Love
Tuesday, September 14, 1999

Mike never implicated me in the crime. He had destroyed his flip phone and thrown it away. The police never linked me to Royce's assault. I had no idea whether Royce would recall his momentary meeting with Mike a couple of years back. Without his glasses and with his eyes swollen shut, he was unlikely to have been able to identify his attacker anyway. Although Mike had never specifically informed Royce of why he was being tormented that night, he did accuse him of "faggotry and bullying."

I was guilty of crimes against Royce but not assault or attempted murder, although I knew that had it not been for me, Mike never would have brutalized Royce as he had.

But Mike had the free will to do as he chose whether I had somehow encouraged it or not.

A week and a half after the attack, Royce was still in the hospital. He was suffering from a fractured skull and a severe concussion. He had woken up a few times, but his wounds were so substantial that he wasn't able to give the police or hospital staff any usable information. The doctors had had to drill into his skull to relieve the pressure of the blood building up in his brain. They stated that they were "cautiously optimistic."

As wicked as it sounds, I found this relieving.

Mike was in prison and I was still deathly afraid of being linked to the crime.

I kept it all inside. It was constantly preying on my mind—I hadn't had a good sleep since Mike had called that night when he had beaten Royce. I even kept Kat's knowledge as minimal as possible. I didn't want her implicated in any way.

A few weeks after the attack, the assault on Royce had begun to settle into the back of my mind. I still felt horrible, but with Mike in prison and keeping quiet my fears were pacified. One afternoon I went to McDonald's with Dad for our daily outing. There was a local newspaper sitting on the table beside us.

Reality came crushing down on me. This must be some trick, but who would want to mess with my head after so many months had passed? I hadn't seen or spoken with Royce for numerous months.

Still, I was a lifetime away from coming to terms with the ordeal he had put me through.

I felt instant excitement followed quickly with relief, and then sheer terror.

Right there on the front page of the newspaper was a cameo of Royce in the bottom section with the statement in bold: "Victim of Brutal Assault Dies of Injuries."

I don't know why I was so surprised. I knew what had happened and when it had happened. Even with my constant worry that I would be brought into police custody at any time, even if just for questioning, I was still surprised. I supposed that I simply hadn't let the cold stark reality of Mike's confessed crime really sink in.

It was the cameo of Royce's pasty Augie Doggie face that my eyes were drawn to. Those sunken cheeks. That balding blond crown. Those depressed raccoon eyes. That whiny smile.

A smirk crept across my face.

At last it was real. He was gone.

I could list dozens of people Royce had offended and bullied over the years, with myself floating somewhere around the top of the list. But how many other than me had been reduced to the mindset that would allow me to contemplate carrying out a horrific act as Mike had?

Officially, I'd had homicidal ideation, and I had been hospitalized and released accordingly. My mind wasn't as sharp as it had been before the doctors started doping me up, but I'm pretty sure that neither Kat nor I had specifically named Royce to Dr. Edwin, although I had told her that my thoughts were about my boss. Only Kat and Mike knew the truth of what I had done at Royce's. And Kat had been in bed with me when Mike called that magical night a few weeks ago. Kat was concerned that I would be linked to Mike's crime and that she too would be implicated. But we were each other's alibi. I did realize that using my wife as justification wouldn't exactly bolster my defense if I needed one.

I wondered if Dr. Edwin would be approached by the police, and if so, what she could legally divulge to them.

And what of Mike? God forbid that he linked me to this act of aggression. I felt tremendous guilt, although anonymously I had betrayed him, and he never implicated me in any way. I should have turned myself in to the police as well.

I was willing to let Mike go down alone for a crime that I had dreamed up.

I was a hypocrite.

I despised myself. I was doing everything that I stood against.

My integrity ached.

Mike's charges were amended to include first-degree murder. As with the first case, he pled guilty and this time he was sentenced to life without the possibility of parole. I don't know why, but he still refrained from implicating me in any way.

I went to visit him at the prison twice.

The first time, before I could elicit an utterance, he put his finger to his lips and told me to never speak a word of what had happened to anyone else. He then stood up and walked away.

The second time the prison guards informed me that he refused to even see me.

I never saw Mike again.

Despite my paranoia, the door never did come crashing in.

I was entering a dark mental place. Bleak and disparaging. The feeling of listless loss was insurmountable. I felt powerless. I felt so sad. I was embittered with sweet depression. I didn't want to move. I didn't want to speak. I didn't want to do anything. I was not motivated. I prayed for the end to come.

I had betrayed Mike, and the only other person in the universe who knew was Kat.

I had numerous pills. Perhaps a handful would end my life. I was on Valium and clonazepam, among several other antipsychotics and antidepressants. I could swallow all of them. I would die peacefully, sleeping my way back into Father's realm. Would I find pure peace? What would Father say about cheating my destiny? What *was* my destiny? Was there such thing as destiny?

I realized that I was not to die by my own hand.

Was I meant to be a prophet or leader? Perhaps even a master?

I had no idea.

Royce had weakened if not nearly destroyed me by manipulating my thoughts.

Maybe I was creating these feelings of anxiety and depression to justify feeling sorry for myself. Perhaps if I masked my true nature with these thoughts and feelings of desperation I would not have to face the stone-cold reality of daily life.

But still the feelings existed. They were real.

Even knowing that he was dead, I was still scared shitless of Royce. I couldn't explain the power he had over me. I sensed him. I was so terrified. I would wake up sweating in the middle of the night. Sometimes my nightmares were so realistically horrible that I would wet the bed.

I begged, *Please Royce, just leave me alone. What did I ever do to you?*

I still believed that he must have seen something of himself in me. Something he disliked or lacked. Perhaps it was kindness. Perhaps it was his initial impression of my brash youth and self-confidence.

Perhaps it was my apparent feigned ability to be keep from being easily trodden down. Or perhaps it was as I had thought all along: he envied me in some way.

Or maybe he just wanted someone to feel more miserable than he felt. He wanted someone else's life to be as empty and meaningless as his was.

I was close to the answer. I was convinced of this.

Soon Father would reveal all.

Goodbye Mrs. Sunshine
Early October 1999

After my last psychotic break, Kat walked on pins and needles around me. She slept in the spare room, the room that had been intended for our never-to-be offspring. A lock was installed on the door, and it was always locked when Kat was inside.

Finally, after all the noise around Royce's death subsided, Kat broke down and asked my parents if I could stay with them through the weekdays and come back to see her on the weekends. She had reached the end of her rope. Her doctors had been telling her to leave me for several months—I was contributing to her mental health issues. My parents understood this.

After a few more weeks, Kat asked my parents if they minded not bringing me out to see her on the weekends as well. I couldn't understand. I grew angry and frustrated, but not in a violent way. I wanted to talk to her but she refused. She claimed that she needed some time to herself.

The first couple of years after my diagnosis left many voids in my memory. But as clear as day I can remember sitting in my parents' living room with Mom, Dad, and Kat. The room seemed to have a satiny felt-like air about it. It was like a dream. I had tunnel vision, focusing on Kat's lips. Her visage was fuzzy. The curtains were gently shifting back and forth with the breeze from the open window. I was sitting on the couch, swaddled up in a light blanket and holding a pillow to my chest.

My wife looked terrible. Not ugly, but exhausted and worn out. I'll never forget what she said next: "Tomorrow I am going to see a lawyer to get a legal separation."

I could feel my hope drain. I was in a state of disbelief. I didn't know what to say.

"What do you think about that?" my mother asked me.

I broke down.

"Please no! Please no, Kat!"

I started begging Kat to reconsider. "I'm getting better. The medicine is working. Please don't do this!"

"I've made up my mind," Kat said. "I'm not rejecting you, I just can't handle you or meet your needs anymore." I saw tears in her eyes, those big blue eyes—this had been a decision not made easily.

I suspected that my parents had discussed this with her prior to that moment. We had been married for just over three years, and together for five.

The only other thing I remembered from that day was hugging—no, *clinging* to my mom and telling her how much it hurt.

I was crushed. My goal had been to get better with the clozapine and return to weekends, and ultimately weeks, back with my wife, so I promised to work harder to improve my mental health.

My parents owned a condo on the ground floor of a high-rise. They made room for me on an air mattress in the smaller bedroom. Once Kat and I were legally separated, I moved my furniture into my parents' place.

I vaguely remember putting our house up for sale and moving out.

Kat and I kept in touch, but not on a regular or routine basis. At first I called her every day, but Mom convinced me to leave her alone. I had to accept that she needed to move on with her life, and that meant I had to move on with mine.

I slowly got used to my new routine, but I missed Kat terribly. She was all that I had known for the past several years. I was doing well on the clozapine and other meds. I started meeting with a pair of occupational therapists. They were great with helping me deal with and overcome many of my numerous anxiety-driven phobias.

Early on, my mother was still washing my hair—I was still completely afraid of the water. When it came to bathing, I was still deathly afraid that I would slip in the tub. When I showered, I started to feel dizzy as the water cascaded down over my head. When it came to brushing my teeth, I was still afraid of gagging and choking to death on my own sputum.

There was no rhyme to my reason.

It just was what it was.

I remember living in my parents' condo, just sitting outside on the balcony smoking cigarette after cigarette—I wasn't allowed to smoke in their home. It was early autumn, so I enjoyed the crisp air as I inhaled the cigarette smoke. But winter was just around the corner, and it wasn't going to be as pleasant sitting outside. To top it off, my mother complained that I reeked of cigarette smoke after I'd been outside. She insisted that I stand outside for an extra five minutes after each smoking session.

Soon five minutes after a cigarette turned into ten. And next she wanted me to walk around the courtyard in the freezing cold. My mom, despite her faults, was a good, well-intentioned person. I think that after the falling out between us the previous summer we were all able to move on and forward. We were in a good mental space as a family for the first time in a very long time.

Mom was very sly and clever as well. I started to figure out what she was attempting to do with respect to my smoking. Finally, one day she dared me to quit smoking. She played on my anxieties—she knew I would never leave the building to go to the store on my own to buy smokes.

I asked her what the stakes were, not if, but when I succeeded.

She responded: steak and lobster at the finest restaurant in town.

I was in.

A Year of Growth and Well-Being
November 1999–November 2000

Mom was still working, but Dad had been retired for about eight years.

Every day Dad would take me out for coffee at our favorite café. Dad and I had quickly established a routine just as we'd had the previous summer.

I realized early on that I was quite lucky that I had my parents.

That year I began to thrive for the first time in a long time. It was still going to be a long journey, but I felt as if I was returning to my old self. My mood was generally positive and calm. My anxieties, although still present, were no longer holding me back. I was no longer hearing or seeing things. My thoughts were much clearer, and although I did still subscribe to many of the theories that I'd come up with when I was delusional, there was a significant decrease in the paranoia that I had associated with these ideas.

Chapter 27

Goodbye

All the Money in the World
January 1, 2001

It was just after dinner on New Year's Day, around six-thirty, when the phone rang. I answered—it was Mom. Dad had been in the hospital since the day after Christmas with fluid in the lining of his lungs. She had been at the hospital sitting with him as the doctors and nurses went about their business. Ellyn had met with her at the hospital just before dinner—they were just going for a short visit to alleviate his boredom.

They weren't there very long before the hammer dropped.

"Dad just had a stroke," Mom's unwavering voice said into the phone.

I could sense a well of tears building up in the corners of her eyes. I dropped the glass of milk that was in my hand. It bounced, spilling out its contents without breaking. I started to choke on a dry, slightly stale chocolate chip cookie that I had just shoved into my mouth.

It was as if I had been struck by a freight train. My fears were becoming my reality. Although I had envisioned and accepted the inevitability of this for several years, I had no idea how to react or respond. I had purposefully deceived myself into believing that he would be around forever. That was the easiest solution, and the only one that put my mind at rest. At the core I know that I was being illogical and unrealistic, but I couldn't make sense of a life without Dad.

Over the previous several months I had at least learned to treasure every moment we had together.

In my late teens and early twenties, more than a few times while sitting in my car in my parents' driveway getting stoned I would start thinking about Dad. In my relaxed world in which only I could see and exist, I would close my eyes and let the thoughts flow.

In one marijuana-enhanced vision I had seen him in a casket. I watched as if I were a fly on the wall—all those people walking up to his body and their tears spilling onto him as they leaned over to kiss or touch him.

This vision brought on a sad, depthless feeling in my gut. With my eyes closed from the haze of marijuana smoke I watched myself walk up to the casket embracing his lifeless body and kiss him on the forehead. I touched his cool folded hands and whispered, "Goodbye for now. I love you."

I felt a chill run up my back.

He was dressed sharply in his best church clothes. His skin was a bit waxy in appearance, but the man lying before me *was* my dad. In my stoned mind I heard his voice tell me that he loved me too. I prayed to Father that this was simply a figment of my imagination and would never happen.

My buzz started to feel more like a low rather than a high. I sat back and lit a cigarette, put a Sarah McLachlan cassette into the car stereo, and let my mind drift.

In another marijuana-enhanced prophecy, I recall hearing a soft banging noise at the side door of a house. I ran to check it out. It was winter and Dad was lying on a thin carpet of snow. His face looked old and was flushed bright red as he fought for air. His eyes were red and bulging. The blue veins in his head and neck were swollen and throbbing. He was wheezing and gasping for breath. I thought he was having a heart attack. I watched myself fretfully trying to figure out how to alleviate his pain and distressed body. His lips were moving but only slight wheezes were coming out.

I was the only person around. I was panicking.

I heard my voice scream, pleading with him, "What do you need me to do?" I watched myself howl into the empty house. My cries echoed through my otherwise quiet mind. Just thinking about this made my smoke-hazed mind ache. This vision had taken on a life of its own. It was as threatening as a rabid serial killer let loose on an orgy of kids who just wanted to party and fuck.

As the howls in my mind seemed to increase by the decibel, I began to feel extremely anxious. It felt as though the smoke that filled the car where I was sitting was thickening and morphing into a solid that was disabling my lungs. I couldn't breathe. My head ached and it felt like a hunk of lead was on top of my shoulders.

In a panicked state I opened the car window and stuck my head outside to catch a breath of clean air. Slowly I felt my heart slow down and my breathing ease. The pressure within my skull began to recede. After my panic attack subsided, I rolled up the window and lit a cigarette. I put a Sarah McLachlan cassette in the stereo deck, closed my eyes, and just let my head slump backwards against the headrest.

I never forgot that feeling of dread that I had imagined, that inexplicable terror of losing my dad.

And now it was happening.

I don't know why, but I had been sensing that Dad wasn't going to be around much longer. We'd had such a great summer. Mom, Dad, and I had rented a mobile home from July to October. I hadn't seen Dad that happy in a long time. Everything was so perfect that the bad had to follow sooner or later.

I had visited a medium named Angelica the previous year; she had proven to me beyond a reasonable doubt that she was the real thing. Without going into detail, she revealed to me things that no one who wasn't close to me could have known. Initially a skeptic, I was an instant believer.

I visited her again a few months before Dad had the stroke (at the time Dad had nothing out of the ordinary wrong with him), and I asked her if I had any psychic gifts, as I had always thought I had. She cautiously asked me why I wanted to know. I explained my visions to her and asked if they were legit. I was particularly concerned about the winter and Christmas season, because that was when he was at his most vulnerable to having complications due to his COPD—chronic obstructive pulmonary disorder.

Her lips tightened into an awkward "O" and she wiped the side of her mouth with her pinky finger. Her eyes darkened and her pupils dilated. I knew right then what the answer was. But I had put it out there. She asked me if I really wanted to know. I said I did. I should have left it alone. Angelica told me that when bad news like a death is going to occur, she would usually feel nauseated or ill. She looked nauseated to me. She unconvincingly said she couldn't sense anything bad happening.

In early November Dad had been complaining of back pain. We brought him to the hospital, where he was admitted for almost a full week. He had fluid surrounding the lining of his lungs. The doctors ran dozens of tests to determine the cause and source of this fluid. The results all showed that there was no specific cause—it was an anomaly. After a week, the fluid had been drained and was no longer being generated. He was given a clean bill of health and sent home.

Dad was generally a pretty easygoing guy, although he was a pretty OCD when it came to tidiness. He rarely complained, especially about his own woes. We went to Ellyn's for Christmas that year. He was jolly and we all had a great time.

We had no idea at that time that behind that big bright smile he was miserable with pain—the fluid on his lungs had returned. He was admitted to the hospital on the morning after Christmas.

That was his last Christmas ever.

The night before Dad had the stroke, Mom and I had welcomed in the new year with a round of cheers and hurrahs. This year was going to be one of the best ever. Usually at some point in the winter, Dad would end up in the hospital because of his COPD. He'd suffered from bronchitis every year going back to the years when he'd been a smoker—that was almost twenty years before. He was super-vigilant if not outright obsessed about catching a cold, because it always landed him in the hospital around the Christmas season. The previous year he had completely missed our Christmas celebrations because he'd had to be hospitalized. I remember thinking that it was a practice run.

This year he was determined to celebrate Christmas with all of us.

I hoped and prayed that Rusty would be allowed to enjoy Christmas with my entire family, but that didn't happen—my legal battles with the O'Reillys were far from over because of my mental health issues and Kat was no longer in the picture, so Rusty still wasn't permitted to see me or any of my family.

Despite all my ruminations and attempts to prepare myself mentally, I hadn't predicted that it would happen this way. To top it off, my sweet Rusty would never get to experience just what a great man his Gramps was.

I picked up the phone. Mom was on the other end. She was unnervingly calm.

"His right side is paralyzed, and he can only speak in a whisper."

I asked Mom if I should come to the hospital, but she said Ellyn was with her and she was fine. Mom's sister, my Aunt Ruth, called me about an hour later to see how I was doing. I told her that I was freaked. I also told her that the psychic, Angelica, had told me that everything was going to be fine. Aunt Ruth knew Angelica and knew that she was genuine. She had gone to see her several months before and the psychic had predicted that one of my uncles (again, on Mom's side) had a medical issue and that he should see a doctor. Aunt Ruth then told my mom and my uncle. He went to see his doctor and they discovered that he had skin cancer. So when I told my aunt what the psychic had said, she said that Dad would be fine.

The next day I had an appointment to get another tattoo. I asked Aunt Ruth if I should cancel my appointment. At first she thought it would be fine, but when I told her that I would be out of town for four to six hours she suggested that perhaps I should cancel—she was concerned that if something else happened to Dad and I wasn't around that I would never forgive myself.

I canceled my appointment.

I spoke with a few people and was reassured that numerous people recover from strokes. That gave me a sense of hope. And then Mom called again around midnight.

"Your father has bleeding tumors in his brain."

I began to tremble.

"They are cancerous and inoperable."

"Is there anything I can do?" I asked. My heart was aching. This was one of my greatest fears—I loved Dad, and I wanted him to live with me and Mom forever. Mom said she was hanging in there. Ellyn was with her, and there was nothing I could do. Mom told me to get some rest and that Aunt Ruth would bring me down to the hospital in the morning.

I hung up the phone. I was sobbing.

"My daddy is going to die!" I cried out into the air.

I had just started a lucrative short-term business venture a couple of months before. I was selling off my old '80s heavy metal records and I was making money like a maniac. I had been so happy to have been so fortunate, even though it was only going to be for a few months. For the first time since I had left the corporate world I was making more money than I needed.

But now I felt nothing.

All that money meant nothing.

That night I tried bargaining with Father—I would trade all the money in the world for my dad to be well.

But it just wasn't meant to be.

After that, my memory was pretty much a blur until the next day. I just remember crying off and on all night. I wished that I had Kat there to hold and reassure me that she would be with me through everything. We hadn't seen one another for well over a year.

The next day I went to the hospital. I hadn't had much sleep the previous night. Mom greeted me at the hospital entrance, and I followed her through a maze of corridors and elevators until we reached Dad's room.

I didn't know what to expect when I saw him.

I didn't know how or what to feel.

Mom hadn't said a word since she'd met me. She had her tough-guy face on. I had watched Mom when her parents had passed—she had remained stoic and calm. She had told me that she had grieved in private. I felt so terrible for her. I couldn't imagine seeing my soulmate suffer.

We walked into Dad's room. There were four beds inside. The screens were pulled around each bed. The room reeked of death and shit. The woman beside Dad was moaning and kept buzzing the nurses. The man kitty-corner to Dad was mumbling to himself, and he kept pulling back the curtains—he was covered in his own feces. The woman across from Dad was awake and friendly.

I had promised myself that I wouldn't cry when I saw Dad. I didn't want to upset him.

I kept my promise for the first five minutes.

I cautiously walked up beside him and I hugged him. He pulled me in with his good arm and buried my face into his chest. He started to tremble. I could feel his sobs. I kept my head pressed tightly to his chest and kept whispering, "It's okay Dad. It's okay."

That's when I caught the feels.

We must have held each other for over five minutes, the longest we had been in direct contact for as long as I could remember. I let him go and stood up. He looked odd with his entire right side being immobile. My dad had always been a boisterous speaker, mainly because of his thirty years of yelling over the noise to his coworkers at the steel mill. Now his voice had been reduced to a barely audible whisper.

I looked at him. His eyes were red from crying. His cheeks were swollen and covered in tears. Mom and Ellyn had left me to be alone with Dad. I laid my hand on his paralyzed right arm. I quietly stood beside him for over twenty minutes. We were both speechless.

"How are you?" Dad finally whispered.

How the hell do you think I am? I thought.

"I'm okay," I said. I smiled, took his hand in mine, and gave it a gentle squeeze.

Mom and Ellyn returned to the room, followed by a doctor. The doctor had olive skin and a full black beard, with a shock of black hair waving across his forehead. He was holding a clipboard filled with several file folders. He pulled the curtains around my dad's area.

I let go of Dad's hand and moved out of the way for Mom to move in beside him.

With complete professionalism and an absolute absence of emotion, he promptly told us Dad's diagnosis. He had stage 4 lung cancer, cancer of the liver, plus the cancerous tumors in his brain. Before we had a chance to ask the doctor what the prognosis was, he told us that there was nothing that could be done except to make him comfortable, but he said that he would return in an hour to discuss what we would have to look forward to and how we would best treat him.

Just as quickly as this new information was sinking into our heads, the doctor slipped away from the room.

All eyes were on Dad. He was looking directly at Mom. He was bawling his eyes out. His entire bed was quaking. I looked at Mom; she had cupped her hands over her mouth in grief and disbelief. It was rare for Mom to emote in front of anyone. She was quivering with sorrow as tears fell. Her knees buckled—for a moment I thought that she was going to fall or pass out. She moaned quietly and straightened herself up. She leaned over Dad and hugged him. Ellyn and I left the room. As we were leaving, I heard them whispering that they loved each other.

We left our parents alone and headed down to the coffee shop. We didn't speak a word to one another.

After thirty or forty minutes we returned to Dad's room. He was sleeping. Mom was holding his left arm and her eyes were closed as if in prayer. She looked exhausted. I know we all looked shaken up.

The doctor returned after an hour, as promised. We left Dad while we spoke with the physician outside of his room. We all had so many questions to ask that he had to shush us. But it all boiled down into three basic questions.

Our first question was how they were going to keep him comfortable. The doctor explained that once the fluid around his lungs was cleared he would be moved to a hospice for palliative care. Over time Dad would be subjected to a morphine drip, which would be adjusted depending on his level of pain. We insisted that he would not want to be stoned to the point where he couldn't communicate during his last days, but we didn't want him to suffer either.

The next thing we wanted to know was why the cancer hadn't been detected sooner. The doctor explained that it was a very aggressive and fast-moving form of cancer. Back in November, when Dad had first been treated for the fluids on the lining of his lungs, there was no cancer. He told us that this was a blessing, because this way we wouldn't have to see him suffer through operations and chemotherapy, which may have increased his lifespan a little but would have simply dragged out the misery within everyone, especially Dad.

Our last question was how long he had to live. His answer sent an atomic blast through each of us. He said three weeks, give or take a few days. He believed that Dad would die of a heart attack or another stroke much sooner than it would take for the cancer to take him.

We were all dumbfounded. Any further questions became irrelevant.

Mom asked us to go home and contact all his family and friends that night. Everyone who needed to be contacted was written in Dad's all-important day planner.

Dad was sitting up when we reentered the room. I motioned to Ellyn that it was time to leave. We each took a turn giving Dad a gentle hug and kiss and left him alone with Mom for the night.

I wished that I had Kat to sit at my side that entire night, through every phone call, through every moment of grief, through every tear. She could be my anchor. She could help keep me sane.

That night I finally did sleep. I squeezed a spare pillow, clutching to it as never before, as if I was afraid that if I let go it would leave me too.

The next morning Ellyn and I returned to the hospital. Mom told us that through the night Dad had slept off and on. Most of the time when he was awake, he would cry and whimper that he didn't want to die. It was heartbreaking to hear. Still, she didn't want us to tell him how long he had.

Dad lived exactly three weeks and two days after his diagnosis.

He passed peacefully with Mom at his side.

Part VIII

It's a Long Way Down

Chapter 28

This is the End

The Runaway
February 2001

After Dad passed, I stayed in the condo with Mom. I shared a mortgage on the condo, so when Mom passed I would inherit three quarters of it, and my sister would inherit the remaining quarter, although she had her own place with her boyfriend Geoff. My sister had been made aware of my mental illness from the start, but she had never had to really face it. On the occasions when she saw me, I was medicated, lucid, and calm.

Ellyn had suffered through her own demons and disappointments, and she had come out fighting. We were both strong individuals, just in very different ways. We both understood and had experienced workplace politics and bullshit. We both knew the pain of betrayal. We had both experienced depression and anxiety. One difference in our inner strengths was that she had the personality type that enabled her to internalize her issues, even better than me. But she wasn't completely broken by her experience after a major betrayal at work; she had encapsulated herself behind an inner wall that took a long time to knock down.

Beyond her personal experiences, she was uninformed about mental illness. Like most people when they learned of my illness, she didn't know what to say or how to act around me.

All she truly knew was the stigma.

The TV and movies make schizophrenics out to be a menace to society, and I got it—it was generally a misunderstood illness. I endured many jokes asking, "Which one am I talking to now?"

Almost every time something tragic occurred, like a school shooting, the news and authorities would blame the tragedy on the mentally ill. That shit sold. Even I had found myself fulfilling that stereotype in the past. The truth is we schizophrenics are generally more afraid of others than we are violent against them.

With the loss of Dad, I felt empty. He had been one of my closest friends for quite a while. We had spent our entire days together since I had returned home after Kat. In many ways I was fortunate that I couldn't work, because it gave me the opportunity to really get to know him.

A couple of months after Dad had passed, I felt like I was becoming more of a burden than a blessing to Mom.

Every winter since I'd been sick, I slipped a little with my spending habits. Over time I had learned that when I screwed up financially, Mom would help me fix it, and we usually caught it before it was more than two or three hundred dollars.

This year, I was making a lot of money selling my old records and I renewed my relationship with eBay. It was just as it had been so many years ago. Mom had noticed the increased frequency of packages arriving, but I insisted that I had a good hold of things. It didn't take long until I had maxed out my line of credit, which was held up as collateral for the ownership of my condo. If it came to it I had my retirement savings, but I dared not touch that money unless absolutely necessary.

Mom had trusted me to control my spending, and I let her down.

I started to really beat myself up. The guilt was overwhelming. I knew that I had to inform her of my spending habits, but this time I had really hit rock bottom. I couldn't face her and admit defeat yet again.

I had been stable for so long that Mom had stopped watching over me. I had my shit together—or so we thought. I had convinced her that I was doing well. I had promised her that if I started to slip, I would call a doctor.

I didn't.

Instead, my guilt triggered me to delve into a state of mild depression. Soon, my anxieties kicked back in, to the point that I became too anxious to leave the house to go to see the psychiatrist, or even my family physician. All I had to do was talk with Mom, but I just couldn't admit that I had failed so miserably.

I slowly stopped taking my meds properly, until I stopped taking them at all.

After all our hard work over the past few years I had come undone, and all the old symptoms crept back in.

The voices started up again, louder than ever. I became convinced that the doctors were going to rescind my sick-leave benefits and force me back to work at W.V.H. Steel, and then I was going to be fired and left to drift amongst the unemployable. I started canceling my appointments. Once again, work and Royce came to the forefront of all my thoughts and actions.

Royce was dead, yet he was more alive than ever within my mind.

The problem was, once the delusions, voices, and other symptoms started back up, I was too afraid to speak up. I believed everything my mind told me.

After only a few short months, I was trapped in purgatory. Finally, I called my sister and fessed up. She freaked out. I should have known better—she had no idea how to deal with this. In my room in the condo there were packages piled upon packages.

Ellyn thought that I had become a hoarder.

I insisted that I was not a hoarder—I was a *collector*. I collected CDs, LPs, plastic model kits, video games, comic books, and all kinds of memorabilia. I had even spent $25,000 on a pickelhaube—a rare German helmet from World War I.

I was still collecting my disability pension, but I had it spent months before I even received it. My line of credit was maxed out at $20,000. Ellyn decided that it was time to tell Mom what was happening. I had some substantial retirement savings, but if I started to withdraw from those funds I would be heavily taxed and left without enough of an income to survive once I was a senior.

The entire time, Ellyn's boyfriend Geoff was self-righteously complaining. I heard him recommending to Mom and Ellyn to wash their hands of me and let me live in my own stench. At least that's what I thought he was saying. I couldn't trust anyone or anything, especially when I had to rationally process it.

I just couldn't admit defeat to Mom yet again, so decided I only had one choice: I ran away from home.

I ran, and I ran, and I ran.

I ran to the deepest bowels of the city's downtown.

I ran until I felt that I would never be a burden again.

And then I ran some more.

I just wanted to die.

My Home Once Held a Refrigerator
March 2001

My box. My home.

It was rather beaten up already. The cold, snowy winter had made the corrugated cardboard pliable and weak. Soon I would need to get another; luckily that wouldn't be too hard. All I had to do was go to the department store on delivery day. That was every Tuesday. They were not very kind to me at the department store. They all looked at me strangely. They looked upon me in their various ways, some with feigned pity, others with blatant apathy, although it depended on who was doing the looking that determined which emotion was shown.

One worker, Jimmy, always gave me a new box. I usually got a new one every couple of weeks. He was just a young kid. Not too bright, but a really nice kid. I think Jimmy was mentally challenged or autistic. He never judged me. He never told me to get a job. He never acted like it was a big deal to give me a box that they were just going to throw away anyhow.

I had no sense of vanity anymore. I'd been through so much that I'd come to realize appearance doesn't really matter. Kat. She was so beautiful. I lost touch with her what seemed to be a lifetime ago. I wonder what she would say to me if she saw me right now. Would she be able to see through the matted hair and beard, and look me in the eye with dignity and respect? Would she look upon me with awe as she once did? At one point in my life I could have asked her to follow me off a bridge into dark murky waters, and I believe she would have.

I hid in my box and I thought back on my life, on what could have been.

Brian A. Plank

Rusty Is a Real Boy Now!
Saturday, August 5, 2001

It was Rusty's seventh birthday, but I had no idea. Time stood still when you lived on the streets. It was either hot outside or it was cold. The days were either long or they were short.

I still wondered if he was ready to call me Daddy yet. Every day, I prayed for his safety and that he was flourishing. I tried not to think about the custody case; I felt that since I'd run off I'd blown it. It was just another reason for Mom to be disappointed in me.

I had only been on the streets for just over six months, but I was well established within my community of the dregs. Most of my peers were addicted to alcohol and cigarettes. Many of them were here with me because they abused these substances. I was fortunate; I had given up smoking cigarettes years ago and had no intention of going back. And as far as the drinking went, I would get loaded every now and then but I didn't have an addiction.

I often wondered how everyone back home was doing.

Before he died, Dad showed up at almost every visitation. He watched Rusty through the window, but he had never had the joy of hugging him or hearing him say the word Grandpa.

He proudly carried a picture of my boy in his wallet, and often said how he looked forward to picking him up and hugging him.

Once Dad was in the hospital and he had accepted that he was never going to meet Rusty, Dad had Mom find a recent picture and write a letter to accompany it. He asked Mom to give it to Rusty when he finally came home to stay with us.

Dear Rusty, my one and only grandson,

We never got to meet, so please let me introduce myself to you. I am your Grandpa. I am your daddy's dad. I've seen you with your daddy. I've watched you every chance that I could since you were a two-year-old toddler. My only regret in life is that I never had the opportunity to meet you in person and shake your hand or give you a hug.

I know that you are an amazing boy. And if you're anything like your daddy, you're on your way to being an amazing man. He is so proud of you, as am I. He brags about you all the time. When he thinks of you, he smiles. You are the sparkle in his eye. When you are in pain, he feels it. You are the twinkle of hope in his tears.

Please remember: Your family is the most important thing that you have. Your grandma and daddy love you so much! I don't know if you will ever have any idea how much. I know that you love your Grandma and Grandpa O'Reilly and your mommy too. Don't ever stop loving any of them, no matter what happens.

I hope that you will always remember to treat yourself and others with dignity, respect, and love. You will have your ups and downs, but no matter what stay true to yourself. Love is the key to happiness. It is important you know you are always surrounded by it—always know that. And do not be afraid to show your love. Be sure to spread your joy. Listen to your heart—do what feels right for you, not what others tell you is right.

Always stand tall beside your daddy and be proud to know that we three all share our blood. You are a piece of me, and I will always be at your side, even though you may not know it.

I want so much for you to live a life of joy and happiness.

I love you now, and I will until we meet in Heaven some day!

Love, Grandpa

Quiet Time
February 2001–December 2001

I was living in the entrails of my birth town, Pittsburgh, where my family still lived. I had fallen off the face of the earth. I didn't know if I was missed. I didn't know if my family was searching for me.

I had never imagined such sadness and depression as I witnessed here amongst the homeless. Most of the people around me were on the streets due to mental illness or drug addiction, or an addiction due to mental illness. Many of my peers drank to quiet their souls and/or to numb their bodies from the cold harsh reality of life. Most of them preferred to be left alone. They suffered from extreme anxiety and depression. I met many others who also suffered from delusions and paranoia.

We were the ones forgotten and ignored by society.

Many of us had once had successful careers and jobs. I lived with ex-engineers, ex-doctors, ex-lawyers, etcetera. Until I'd ended up here, I couldn't comprehend how a well-educated contributor to society could end up wasting away, drunk or stoned, on the streets wearing the same clothes every day. I was now living proof that it could happen.

I spoke with many of my homeless peers. Those who were willing to speak over a bottle of cheap wine would describe situations akin to my own. Post-traumatic stress disorder. Working for companies that were not the least bit concerned about their mental health or stability. There were government provisions and guidelines which the companies were supposed to adhere to, but these rules were applied with complete apathy. It was all about results and the bottom line. If you weren't actively producing, you were hindering. Maybe you were eligible for a company-dictated number of bubble-gum psychologist visits. If it got so bad that you were missing time you could be disciplined, or even fired, unless you were fortunate and there was a long-term disability pension available, like I'd had.

I also learned that a great number of my homeless friends had also been on their path to enlightenment. They too had been for blackballed for being whistleblowers and/or telling the truth.

A lot of these people were ex-military. Once the military was done with them, they were sent out to ferret out their own future with little or no support.

Some of us had families who probably missed us.

Some of us had no families or friends.

We were a community. There was an initiation to the group; you had to prove yourself by stealing from or distressing the "normals." The general rule, once you'd been accepted, was that everybody shared their daily delights.

There were the outsiders who were other homeless people but not a part of our group. They would often raid our groups and steal our sundries. I was never one to fight, but I was forced to toughen up. In the workplace, bullying and gaslighting were horrible, but there was never physical violence. I grew accustomed to being physically challenged by others while on the streets.

I was lightyears from the workplace and I still had nightmares. I wondered what someone like Dr. Royce Pincer would say to me if he was to bump into me now.

Would he pity me? *Probably not.*

Would he feel shame for his part? *Probably not.*

Would he buy me a coffee, or a sandwich? *Probably not.*

Would he run from me, frightened? *Probably.*

This was a terrible life. During the day, you had to beg for nickels and dimes. If you were lucky you received a quarter. If you got a dollar, you'd hit the jackpot. I felt so humiliated. I was willing to do almost anything for enough money to get at least a cup of coffee each day, let alone a sandwich. Often, if you timed it right, you could ransack the fresh garbage from the vermin-infested alleys behind the restaurants. As I said, the idea behind our community was that we share all our daily spoils, but the reality was that each of us would scarf down a half-eaten hamburger or pizza crust in private if we knew we could get away with it.

I learned that not all people were offended by my appearance and smell. On more than one occasion a good Samaritan would invite me out to lunch. At first it was difficult to accept charity, but I had to learn to swallow my pride, else I would perish.

Sometimes there was an expectation of sexual gratification after a meal—I am ashamed to say that sometimes I simply did what I had to. I'd learned that objecting could lead to a beating.

Winter had been the worst. My home, like most of my peers, was barely shelter during a summer rain. It wasn't well suited for the chilling winds of winter. It was constantly damp and dilapidated. My only belongings were the clothes on my back and an old Toronto Blue Jays baseball cap. We would use old wooden skids that were left behind the restaurants as firewood, and we would build small fires in trash cans for warmth. Many passed a bottle back and forth to help keep warm, but I generally refused, except on rare occasions.

I learned to have no pride. If you had to piss, you just walked a few feet away from your home and found a nice piece of wall. Taking a shit was the same—there was no place for humility. When you had to go, you just dropped trou and did your business. There was no toilet paper, so you hoped you could find a newspaper that could serve your purpose. All of this occurred hidden in the back alleys, of course.

As lucid as I may sound now, believe me, I was far from it. I could not remember the last time I had any of my medications. So even though I seemed to fit in with my small community, I was still terrified that the government and police were after me, and that they wanted to put me back in the workplace. I saw terrorists every day. I stared death in the eye. I sat beside Father sipping coffee, like the good son he expected me to be. At first I kept to myself, and like any community the locals came over to check me out. Slowly I found my niche.

One night, I looked up through sleep-blurred eyes to see a hand reaching out toward me. The hand was glowing in the dark like that of an angel. Was this my angel who had visited me so long ago? Was my life to be changed again? As the glamor of this beautiful hand shone in front of me, I nearly shit my pants—it was Kat's hand. When she recognized me through my disheveled appearance she crouched down and took my hand in hers. There was a tear in her eye. She helped me up and hugged me so tightly I couldn't breathe.

After we had separated, we'd gone in our own directions. She became a successful college professor, and I had become a tiny louse feeding off the blood squeezed from the streets.

"I never stopped loving you," she choked. Tears ran down her cheeks and she patted my long straggly beard.

I couldn't believe it. Surely, I was hallucinating.

What an evil plot for my mind to play on me.

This was some sick trick.

Someone was setting me up.

Redemption
December 3, 2001

She took me by the hand and helped me to my feet.

She didn't comment on my guise.

She didn't talk down to me.

She didn't coddle me.

She was just there for me.

We walked without speaking for about fifteen minutes until we reached a parking lot. She pulled out a set of keys and pointed to a silver Buick SUV. "I'm over there."

I hesitated. What about my community? What about my friends who shared the streets with me? She had rejected me once a couple of years ago; who was to say that she wasn't going to do the same again? I didn't feel delusional, but I did feel quite paranoid.

As a schizophrenic, I had learned that when you feel normal, the odds are that you were not.

"They are everywhere," I emphatically whispered. I didn't even know who "they" were anymore.

"You are safe with me," she confidently replied.

I didn't know if she was real or not, but my gut told me that she was legit. Still, I had to test her. I hadn't seen her for two years. The question could be answered by anyone who knew us as a couple, but not anyone else.

"What is my nickname for you?"

She chuckled. "Giggles!"

She was correct, but to be sure I tested her again.

"When I say 'ready Freddy?' what do you say?"

"Sure am, Sam!" She chuckled again.

I was satisfied. This was my Kat.

She helped me get cleaned up and provided me her couch to sleep on. When we had split, we swore to each other that we would always be best friends. She was now fulfilling her oath.

Over the next couple of weeks she got me set back up with a permanent address, and I started collecting my disability pension again.

Upon rescuing me, she had immediately notified Mom.

Naturally, Mom had missed me and was anxious to reunite. However, I didn't feel stable enough to see her so soon. You can take a man from the streets, but you can't take the streets from the man.

After a few weeks I felt ready to face my family again. I was prepared to hear the worst—I knew that I deserved a good tongue lashing.

Most importantly, Kat was able to crack through my thick skull that I needed to be medicated. When I first came to live with her, I was so used to life on the street that when she took my clothes to the laundry I thought that she had stolen them, as I had grown accustomed to others doing on the street.

I started to panic and began hearing voices again—I was having a psychotic episode.

Kat did her best to calm me, but ultimately decided that I needed professional help.

She had me admitted to the hospital. I was working with a team of psychiatrists and nurses. After I had stabilized and was back on my medications, she encouraged me to move on with my life. I had been so used to begging for change that on many days she would have to fetch me from loitering with my change cup out in front of the local mall a few miles from her house.

She told me that she had been searching for me for over a year—as soon as she heard that I had run off. It was just by chance and a little of a nod and smile from Father that she found me as she did.

It was mid-December and I was feeling miserable, perhaps outright depressed. I had returned to a life of television, movies, and video games. At first, I found reading too difficult—my poor short-term memory limited my general learning comprehension. Even watching movies could be a chore if they were longer than ninety minutes.

But I quickly felt that I was wasting my talents and my life.

I felt that it was time to try to get back on my feet.

I was still one academic year from completing my engineering degree and I wanted to complete it, just so I could say that I had seen it through. But my mind was so frazzled from the goings on of the past couple of years that I was scared to death of failure.

I started back to my former psychiatrist, Dr. O'Liam. He didn't say a word about my long absence. He was as friendly as always. We picked up right where we had left off.

When I asked, he said that with my med cocktail I may find university-level academics extremely difficult, if not all-out impossible. One of the chronic side effects from my meds was that my short-term memory sucked. Often, I would answer the phone and take a message but forget it before it was completed, even if I had pen and notepad.

But Dr. O'Liam was ever the optimist. He told me that if I set my mind to it, he was confident that I would succeed. He set me up at a local research institute to evaluate my mental acuity. The tests revealed that I could finish my degree, but it would take an enormous effort. The clinicians recommended I go to community college, where they felt I would have a better chance of success.

I was warned that I would not be achieving A's and A+'s.

Even though I had been warned that the odds were stacked against me, I enrolled in the university to complete the last year of my engineering degree, starting in January 2002.

Reunited
Christmas 2001

I was deathly afraid to see Mom. When I had left home I had screwed up my finances—my life—so badly that I was ashamed to see her. I was afraid that she would tell me that I had disappointed her. Mom had taken money from her personal retirement savings to pay down my debt, but Dad had left a substantial amount so she wouldn't lose the condo.

That Christmas Mom and I were reunited.

Ellyn and Geoff were present as well.

My hair was still long, but it had been trimmed so that it was not as matted and straggly as it had been. Kat had also helped me trim my beard so that I looked presentable.

Instead of reading me the riot act, I was embraced by Mom and Ellyn.

Tears flowed in all directions.

We had never really grieved for Dad as a family.

It had been exactly two years since his last Christmas with us.

That night we all raised several glasses to Dad and shared our stories and memories about him with one another.

I was one of the best nights of my life.

Chapter 29

I See Your True Colors, and That's Why I Love You

It's Time to Raise the Flag of ~~Hate~~ Hope
January 2002

To hell with all the doubters. To those who looked down their fat noses at me. To those who snickered or spat upon me. To those who judged me.

I had persevered. I had survived.

I had returned to society after a life on the streets. I struggled and came out on top. Perhaps that was the quality that Father sought. I felt things. Deeply. I was an empath. I felt what the typical human felt. I understood the plight of the feeble. I recognized the injustice suffered by the poor. I considered how my decisions could impact others.

I had been through Hell and come out on the other side.

I had seen atrocities on the streets that I would never repeat to anyone else.

After all I had been through, I still cared.

Brian A. Plank

I'm Gonna Break My Rusty Cage
Thursday, May 3, 2002

Even while I was hiding from the world on the downtown streets, Mom had never given up on getting custody of Rusty. In my absence, the court had allowed Mom a weekly supervised visitation. Kat wasn't in the picture since we had separated, but she did try to keep in touch with Mom, especially after Dad passed.

Mom was a good Christian woman. If you looked up the term in a dictionary, I swear Mom's image would be posted beside the definition. She was one of the strongest people that I knew. Sure, we'd had our fallouts in the past, and I disagreed with a lot of her methods on how she had treated me when I was a child. But one thing I had to say was, good or bad, Mom was always there for anyone if they needed her. Sometimes she was played, but she never completely gave up on anyone. She told me that, even while I was lost over the past year, she knew that God was taking care of me and that we would be reunited.

Even before Dad passed away, Mom had started to bond with the O'Reillys. While I was away, my sister and Geoff had two young twin daughters, and Mom absolutely adored them. She spent as much time with them as she could. She was an awesome grandmother. I thought she spoiled the girls; in fact, she admitted that she did. She said that it was her grandmotherly privilege.

The O'Reillys had only had one child, Dan, so Rusty was the only grandchild that they had, and ever would have. They were very good to Rusty. At first they were standoffish and cautious because of all the nonsense that Jenn and Dan had been feeding them. Even when Jenn fell off the wagon and got herself addicted to crack, they supported her—that was the type of nurturing personality that Mom had as well.

I think that I got my sense of empathy from Mom, because she would talk to the O'Reillys with an understanding of how much they would be missing when we won custody of Rusty.

Mom had always insisted that the O'Reillys should be given time with Rusty once the custody battle was finally sorted out. On the surface I disagreed with her, but deep down I knew that what Mom was proposing was the right thing to do. It was the Christian thing to do.

Truman said that these types of cases didn't usually last so long—Rusty was almost eight years old. We had been starting and stopping the court battles for six years, mostly because of finances, but also because of issues such as Jenn's drug habit and the mental health issues that Kat and I were suffering through.

Today was the last court date before the final decision was going to be made the following week. For a few years, Truman had been assuring us that we would win full-time custody.

Part IX

Faith: Thursday, May 10, 2002

Brian A. Plank

Unopened presents beneath the tree, a Daddy cries but no one sees
All because Mommy told a lie, the courts won't even bat an eye
He loves his son with all his heart, a false allegation has torn them apart
He has to prove he did no wrong, this has gone on way to long
Another Holiday will come and go, he just wants him to know
That his love for him will never stop, he loves him to the mountain top
All the gifts are put away, waiting for when he can come and play
The day will come and with all of his might, he can say he never gave up the fight
To all the dads who are in this fight, you are not alone on this special night
Your kids will know that you always care, all you have to do, is hang in there.

– Trevor Cobb, Lyrics. Facebook, 17/12/19.

Chapter 30

Perseverance of Time

1:30 p.m.

We were all standing as the judge reentered the courtroom. His black robes flowed with honor and authority. His face was stern and deliberate. His graying hair stood up with a slight tilt to the right. He sported closely trimmed sideburns, but his face was otherwise cleanshaven. His aura had always shown that he was a firm but compassionate and just man.

As he sat, he scanned the room with the wisdom of Solomon in his eyes. We had no idea how this was going to end. My family had spent tens of thousands of dollars on Truman Kush and his legal team over the past seven or so years. The O'Reillys had also invested a great deal of time and money into cultivating and providing for the boy, in addition to taking Jenn in with her issues.

I felt for them. This had been such an anguishing ordeal. They had lost their son, and in many ways their daughter-in-law too. They only had Rusty to cling to. I looked across the courtroom at Jenn. She looked like shit. I couldn't tell if she was jonesing for a fix or if she was already high. I pitied her and her late husband's family. She had royally screwed up everything. To this day she was still claiming that I was not Rusty's biological father.

I imagined that the O'Reillys felt for us as well. At the same time they had tried blocking us from any contact since his birth, even when Dad was in the hospital dying.

The judge leaned forward and began a brief but emotional diatribe about the difficulty of meting out justice with mercy. We were almost delirious with anticipation as he continued to speak. None of it really sank in for me until he reached his summary.

"I hereby award full custody of Russel Daniel O'Reilly to the complainant."

With a deafening thud the judge's gavel pounded down.

There was a moment of complete silence, hastily followed by taunts of outrage from Jenn as his words sunk in. Mom was standing on my right and Kat was on my left. I squeezed each one's hands. Our eyes brimmed with tears.

Rusty was not in the courtroom. He had been kept out of all the legal and family issues by the O'Reilly family. He was almost eight years old and I had no idea how we would bring him into our fold. All he knew was the O'Reillys, and me from our visits.

1:50 p.m.

Jake was in court with the entire Prue family except for Chucky when the judge ruled. In fact, they had been very supportive of us during our entire plight to gain custody of my son. They had seen how Jenn's life had spun out of control following Dan's death. They had been instrumental in having Jenn declared an unfit mother. Chucky had suffered from the effects of her addictions and general neglect and was getting counseling.

Jake and his family had been awarded full-time permanent custody of Chucky. Jenn had been awarded supervised two-hour biweekly visitations with him, which she missed half of the time. Chucky was almost twelve years old now. Jake told me that he had no memory of me, which calmed my heart a little. The last thing I wanted was to be a contributing factor to his mental well-being.

After I had been awarded custody over Rusty, while still in the courtroom, Jenn became furious. She began uttering death threats at us. She and the O'Reillys continued to yell out that she had been clean and sober for over five months. I wasn't convinced, but I hoped that for her sake she was being truthful and that she could keep herself clean.

Even though they had never allowed us access to him, we had discussed within our family and our lawyer that we felt it was only fair to allow the O'Reillys monthly visits. This was not court-ordered; we felt that it was simply the right thing to do. Our only condition was that Jenn was not permitted to be there unless supervised by a court-approved social worker.

3:00 p.m.

Upon hearing the judge's ruling, Jenn started hollering that Rusty was not my son. From the very moment that she had learned of her pregnancy she had refused to accept even the notion that he could be mine. She had been shown the physical proof. She had been shown the scientific proof. Still, she remained unyielding.

The commotion she was starting alarmed the court guards. They motioned for us to leave. As we exited the courtroom, she grew even more animated and had a full-on fit.

Kat, Mom, and I stood in the courtroom halls, anticipating our first encounter with Rusty.

I saw him at the end of the hall, holding a court officer's hand. The O'Reillys were with him. The small crowd stopped just outside of the courtroom, about twenty feet from us. Mr. O'Reilly crouched down and whispered to the boy.

It was immediately clear how much the O'Reillys truly did love him. The bustling in the courtroom was almost overpowered by the impact of the O'Reillys' tears hitting the wooden floors.

Mr. O'Reilly twisted his body and pointed to me.

I don't know what he told the boy, but Rusty looked confused and started crying. Rusty clung to him—the only stable adult male figure he had known in his life. Dan had died when Rusty was only two, so his only memories were from photographs.

Mr. O'Reilly stood up, brushed the front of his suit off, and took the boy by the hand. He started walking in our direction. When he was about fifteen feet from us, he let go of the boy.

"Go," he ordered. I could see the tears running down his face.

I crouched down and opened my arms to embrace my son.

Rusty started in my direction but stalled several times, turning his back to me and looking at Mr. O'Reilly. Mr. O'Reilly kept motioning the boy forward, each time wiping a fresh tear from his face.

Finally, Rusty started to run to me, arms outstretched.

As Rusty came within reach, Mr. O'Reilly turned his back to us and returned to be with his family.

For the first time I heard that word I'd been waiting years to hear: "Daddy!"

It echoed through the halls of the building.

3:01 p.m.

I was already dead by the time I heard the gun go off.

3:02 p.m.

Time had all but stood still. As my son reached me his skull exploded, leaving a gaping hole where his face had been. My face was covered in his blood, bone, and brain matter. The bullet had also penetrated *my* skull, leaving a sickly streaked fan of crimson on the floor and walls behind our embraced bodies. I was on my back with my arms wrapped tightly around Rusty.

All I could hear was a high-pitched screech and echoes of the gunshot.

"Noooooooo!"

I was but a shadow watching and listening from above.

I looked down and saw Mom and Kat both standing beside the dead bodies of my son and me. Both women were wearing looks of indescribable horror. The slow-spreading pool of blood that belonged to Rusty and me slowly spread toward their feet.

Kat approached the carnage and knelt in the pooling blood, leaning in to hug us. She held on for several minutes, clinging to us as if for dear life as the courtroom officers attempted to pull her from us. I watched as my beloved raised her gory hands to her face as she looked up to the ceiling of the hallway. Without a word, the officers carried her off to the side of the hallway. They draped a blanket around her.

She had raised her bloodied hands to her cheeks as she screamed, leaving trails of gore running down her face.

As she was being dragged away, I could read her lips: "Why?"

Mom was in too much shock to move. She was a statue. Her mouth was wide open calling out that eternal no. Eventually the officers moved her beside Kat.

The two women held each other and the tears began their endless flow.

With all the commotion exiting the courtroom, Jenn had managed to grab one of the court officer's guns. I couldn't make out what she was screaming, but I watched as the recoil of the handgun made her stumble back a little, nearly knocking her off her feet.

I could see only what could be called pure evil on her face.

I saw Jenn point the gun at her chin and wrap her finger around the trigger a second time. Quickly the court officers grappled her, causing her to drop the gun to the floor. Her eyes never left the grisly mess that she had created. I could hear her crowing like a lunatic as she was cuffed and dragged away.

Everything started to fade.

My son was finally at home with me, his Daddy.

EPILOGUE

The Final Creation

Rusty was dead.

I was dead.

Within an instant we were but a shadow hovering over the scene that was playing out below us. We were together at last, tightly clinging to each other, just a father and his son. Needlessly murdered by a jealously insecure, selfish, drug-addled woman.

I could see the bloody hole which had been Rusty's face.

I could see the back of my skull burst open as if it was a watermelon smashed by a sledgehammer.

Right before my shadow's eyes I watched as Rusty let go of me and began floating and fading into the darkness. He did not fuss one bit as he went onward with his journey. I hoped that we may meet again in another time, in another place.

Next, I felt a gentle warmth embrace me. I felt myself fading into the black. I was all alone, but I didn't feel deserted. I didn't feel sad; I felt free. I was at peace in this odd dimension of existence.

All the individuals whose lives I had in some way impacted were paraded before me. I saw people that I never would have dreamed had given a second thought to my existence. Behind each of their eyes there was a story revealing how I had blessed their lives, many in ways that I had no idea of. I saw people I didn't even recognize.

The stories their eyes told... I felt pure joy.

I had tried to be true to myself. I had almost failed. I realized at that instant that this would be my last creation: my judgement.

My words. My prose.

Was I a liar? Was I a hypocrite?

It was time to take accountability for myself. No blaming others.

I had been responsible for my own misery in life.

I had been lied to by myself.

And then I knew the answer. I knew how to deal with the negativity. The bullies, the politicians, and the false prophets. I not only forgave but thanked all my human oppressors and tormenters. I realized that had it not been for them, I would not be where I was now. Each one had played a role in how I created my experience. The more I forgave and thanked, the lighter I felt, until I felt nothing but Father's all-encompassing warmth.

And with that all my thoughts were completed; all those questions about life, death, and the universe that I sought answers to were answered. I was finally experiencing Father in all His glory. I felt pure joy and happiness.

I was with Father.

I *was* Father.

The Light

I had recently begun hearing muffled voices and sounds. They were usually soft and gentle; I felt very safe. I was floating in nothingness. Occasionally I felt a gentle poke, or a slight resistance to my movement.

Time was accelerating with every day.

I hadn't experienced anyone for as long as I could remember, except for Father. I was constantly ruminating on the meaning of life, death, and the universe. I knew all the answers, but I had no sheep to herd toward enlightenment. I realized that we were all sheep, just in different flocks. But we all bled red.

I had so much knowledge . . .

I knew everything that Father knew.

I had always heard the mediums and paranormal experts telling the spirits to go into the light. There were as many interpretations of what this light was as there were humans. It was like faith: no two people could possibly hold the same beliefs as each other to the same extent.

The muffled voices were becoming clearer. I was able to make out the occasional word or recognize the occasional tune. I was beginning to feel a little trapped. Although I was floating free, I felt a gentle pressure surrounding me.

I started to see a hint of the light.

I loved it here. It was so peaceful. I never wanted to leave.

The next thing I knew, the pressure surrounding me was becoming insurmountable. I did not like this. I could see the light up ahead. I could hear Father cooing in my ear, "Go to the light."

That was the first voice I'd heard for as long as I could remember.

I felt a tremendous force on the top of my head. I was being forced out of my safe haven.

I did not like this. I did not want this.

"Go to the light."

With another unpleasant squeeze, I felt a chill on the top of my head.

I knew exactly where I was.

I was being reborn.

Before I knew it, I was freezing cold. I was quickly handed around from person to person until I was finally placed on a warm breast. This was my introduction to my new mother.

I had so much to share. I knew all of Father's secrets and truths.

I understood the meaning of life.

I was ready to start communicating. With every ounce of my tiny being I tried to speak, but all that came out was a quiet cry. I started to explain how to reach enlightenment. But again, only a feeble cry came out of my mouth. I kept trying, until I finally wore myself out.

All that I knew was that my mother's name was Patricia, my father's name was William, and I was a "healthy baby girl."

My new name was Olivia Taylor.

My parents weren't married. William was a doctor, a cardiologist. He was thirty-one years old. Patricia—or Patty, as William called her—she was a thirty-three-year-old investment broker. I had been born to privilege.

As time passed, I grew stronger. For months I continued trying to tell my parents about the meaning of life and how to craft out a glorious experience. But the harder I tried, the more upset I would get. I was constantly wearing myself out. I slept most of the time.

And I couldn't control my body. I was reduced to soiling myself. I had very poor motor skills. I was dying for a piece of pizza, but all I was given was sweet warm milk.

With time I learned words. I learned to crawl.

But as I met all my milestones, I was forgetting the lessons and deep understandings that I had learned from my previous life experience. By the time I was two years old I was a fully functioning and extremely curious toddler. I was in the process of creating an entirely new life experience.

I had to relearn everything.

Manufactured by Amazon.ca
Bolton, ON